D1756931

WESTMINSTER AND THE WORLD

Commonwealth and Comparative Insights for Constitutional Reform

W. Elliot Bulmer

BRISTOL
UNIVERSITY
PRESS

First published in Great Britain in 2020 by

Bristol University Press
1-9 Old Park Hill
Bristol
BS2 8BB
UK
t: +44 (0)117 954 5940
e: bup-info@bristol.ac.uk

Details of international sales and distribution partners are available at bristoluniversitypress.co.uk

© William Elliot Bulmer 2020

British Library Cataloguing in Publication Data
A catalogue record for this book is available from the British Library

ISBN 978-1-5292-0062-1 hardcover
ISBN 978-1-5292-0066-9 ePub
ISBN 978-1-5292-0063-8 ePdf

The right of William Elliot Bulmer to be identified as author of this work has been asserted by him in accordance with the Copyright, Designs and Patents Act 1988.

All rights reserved: no part of this publication may be reproduced, stored in a retrieval system, or transmitted in any form or by any means, electronic, mechanical, photocopying, recording, or otherwise without the prior permission of Bristol University Press.

Every reasonable effort has been made to obtain permission to reproduce copyrighted material. If, however, anyone knows of an oversight, please contact the publisher.

The statements and opinions contained within this publication are solely those of the author and not of the University of Bristol or Bristol University Press. The University of Bristol and Bristol University Press disclaim responsibility for any injury to persons or property resulting from any material published in this publication.

Bristol University Press works to counter discrimination on grounds of gender, race, disability, age and sexuality.

Cover design by Liam Roberts
Front cover image: Shawshots / Alamy Stock Photo
Printed and bound in Great Britain by CPI Group (UK) Ltd,
Croydon, CR0 4YY
Bristol University Press uses environmentally responsible
print partners

'One of the many reasons why we are in this crisis is that we do not have a codified written constitution. It is only the unwritten, uncodified understandings that protect the body politic from regressing to government with minimal checks, balances and accountability. Up to now we have had to depend on people playing by the rules. Well, now we have a Government who are not playing by the rules.' Caroline Lucas MP, MP for Brighton Pavilion (Green Party), House of Commons (4 September 2019)

'During the long years I fought to promote constitutional reform, I was struck by how its opponents successfully cast any change to the *status quo* as an assault on Britishness. In fact, the liberal tradition of political reform is a quintessentially British one. A first step would be to present it as such.' Nick Clegg, former leader of the Liberal Democrats and Deputy Prime Minister (2017)[i]

'Never has the Commonwealth been more central as a reservoir of comparative constitutional knowledge for the UK than this. Brexit is in more sense than one the belated arrival of the post-imperial moment for the UK. Learn from those that you once taught.' Dr Asanga Welikala (2019)[ii]

'In times of change we need to find the balance … of change and stability. Calling for radical change without being aware of or having respect for the traditions that make up the foundations of our structures and institutions will inevitably leave our society drifting. So, one mistake would be to try and change everything. The second mistake, however, would be to try not to change anything.' Justin Welby, Archbishop of Canterbury (2019)[iii]

[i] Clegg, N. (2017) *Politics: Between the Extremes* (London: Bodley Head), pp 249–50.

[ii] Welikala, A. (2019) Tweet: 11:41, 7 September, https://twitter.com/welikalaa/status/1170271170467368960

[iii] Welby, J. (2019) William Temple Foundation Annual Lecture, 14 May, www.archbishopofcanterbury.org/speaking-and-writing/speeches/archbishop-canterbury-delivers-william-temple-foundation-annual

Contents

List of Tables

Acknowledgements

I wish to thank the many people who have contributed to this book, from initial discussions about the concept, through the writing and review process to the production of the final text. In particular, thanks are due to Dr Asanga Welikala (University of Edinburgh), Dr Donal Coffey (Max Planck Institute), Prof. Tom Ginsburg (University of Chicago), Sumit Bisarya (International Institute for Democracy and Electoral Assistance), Dr Stuart White (Jesus College, Oxford), John Drummond (Scottish Constitutional Commission) and, of course, to my wife Eva Dominguez, who has borne this book with more patience than it deserves.

For my father, John Douglas Bulmer, who inspired me with tales of tropical islands far away.

Note on Cover Image

The cover image shows SS *AMRA* of the British India Steam Navigation Company. Built on the Tyne in 1938, she sailed on the Calcutta–Rangoon mail route until requisitioned for war service in 1940. During the Second World War she served as a troop ship and hospital ship, supporting the landings in Sicily and Salerno in 1943. Released from government service in 1946, she was refitted and returned to commercial use on the Mombasa to Bombay route. She was scrapped in 1966. Her lifespan therefore coincides with both the majoritarian heyday of the British constitution and the peak years of decolonization during which the Empire was transformed into the Commonwealth and Westminster Model constitutions spread around the world.

Note on Author

Dr W. Elliot Bulmer is Lecturer in Politics at the University of Dundee. Formerly he was a Senior Programme Officer (Constitution Building) at the International Institute for Democracy and Electoral Assistance and before that served as Research Director of the Constitutional Commission in Scotland. He is a member of the United Nations Development Program's Expert Roster on Governance – Constitutions and is a regular columnist for *The Sunday National*. He has provided technical assistance in support of constitutional change processes around the world, including Afghanistan, Myanmar, Philippines, Tuvalu and Ukraine.

Rediscovering Britain's Wider Constitutional Tradition

Aims and approach

This book is intended as a work of practical constitutional scholarship applied to an urgent, pressing problem. It is not a book on constitutional history, constitutional law, constitutional theory or comparative politics – although it draws upon each of those disciplines. It is, rather, an attempt to identify the pressing affliction of the British body-politic and to recommend a remedy.

The affliction is a deep constitutional crisis. The 'unwritten constitution', which grew up over the centuries from a hotchpotch of statutes, judicial decisions, disputed conventions and half-remembered traditions, has reached the end of its useful life. The remedy is a new constitutional settlement founded upon a written constitution. Mere cosmetic tinkering is not enough. Further piecemeal, make-do-and-mend improvisation will only confuse, not resolve, the matter. The only hope for the revival of our democracy is a written constitution: a supreme and fundamental law, founded upon a broad political and societal consensus, in which the fundamental principles of the state are declared, the rights of the people are protected, the various institutions of government are defined, and the relationships between them regulated.

Although there are a few novel touches, the constitutional proposals advanced in this book are likely to be familiar – and acceptable – to most supporters of constitutional reform. They reflect the 'Charter 88 agenda' (discussed in Chapter 2) that has motivated constitutional reformers in Britain for the last three decades. The originality of the book lies less in its specific constitutional proposals and more in the approach by which they are reached and the means by which they are justified. The book responds to the new constitutional crisis, unanticipated by the reformers of the pre-1997 era. Then, the main impetus for reform was a fear of what Lord Hailsham called 'elective dictatorship' – the concentration of power in the Prime Minister at the head of the governing majority. This fear has not diminished – indeed, with the return to majority government in the 2019 general election, it might have increased. However, it is now merely part of a wider crisis, which includes a general disintegration and distortion of the unwritten constitution, the erosion of its moral foundations and the collapse of its long-held assumptions. We have passed from the majoritarian heyday of the British system of government, through an era of incoherent piecemeal reforms, to a period of decline and fall.[i]

In these conditions, a written constitution has a number of potential benefits. It could provide a means of 'rebooting' our democracy: starting afresh, clearing the decks. It could do much to improve the quality, inclusivity and resilience of our representative institutions. It could help to preserve an open and pluralist society, promote the common good and general wellbeing of citizens, and provide for a genuine devolution of power away from Westminster and Whitehall to the nations, regions and cities. All this has been understood for a long time, but that is no longer the whole story. In our current confused situation, a new written constitution could also be an instrument of healing, reunification and trust-building. It could restore much-needed clarity and coherence. It could even help a society divided by Brexit piece itself back together and return from the brink of destabilizing political polarization. A shared attachment to the constitution can be an important anchor for national identity, transcending political, as well as class, racial and regional, divisions. In other words, a new written constitution offers a solution both to the institutional crisis of representation and governance, and also to the underlying crisis of national identity, purpose and direction. It has gone from being desirable to essential.

The central argument of this book is not only that a new written constitution can and should be adopted, but also that, contrary to common assumptions, to do so would be entirely consistent with British constitutional traditions. Many would-be constitutional

---

[i] It is convenient, and not entirely ahistorical, to divide the history of the British constitution into seven ages: 1. 1660–1689: English Restoration; 2. 1689–1746: Hanoverian Settlement; 3. 1746–1832: Parliamentary Oligarchy; 4. 1832–1928: 'Struggle for Democracy'; 5. 1928–1997: Majoritarian Heyday; 6. 1997–2016: Incoherent Reform; 7. 2016– Decline and Fall.

reformers reject the Westminster Model and turn to continental Europe or Scandinavia for models of reform. But what if the Westminster Model does not have to be abandoned? What if it only has to be embraced in its fullest, most developed sense?

The crux of this argument is that the British constitutional tradition should not be understood as a merely insular phenomenon, as if it belonged to the United Kingdom alone. It is, rather, a global-imperial inheritance, shared with a worldwide family of 'Westminster Model' democracies, of which the United Kingdom is the first, but no longer the best, example. The Westminster Model – like the English language, the Common Law, cricket and Anglicanism – had its origins in England, but it has flourished and reached maturity only through being propagated around the world by the British Empire and Commonwealth.

We know that the Palace of Westminster is 'the Mother of Parliaments'; what is less well known is that it is also the Midwife of Constitutions.[1] Almost all former British colonies, on independence, adopted a written constitution that faithfully replicated (with such modifications and prudent improvements as they saw fit) the essential features of the Westminster Model. In most if not all cases, they did so willingly, not as an act of British coercion, but out of a desire to emulate a system that many elites in the countries transitioning to independence genuinely admired.[2] [ii]

Today, the Westminster Model is one of the world's most prolific and successful forms of democracy, found on every inhabited continent. It is as vitally manifest in Ottawa, Canberra, New Delhi, Dublin, Valetta or Kingston as it is in London or Edinburgh. From British Colombia at the far edge of the Western Hemisphere to Pacific Islands on the other side of the globe, one can see a family of more or less closely related democratic systems. The constitutional arrangements differ in detail from country to country but, despite the variety of national adaptations, these Westminster Model constitutions continue to belong to the same community of constitutional thought

---

[ii] S.A. de Smith wrote that 'The last voice to incant the slogan "British is best" is likely to be that of a colonial nationalist on an obscure and remote island'. (De Smith, S. A. (1961) 'Westminster's Export Models: The Legal Framework of Responsible Government', *Journal of Commonwealth Political Studies*, 1(1).) I have probably met that person – at the Constitutional Conference on Funafuti Island, Tuvalu, in 2018 – arguing that the Westminster Model has served Tuvalu well for 40 years since independence and that to change it would be a dangerous retrograde step.

and practice. They are held together by common history and by an enduring similarity of institutions, laws, ideas, norms and practices. They share the same lexicon, the same foundational literature, and even a degree of overlapping jurisprudence – all derived, directly or indirectly, from British constitutional foundations. As former Prime Minister David Cameron said in a speech to the Jamaican Parliament in 2015:

> This place feels instantly familiar. These benches, the mace in front of us, the atmosphere – there is much about this place that reminds me of home. But this familiarity is about much more than bricks and mortar. It is a warm reminder of the strong democratic and parliamentary links that bind us together, and the strong links that bind the UK, not just to Jamaica, but to the whole Commonwealth Caribbean.[3]

There is a story to be told about the Westminster Model in the Commonwealth that is both of general academic interest, from the point of view of comparative politics and legal history, and timely in terms of its beneficial influence on contemporary constitutional debates in the United Kingdom. This book sets out to tell that story. In doing so, it argues that the constitutional renovation so desperately needed in the United Kingdom can be achieved not by an abandonment, but by a rediscovery, of Britain's global-imperial constitutional tradition.

The off-spring of Westminster have transitioned to independence, adapting, refining and improving the Westminster Model along the way. Some rejected it, of course (usually in favour of an authoritarian one-party state), but those who have stuck with it provide a vast pool of experience on which to draw. There is much we could learn from them to inspire and inform the overdue refoundation of the United Kingdom's Brexit-beleaguered and Boris-battered constitution.

To renew our constitutional settlement in this way, adopting a written constitution that draws extensively on examples from the old British Dominions, the Commonwealth realms and other countries where the Westminster Model has taken root, is not, therefore, to reject the inheritance of Britain's own tradition, but to seize hold of it, apply its lessons, and make it our own. A written constitution is not a revolutionary break with the British constitutional tradition, but the natural culmination and completion of that tradition.

This approach enables the case for a written constitution to be framed in ways that are acceptable not only to those of Whiggish or Radical sensibilities, but also to those moderate, pragmatic conservatives whose longstanding faith in the unwritten constitution has been sorely tested. A generation ago, conservatives could mount a coherent and principled defence of the status quo. Aside from the partisan advantages that the existing system afforded them, and a general disposition not to fix things that appear not to be broken, Tories have tended to admire the crude but brisk efficiency of the pre-1997 British system. When in office, they gladly relished the power that it gave to the government, while respecting, for the most part, informal restraints on that power. British system of government in its majoritarian heyday had many faults, but it had a certain undeniable logic. The rules, although unwritten, were fairly clear and widely accepted. That position is no longer sustainable.[4] The muddle, confusion, uncertainty and disarray of Brexit has been followed by Boris Johnson's game of 'constitutional hardball' – pushing the legal rules to their limits, attacking the judiciary, Parliament, civil service and media, and defying traditional norms of respect, tolerance and forbearance.[5] This should convince sensible and moderate conservatives, who might never have considered major constitutional change before, that the institutions they hold dear are more fragile than they thought. When the 'good chaps' theory of government is stretched beyond breaking point, the time for making do, muddling through, tinkering, fudging it and winging it is over. A written constitution, rejected so vehemently in the 18th, 19th and 20th centuries, may be the best way for decent conservatives, embarrassed and ashamed by right-wing populism, to preserve and defend all that is good in Britain's constitutional heritage.

This spanning of the centre ground, from the democratic left to the mainstream right, is essential to the success of constitutional refoundation. Working constitutions are rooted in cross-party agreements underpinned by broad societal consensus.[6] A constitution has to be a national compact, intelligible (in its basic principles) and acceptable (taken as a whole) to the vast majority of people. It must define the common ground we share and on which we will base our common life together as a *res publica* or political community. We might have healthy disagreements on policies, priorities and personalities, but at least we can agree to play by the same basic rules and to adhere to the same overarching principles of democratic decency: rules and principles that are generally accepted, as near universally as possible, as basically legitimate, fair and reasonable.

Rooting a constitutional re-foundation in the Westminster tradition means that this book is perhaps more realistic than other books advocating constitutional change, both in its expectations of what a constitution can achieve and in its recommendations as to what the future written constitution should contain. There is a tendency in my proposals – although only a mild one – towards a degree of constitutional reticence and parsimony. While rights, principles, and perhaps even socio-economic provisions can have their place in a Westminster Model constitution, we ought to see the constitution primarily as a framework for democratic self-government, through which ordinary parliamentary politics plays out, rather than as a transformative programmatic manifesto. This may disappoint some who might be tempted to see the constitution as a shortcut to radical social change. Controversial topics, hot-button issues of the moment, and provisions of a merely legislative or policy-making character are sometimes better left out of the constitution. It is important to nail down the institutional and procedural rules, and the most fundamental rights, without overloading the constitution with a partisan agenda. Aside from any considerations of constitutional theory, this might just be the pragmatic compromise that enables common ground between the parties to be found.

Background and foundations

There is a small but growing body of British 'constitution-building' literature – works that go beyond both the dispassionate analysis and partisan critique of the unwritten British constitution, to lay out positive plans for its reform or replacement. Early contributions to this genre include a lecture given by Lord Scarman to Charter 88 in 1992[7] and two books setting out draft constitutions: *Common Sense: A New Constitution for Britain* by Tony Benn and Andrew Hood,[8] and *The Constitution of the United Kingdom*, published by the Institute for Public Policy Research (IPPR) in 1991.[9] The IPPR's draft constitution, in particular, is a solid and sound document; one might quibble with it here and there, but on the whole it still stands the test of time.

A more recent contribution is the report entitled *A New Magna Carta*, published by the House of Commons' Political and Constitutional Reform Committee in 2015. This report was largely the achievement of the chairman of the committee, former Labour MP Graham Allen, whose commitment to democratic constitutional change was a constant theme of his political career, with technical assistance from Professor Robert Blackburn QC. It contains a draft for written constitution which is technically sound, although it does make some odd design choices, such as a partial retrenchment of devolution and a replacement for the House of Lords.[iii] Other recent works on constitution-building in the United Kingdom include those of Jeff King (*The Democratic Case for a Written Constitution*, 2019), Vernon Bogdanor (*The New British Constitution*, 2009) and Andrew Blick (*Beyond Magna Carta: A Constitution for the United Kingdom*, 2015).

This book draws upon a canon of constitutional literature that has, for several centuries, sought to define, explain, analyze, advocate and reform the Westminster Model. This canon once formed the basis of any serious education in British politics and constitutional law. It includes Sir Thomas Smyth's *De Republica Anglorum* (1583), the works of Sir Matthew Hale, Sir William Blackstone's *Commentaries on the Laws of England* (1765), Jean-Louis de Lolme's *Constitution of England* (1771), Lord John Russell's *Essay on the History of the English Government and Constitution* (1825), John Stuart Mill's *Considerations on Representative Government* (1861), Walter Bagehot's *The English Constitution* (1867), William Stubbs' *Constitutional History of England* (1875), A.V. Dicey's *Introduction to the Study of the Law of the Constitution* (8th edition, 1915), and Sir Ivor Jennings' *Cabinet Government* (1936) and *Parliament* (1939). Those inclined to comparative studies might include Lord Bryce's *Modern Democracies* (1921) and Fossey Hearnshaw's *Democracy and the British Empire* (1920), both ripe with insights into the dominion constitutions.

To this list might be added more recent works examining the operation of the British system in the second half of the 20th century from Vernon Bogandor's *The Monarchy and the Constitution* (1997) and Peter Hennessy's *Cabinet* (1986) and *Whitehall* (1989), to Geoffrey Marshall's *Constitutional Conventions: The Rules and Forms of Political Accountability* (1997).

The wider cannon includes some of the philosophical works that have shaped thinking on political institutions in the Anglo-British tradition: John Locke's *Second Treatise of Government* (1690), Edmund Burke's *Reflections on the Revolution in France* (1790), Thomas Paine's biting rejoinder *The Rights of Man* (1791), Harold Laski's *Liberty in the Modern State* (1930). At a stretch, it might also include *Christianity and*

[iii] The second chamber in that draft constitution would be elected for 15-year terms, with one-third of its members being elected at each general election; this reflects certain proposals of the Wakeham Report (Royal Commission on the Reform of the House of Lords, 2000, *A House for the Future*), but it seems an unsatisfactory way to balance representativeness with independence; members elected on such long terms are partisans, without being in any sense accountable to voters.

Social Order by William Temple (1942) and *Social Insurance and Allied Services* by William Beveridge (1942), which together laid the moral and philosophical foundations for the welfare state after the Second World War and provided much of the policy impetus behind the British system in its majoritarian heyday.

Above all, this book rests upon a body of writing that set out to study the transmission of the Westminster Model around the world, and its development in different soils and climes. Of these, the foremost names of the decolonization era are Sir Ivor Jennings, Stanley Alexander de Smith and Kenneth Wheare. Jennings' *The Constitution of Ceylon* (1949) and *Approaches to Self-Government* (1958) are classics, as is S.A. de Smith's *The New Commonwealth and its Constitutions* (1964). The latter, especially, has been a constant table-top companion throughout the writing of this book. In *The New Commonwealth and its Constitutions*, de Smith not only describes the constitutional provisions of newly independent Commonwealth countries, but also makes subtle, parenthetical recommendations for reform of the British system of government. From time to time, after describing various contrasting Commonwealth practices, he reflects that some solution found by constitution makers in a far-flung part of the Empire is a very good one, and one that would be well worth copying if ever in a position to write a constitution for the UK. It is de Smith, for instance, who recognizes that federalism, far from being alien to British thought and practice, is a characteristically British institution.[10] He also recognizes both the value of being explicit, in translating constitutional conventions into written constitutional texts, the usefulness of formally recognizing the role of the Leader of the Opposition, and the need for 'neutral zones' (like Electoral Commissions, Public Service Commissions and Judicial Service Commissions) in preserving constitutional democracy. When this book looks to, say, the Solomon Islands for a rule on the granting of royal assent, to Fiji for the right of the Speaker to summon sessions of Parliament, to Belize for the rule on how to form a government, or to Malta for provisions on the dissolution of Parliament, it is pure *de Smithery* – in intent, in methodology, and in materials, it owes much to de Smith's example.

Later generations of comparative constitutional scholars have done much to further our understanding of Westminster Model constitutions. It is neither possible nor necessary to provide an exhaustive list, but some notable examples are worthy of mention because they have either been influential in shaping the thinking behind this book or have contributed to the baseline of knowledge on which much of the book rests. A shortlist of titles would include: *Exporting the British Constitution: Responsible Government in New Zealand, Canada, Australia and Ireland* (A. Ward, 1987); *The Making and Remaking of Commonwealth Constitutions* (W. Dale, 1993); *Sovereigns and Surrogates: Constitutional Heads of State in the Commonwealth* (D. Butler and D. Low, eds, 1991); *Westminster Legacies: Democracy and Responsible Government in Asia and the Pacific* (H. Patapan, J. Wanna and P. Weller, 2005); *Post-Independence Constitutional Change in the Commonwealth* (Leslie Wolf-Philips, 1970); *The Codification of Constitutional Conventions in the Commonwealth Caribbean Constitutions* (M. De Merieux, 1982); *A Political Legacy of the British Empire* (H. Kumarasingham, 2013); *Bills of Rights & Decolonization* (C. Parkinson, 2007); *The Constitution of Independence: The Development of Constitutional Theory in Australia, Canada, and New Zealand* (P. Oliver, 2005); Brian Galligan and Scott Brenton's edited volume *Constitutional Conventions in Westminster Systems: Controversies, Changes and Challenges* (2015); and *The Veiled Sceptre: Reserve Powers of Heads of State in Westminster Systems* (A. Twomey, 2018).

There are also notable works on constitutions and constitutionalism in specific periods, countries or regions: Donal Coffey on the origins of the Irish constitution and inter-war Commonwealth developments, Derek O'Brien on constitutions of the Anglophone Caribbean, Peter Russell on constitutional politics in Canada, Geoffrey and Matthew Palmer on New Zealand, Yash-Pal Ghai and Jill Cottrell on the South Pacific – and many more.

Such rootedness in the traditions of British and Commonwealth constitutional scholarship is integral to the project of re-founding the constitution. Constitution makers should adhere to a Hippocratic Oath: if you cannot do good, at least do no harm. If we are to rebuild the constitution from first principles, we must first have a thorough understanding of how the Westminster Model works, its historical origins and development, its fundamental principles and practices, and its adaptation to a variety of different contexts and circumstances. This understanding keeps us from proposing unsuitable changes that might unbalance the constitution, undermine its coherence, or have risky unforeseen consequences.

However, to be rooted in a tradition is not to be bound to a narrow interpretation of that tradition, or to its unimaginative application, such that the door to innovation is closed. The Westminster Model is broad enough to allow for meaningful democratic change, with a written constitution embodying the reforms necessary to restore faith in our institutions and to secure the common good in our public life. The whole 'Charter 88 agenda' can be encompassed within it. It simply means: (i) that reform should build upon, and not reject, our Westminster heritage, and (ii) that the new constitution should be presented and portrayed not as threateningly alien to British constitutional traditions, but rather as the fulfilment and guarantor of those traditions.

Imperialism, anti-imperialism and post-imperialism

The Westminster Model of constitutional democracy draws upon a long stock of English history, from the Magna Carta to the Glorious Revolution. It cannot be properly understood, however, through the lens of English exceptionalism. The defining characteristics of the Westminster parliamentary system developed not in an English state or even a British state, but in a British-imperial state. The 'struggle for democracy' from 1832 to 1928, during which the franchise was extended and parliamentarism consolidated, was also the period of greatest imperial expansion. Democracy and Empire grew together. The 'majoritarian heyday' of the British constitutional system – from the achievement of universal adult suffrage in 1928 to the beginning of the Blair-Brown reforms beginning in 1997 – spanned the period from the British Empire's greatest extent, through its gradual transformation into the Commonwealth, to its precipitous decline (with an end point marked by the transfer of Hong Kong to China in 1997).

A project such as this, drawing on British-imperial and Commonwealth constitutional history, opens itself up to accusations of imperialism, as if by writing about the Empire and Commonwealth in anything but condemnatory tones, one is thereby justifying imperialism's worst excesses, hankering after bygone days, and glossing over the racism, greed, class hierarchies and abuses of power that characterized the Empire. That is, of course, unfounded.

The British Empire was a vast enterprise – commercial, political, military and administrative – that touched every inhabited continent and continued for several centuries. The failings of the British Empire are easy to list: concentration camps in the Boer War, the Bengal Famine, the Irish Famine, the Amritsar Massacre, the repression of the Mau Mau rebellion, the whole system of extractive economics, indentured labour, penal transportation. We must acknowledge the damage done and not seek to marginalize the bloody and brutal aspects of imperial history. On the other hand, the British Empire was not driven by wickedness and exploitation alone. The Empire did bring many tangible benefits, not least in the establishment of political, legal, administrative and financial systems.[iv] Although the process of granting independence was not everywhere smooth or gracious, and the results were not always favourable, such institutional foundations did eventually enable many former colonies to become viable independent democratic states.

This is not to mask the misdeeds of empire with an exculpating 'All's well that ends well'. It is simply to recognize that 20th-century British imperialism, although infused with 'an effortless sense of cultural and racial superiority', was also sustained by liberal and Christian values and 'took sincere pride in its commitment to law, democracy and human equality'.[11] It would be wrong to overlook either side of this complex equation.

In any case, the purpose of this book is not to pass judgment on the British Empire, neither to praise it nor to condemn it. The totaling up of its historical balance-sheet and the sorting out of its mixed legacies must be left to higher tribunals.[v] Rather, it simply tries to recognize our post-imperial reality and to relearn from the former Empire and Commonwealth certain lessons on constitutional subjects that we have forgotten, or never fully applied, at home.

In the 20th century, constitutional learning went from Britain and the old dominions to the colonies – training up what Jennings described as 'politicians as eloquent as Burke, and in Burke's own language' and producing lawyers 'as ready to quote Coke's *Institutes* or Blackstone's *Commentaries* or the Law Reports as any young man in the Temple.'[12] Now the learning has to be the other way. To restore and reform the British constitution, we need to learn from Nehru and Bustamante, Mandela and Senanayake.[vi] These are of course only representative

---

[iv] For example, according to Muang Muang, who eventually became Chief Justice and later briefly President of Burma, 'The Burmese villagers discovered to their surprise that the British', unlike previous rulers, 'did not kill and plunder at random'. British rule brought 'law and order and liberal ideas', and every British administrator 'had been taught as a boy that he must not steal, must not rob, must not tell lies'. (Maung, M. (1961) *Burma's Constitution*, 2nd edition (The Hague: Martinus Nijhoff), pp 5–6).

[v] Broadly sympathetic – and popular – accounts of the Empire include Niall Ferguson's *Empire: How Britain Made the Modern World* (2002) and Jeremy Paxman's *Empire* (2012); more critical – and scholarly – accounts include Bernard Porter's *The Lion's Share: A Short History of British Imperialism, 1850–2004* (2004) and Richard Gott's *Britain's Empire* (2012).

[vi] Jawaharlal Nehru, first Prime Minister (1947–1964) of India; Sir Alexander Bustamante, first Prime Minister (1962–1967) of Jamaica; Nelson Mandela, President of South Africa (1994–1999); Don Stephen Senanayake, first Prime Minister (1947–1952) of Ceylon.

names – the list goes on, and should not be limited to Prime Ministers and Presidents. We need to learn from the constitutional scholars of the former Empire too – from the likes of Yash-Pal Ghai in Kenya, Justice Cherno Sulayman Jallow in the Gambia, U Ko Ni in Burma, and many others.

Since the 2016 Brexit vote, there has been a renewed interest in the Commonwealth. It is regrettable, however, that such interest has largely been limited to the pro-Brexit right, who have unrealistic expectations of what the Commonwealth can, or is willing to, deliver. Britain has lost a lot of international prestige and attempts to 'get the old gang back together' are unlikely to succeed. Residual goodwill has been strained by the United Kingdom's 'hostile environment' immigration policies, which fall hard on descendants of Caribbean immigrants. The centre and centre-left of the political spectrum have tended to ignore the Commonwealth, and so have overlooked its contribution to democracy, good government, human rights, the rule of law, education, and sustainable development. As Donal Coffey notes, 'The tendency within the United Kingdom for those enamoured with the Commonwealth to be drawn from a particular ideological bent should not obscure the kaleidoscope of constitutional designs, case law, and histories which it encompasses.'[13]

Here is the post-imperial paradox. On the one hand, we must learn from the Empire in order to get over it. To reconstitute the state as a modern constitutional democracy we must re-discover the constitutional principles and designs of Westminster Model constitutionalism, as these developed in the Empire and Commonwealth. On the other hand, we must get over it in order to learn from it. To learn from those we once taught – to accept that countries we once ruled over might have a thing or two to teach us – requires a certain humility. We need a frank (neither boastful nor cringing) engagement with our imperial history, which must be balanced by an equally frank assessment of our current reality: an unexceptional and under-performing peripheral European country, sliding down the middle rankings, facing the worst economic, diplomatic and constitutional crisis since Charles I fell out with Parliament four centuries ago.

This book is an attempt to contribute to that process of post-imperial re-foundation. It is written in the hope that one day we might have a written constitution that meets aspirations for a reformed democracy and a renewed social contract, and yet preserves and restores all that is good and worthy in our constitutional heritage.

Structure of the book

The book is divided into 12 chapters. Chapter 2 diagnoses Britain's constitutional crisis and sets it in its historical context. Chapter 3 makes a case for a new written constitution. Chapter 4 answers some common objections to that case. Chapter 5 then defines the Westminster Model, describes its historical development, and argues that a Westminster Model constitution is most suitable for our needs.

The middle chapters of the book discusses the particular constitutional design choices that are likely to arise in the United Kingdom, in each case examining comparative practice from other Westminster Model democracies before making recommendations for the United Kingdom. The aspects covered include foundational principles, rights and religion (Chapter 6), the Crown, Prime Minister and government (Chapter 7), Parliament (Chapters 8 and 9), nations, regions and localities (Chapter 10) and judicial, administrative, electoral and miscellaneous provisions (Chapter 11). Finally, Chapter 12 covers the processes and politics of constitutional refoundation and concludes with some reflections on the need for a broader revival of civic and democratic values beyond the constitution.

2

The Decline and Fall of the British Constitution

The heyday of majoritarian democracy (1945–67)

There was a time when belief in the wisdom and greatness of the 'British Constitution' was an uncontroversial assumption of political life. The generation now at or near retirement age was born and socialized into a system of government that was almost axiomatically good. It might have been littered with strangely archaic titles, rules and rituals, all opaque to the uninitiated, but it worked. It delivered government that was stable and effective, responsive and responsible, honest and capable. It could win world wars and build the National Health Service. It could defeat Nazis and slumlords with equal vigour. It was encased, of course, in a persistent class system of status and privilege, but there was a prevailing sense of public duty and mutual obligation that tied those at the top to those at the bottom. The civil service was generally competent and honest, the justice system fair and reliable, and corruption a foreign concept. The two main political parties (who between them comfortably won more than 90 per cent of the votes at every election) represented different classes and interests, but were both committed to full employment, the cradle-to-grave welfare state, and rising living standards.

With quietly-spoken triumphalism, the dominant constitutional narrative celebrated Britain's long democratic evolution, beginning with the Magna Carta and proceeding through milestones such as the Glorious Revolution and the Great Reform Act, until it reached its perfect conclusion. It was fair game to disagree with this government or that party, to think that the Prime Minister was doing a bad job, or to object to particular policies, but the essential soundness – indeed the brilliance – of the system as such was practically unassailable.

This was not an altogether unreasonable view. The constitutional difficulties that are now so apparent had not yet surfaced. There was no Welsh Assembly or Scottish Parliament. The Northern Irish Parliament existed, but few in Great Britain gave that lonely province a moment's thought. The House of Lords, defanged by Parliament Acts 1911 and 1949, appeared to do no harm; rendered ever so slightly more meritocratic by the Life Peerages Act 1958, perhaps it did a little good. The First Past the Post electoral system – despite an anomalous result in 1951, when the Labour Party won more votes but the Conservatives won more seats – seemed to deliver decisive and responsible government. The conventions surrounding the relationship between the Crown, Prime Minister, Cabinet and Parliament were generally understood and universally applied. The absence of a written constitution did not undermine the country's sense of self; we knew who we were and what we stood for. The lack of judicially protected fundamental rights had not prevented the development – through the democratic operation of parliamentary sovereignty and the principles of the common law – of an open society backed by an enviable array of civil liberties. To criticize such a system, which existed as a solid, dependable, tried-in-the-fire historical reality, must have seemed ungrateful, utopian and unpatriotic.

Compared to the record of Britain's near neighbours, the excellence of British institutions in the post-war decades was self-evident. France in that time had exhausted two republics (the Third and Fourth) and hosted a puppet fascist regime. Its Fourth Republic lasted only 12 years and cycled through 40 governments. The Fifth Republic was headed by an old General whose democratic intentions, although sincere, were as yet unproven. German democracy had collapsed in 1933 and the new democracy established in the western two-thirds of the country was still in its infancy. Italy had had a similar collapse into totalitarian rule, followed in 1946 by the establishment of a turbulent corrupt republic.[14] Spain and Portugal were still dictatorships. All of Europe east of Vienna was under the fist of Stalinism. All these countries had written constitutions – some rather elaborate and optimistic ones – which had either appeared impotent in face of the rise of authoritarianism, or served chiefly as a mask for it. The small countries of Northern and Western Europe (Belgium, the Netherlands, Luxembourg, Norway, Sweden, Denmark, Switzerland and Finland) fared better in terms of their record of democratic stability, but these were of marginal interest. At best, they were seen as benign but ineffectual countries, far removed from the first rank of great powers – to which the United Kingdom, despite the loss of India and the humiliation of the Suez Crisis, still claimed to belong.

Britain's greatest constitutional achievement was to have reached this happy state of affairs without having ever had to think very hard about it. History, tradition, fortuitous circumstance – some might even call it divine providence – had produced a system without theory or grand design. Incremental and pragmatic change, managed by 'good chaps' with a clear sense of what was 'done' and 'not done', resulted in a living constitution, consisting of an elaborate patchwork of statutes, conventions, rules of common law, institutional traditions and ingrained habits. It was incapable of ever being written on tablets of stone, but so long as it was written on the hearts of men all was well. Of course, it was achieved through political struggles – the Peterloo Massacre of 1818, the Tolpuddle Martyrs transported to penal colonies for pioneering a trade union in 1834, the Chartists arrested for demanding democratic reform in the 1840s, the force-fed suffragette hunger strikers, and so on. Yet the prevailing narrative was that we had stumbled into democracy just as we had stumbled into empire – more or less by accident, with an effortless, gentlemanly nonchalance and a natural sense of superiority.

Pressures for change (1967–97)

By the late 1960s – just as the British system in its majoritarian heyday was being exported around the Commonwealth, cracks were starting to appear. It was not from England, but from Wales, Scotland and Northern Ireland, that the pressure for change first came: Plaid Cymru's victory in the Carmarthen by-election of 1966, the Scottish National Party's (SNP) victory in the Hamilton by-election of 1967, and the outbreak of 'The Troubles' in Northern Ireland in 1969.

These events revealed that there was an unresolved, and previously unacknowledged, territorial problem. For much of the previous half century, it had been assumed that there was only one dimension to British politics – namely that of class, expressed through economic and distributive preferences and articulated through a two-party system.[15] These new developments showed that territory and identity were to become politically salient, too. The UK Government's response was the 1972 Royal Commission on the Constitution, usually known as the Kilbrandon Commission. This recommended a cautious devolution of power to assemblies in Scotland and Wales, which led to the (unsuccessful) Scottish and Welsh devolution referendums of 1979.

Also in 1979, Margaret Thatcher came to power as a new brand of Conservative Prime Minister, motivated by a zealous free market ideology. Although Thatcher had no policy of constitutional change, her premiership had profound and lasting effects on the way the United Kingdom was governed. Thatcherite concern for market liberty and entrepreneurial endeavour had strangely paradoxical effects. At the root was a new concept of humanity: the *homo economicus* – the rational, self-interested, 'utility maximizer' of neo-classical economics.

While rhetorically seeking a return to traditional morality against the liberal sexual attitudes of the 'permissive society', Thatcherite belief in the values of the *homo economicus* corroded the moral basis on which the unwritten constitution had rested. This was unintended, but not unpredictable. In a political system dependent upon conventions and self-restraint, it is institutional vandalism to encourage economic attitudes in which breaking conventions and acting in selfish ways becomes laudable. The mantra of 'greed is good' cannot be contained in the economic sphere, but must necessarily spill over into public life. The resultant hollowing out of public ethics and civic virtue has been noted by thoughtful critics from both the communitarian left, like David Marquand,[16] and the traditionalist right, like Philip Blond.[17] The constitutional 'hardball' we see today, where unwritten rules are being pushed to their limits, and the general lack of decorum and decency that has broken out in our public life since the Brexit referendum, have their roots in this swashbuckling 1980s radical capitalism.

Another paradox was that the market liberty of *homo economicus* could only be expanded by an erosion of political and civic liberty. The 'free market' needed a strong and efficient (but brittle, impersonal and aloof) state to enforce its demands against anything that might stand in its way. The informal checks and balances and internal restraints that had moderated the otherwise immense power of the Prime Minister and Cabinet were increasingly pushed aside. Power was centralized, with control over policy areas such as education taken away from local authorities and given to the central government, so that Whitehall could impose 'efficiency measures' such as compulsory competitive tendering for outsourced services, or promote mechanisms of 'consumer choice' such as school league tables. Venerable institutions like universities, the civil service, and even the Church of England, which were motivated by a public service ethos or by the pursuit of any higher aims than profit-maximization and shareholder value, came under attack as bastions of old fashioned (that is, communitarian, solidaristic, non-neoliberal) thinking, for which there was no longer any room.

By the early 1980s, dissatisfaction with the system of government was growing. Faced with high unemployment, pitched battles between police and trade unions, and a political system deeply polarized between the Thatcherite hard-right and Labour's hard-left Militant Tendency, there was room for a new party of the 'soft-centre'. Thus emerged the Alliance – a pact uniting what remained of the Liberal Party with the new Social Democratic Party, a centre-left breakaway from Labour.[18] Formed in 1981 and contesting a general election for the first time in 1983, the Alliance recognized in its manifesto the connection between Britain's divided winner-takes-all economy and its divided winner-takes-all politics.

The Alliance's proposed solution was not only to seek a more centrist and moderate economic course, but also to moderate the political system. Traditional liberal concerns about the excessive powers of the Crown, the lack of transparency and accountability in the executive, and the fragility of civil rights in the absence of judicially enforceable guarantees were combined with a radical plan to deconcentrate power through regional devolution, localism, a reformed (elected) upper House, and the adoption of proportional representation for the House of Commons. Proportional representation could be portrayed as a self-interested gambit by a small party. Yet even if some measure of party interest was involved, the terms in which the SDP-Liberal Alliance advocated for proportional representation demonstrated their understanding of the close interrelation between more consensual politics and more moderate policies.[19]

As it turned out, the result of the 1983 general election was a resounding Conservative victory.[i] Constitutional change was frozen. Nevertheless, demands for constitutional change continued to swell throughout the 1980s. Two civil society movements, one in Scotland and one UK-wide, emerged during this time: the Scottish Constitutional Convention and Charter 88. Although banished into the political wilderness for as long as the Conservatives remained in office, these were later to provide the intellectual foundations for the Blair-Brown reforms.

The major Scottish initiative was the Scottish Constitutional Convention. This gathering, which first met in Edinburgh in 1989, was convened by Canon Kenyon Wright, an episcopal priest and sometime Liberal Democrat parliamentary candidate. It sought to represent both the political leadership and the wider society of Scotland, bringing

---

[i]   In the event, the SDP-Liberal Alliance won 25.4 per cent of the votes, but only 23 seats (3.5 per cent of the total membership of the House). The Labour Party, with only a few more votes (27.6 per cent) won 209 seats (32 per cent of the total). Source: Adam Carr Election Archive.

together all the political parties in favour of home rule (Labour, the Liberal Democrats, and the Greens), along with the Scottish churches, the Scottish Trades Union Congress, the Scottish Federation of Small Businesses and other civil society organizations, to work out a detailed plan of devolution.

The first symbolic act of the Convention was to issue a 'Claim of Right', a proclamation of 'the sovereign right of the people of Scotland to determine the form of government best suited to their own needs'. In other words, the Scottish Constitutional Convention asserted that, no matter what the Westminster Parliament might say or do, there was a distinct, independent, inherent repository of sovereignty in Scotland that had to be respected. The Claim of Right, although not recognized by any court, has become central to Scotland's constitutional self-image as a nation and a political community.[20] While the Claim of Right does not necessarily demand Scottish independence, it does make any simplistic, unitary understanding of the United Kingdom untenable in Scotland.

Beyond Scotland, the major UK-wide movement for constitutional change was Charter 88. Its name denoted the year in which it was issued (1988) but also had historical resonances: to the Glorious Revolution of 1688, the tercentenary of which was then being celebrated; to 'Charter 77', a reform manifesto issued 11 years previously by civil rights activists behind the Iron Curtain; to the 19th century Chartist movement with its demands for the reform of Parliament; and ultimately to the Magna Carta itself. The ten demands of the original Charter 88 are worth quoting in full, because they reflected a growing consensus among the reform-minded minority about what the priorities for change should be:

1. Enshrine, by means of a Bill of Rights, such civil liberties as the right to peaceful assembly, to freedom of association, to freedom from discrimination, to freedom from detention without trial, to trial by jury, to privacy and to freedom of expression.
2. Subject executive powers and prerogatives, by whomsoever exercised, to the rule of law.
3. Establish freedom of information and open government.
4. Create a fair electoral system of proportional representation.
5. Reform the upper house to establish a democratic, non-hereditary second chamber.
6. Place the executive under the power of a democratically renewed parliament and all agencies of the state under the rule of law.
7. Ensure the independence of a reformed judiciary.

8. Provide legal remedies for all abuses of power by the state and the officials of central and local government.

9. Guarantee an equitable distribution of power between local, regional and national government.

10. Draw up a written constitution, anchored in the idea of universal citizenship, that incorporates these reforms.[21]

The first and tenth of these points were, by insular British standards (although not by Commonwealth standards), the most radical. They demand a change to the very nature and basis of power. Instead of entrusting absolute power to a sovereign Parliament, a written constitution – superior to ordinary law and harder to change than ordinary law – would limit and direct Parliament's actions.

The mixed legacy of piecemeal reform (1997–2016)

With the coming to power of New Labour in 1997, a reform programme was inaugurated, committed to the 'modernization' of the British state through the partial implementation of the agenda set by Charter 88 and the Scottish Constitutional Convention. Over the next three parliaments, a number of important institutional statutes were enacted, including: the Human Rights Act 1988, the Scotland Act 1998, the Government of Wales Acts 1998 and 2006, the Greater London Authority Act 1999, the House of Lords Act 1999, the European Parliamentary Elections Act 1999, the Freedom of Information Act 2000, the Local Government Act 2000, the Political Parties, Elections and Referendums Act 2000, the Constitutional Reform Act 2005, and the Constitutional Reform and Governance Act 2010. Further reforms were considered, but not implemented, including a semi-proportional electoral system for the House of Commons (as proposed in the Jenkins Report, 1998)[22] and a partially elected second chamber (Wakeham Report, 2000).[23]

One should not doubt the sweeping effects of these changes. Devolution to Scotland and Wales created new political spaces, in which once minor parties of opposition – the SNP and Plaid Cymru – could form governments and start to shape the policy agenda.[ii] Although

---

ii By 2011, seven parties held government office across the United Kingdom: a Conservative–Liberal Democrat coalition at Westminster, an Scottish National Party government in Scotland, a Democratic Unionist–Sinn Féin government in Northern Ireland, and a Labour–Plaid Cymru coalition in Wales. This would have been inconceivable before 1997.

never fully realized, and not well understood in England, the nature of the Union was changing to one in which the new alternative narratives of national sovereignty, initially expressed only as 'claims' made by civil society, could now find institutional voice.

Aside from devolution, the New Labour reforms also changed the relationship between the state and the citizen. The Freedom of Information Act, for all its weaknesses and loopholes, did subject the workings of the government to a degree of previously unknown public scrutiny.[24] The Human Rights Act, by incorporating European Convention rights into domestic law, has done much to change the culture and the discourse around human rights in the United Kingdom.[25] Its effect has been strengthened somewhat by the establishment, under the Constitutional Reform Act 2005, of a United Kingdom Supreme Court. However, in deliberate deference to the doctrine of parliamentary sovereignty, the Human Rights Act stopped short of the Charter 88 demand for an entrenched, justiciable, supreme-law bill of rights.

The project was hobbled from the outset by contradictory, irreconcilable aims. This contradiction reflected New Labour's muddled thinking about constitutional matters. They could never get beyond the assumption that constitutional change is merely administrative change on a bigger scale. In treating each constitutional issue discretely, New Labour failed to bring about a new, agreed, coherent constitutional settlement. There was no attempt by the New Labour government to connect devolution to other institutional changes. For example, it was not tied to reform of the House of Lords, in a way that could have transformed the latter into a Senate representing the several constituent parts of the United Kingdom. Proportional representation was adopted for devolved legislatures and for the European Parliament, but not for the House of Commons: so multiparty politics was able to flourish at the geographical and political periphery, while two-party dominance continued at Westminster. A Greater London Assembly was established, but not linked to a wider scheme of devolution within England. Indeed, the English question, a lurking, unresolved issue that should have been obvious to anyone thinking in holistic and genuinely constitutional terms, was just ignored. Half-hearted regionalism was considered, but quickly dropped after a failed pilot scheme referendum in the North East of England.

The Blair-Brown reforms also failed to recognize the importance of constitutional conversation. If the constitution is supposed to embody the common foundations on which the state is based, then it ought to be based on political agreement and public consensus. Reaching that underlying consensus is, in fact, perhaps the most important long-term benefit of a constitution-building process. In the absence of such consensus, constitutional reforms are of only fragile legitimacy and remain vulnerable to being rolled back – as we now see with Conservative plans to repeal the Human Rights Act.

The 2010 Conservative–Liberal Democrat coalition also had a moderately ambitious constitutional agenda: to reform the House of Lords, introduce a recall mechanism for MPs, and consider a referendum on changing the electoral system for the House of Commons from First Past the Post to Alternative Vote. These proposals did not get far. The only important achievement was the Fixed Term Parliaments Act 2011, which provided that Parliament would serve for fixed five-year terms, and could only be prematurely dissolved in two circumstances: (a) if the House of Commons, by a two-thirds majority, voted for dissolution, or (b) if a vote of no confidence in the government was passed and a new government could not be formed with the confidence of the House within 14 days. This reform was made possible by the circumstances of coalition government – it gave both parties reassurance that they would not be surprised by a general election. However, some Liberal Democrats might also have been persuaded by principled arguments. The power of the Prime Minister to dissolve Parliament more or less at will had long been recognized as favouring the executive;[26] and those trying to limit executive dominance had seen the power of dissolution as an easy and obvious target.[27]

However, the Fixed Term Parliaments Act sought to regulate dissolution without also codifying the rules of government formation and removal. The appointment and dismissal of the Prime Minister is still governed primarily by convention, and it is unclear to what extent those conventions have survived, or been modified by, the statute. As discussed in the following section, this can give rise to situations in which a government, overwhelmingly defeated in the House on its flagship policy, no longer sees itself as bound to resign.[iii] This is just another example of how relying on *ad hoc* solutions to immediate political problems, rather than systematic constitution-building, has stored up bigger problems for the future.

[iii] In Scotland, where the Scottish Parliament has had fixed terms since its inception, the First Minister must be formally nominated by a vote of Parliament. The Scottish rules, which were consciously designed after careful comparative study, are clear, explicit, and work together in a coherent way. Much confusion could have been avoided, and legitimacy strengthened, had the Scottish example been followed more closely at Westminster.

Between 1997 and 2016, the clarity, coherence and legitimacy that the British system of government enjoyed in its majoritarian heyday was undone – not by too much reform, but by half-baked and ill-considered reform. The things that had once made an unwritten system work – the quiet norms, gentlemanly ethos, self-restraint and informal checks and balances – have gone. No new articulation capable of meeting the ecological, ethical and economic challenges of democracy in the 21st century has been forthcoming. It is now unclear what the fundamentals of our political system are, or should be. The British constitution now exists, according to a 2019 *Economist* op-ed, in a 'half way house which may be the worst of both worlds', in which 'partial codification has removed a mixture of predictability and flexibility while providing neither certainty nor clarity in recompense'.[28] In normal times one might muddle along and make the best of it, but in times of grave crisis and uncertainty it leaves us very exposed. This is no fit way to run a country. In the words of Canon Kenyon Wright, the unwritten constitution which was 'always unacceptable in principle' has now become 'intolerable in practice'.[29]

The British constitution in crisis (2016–20)

Few people today would hold the British Constitution in high regard. Complacency has given way to discontent. Justified pride has been replaced by bemused embarrassment. Brexit has brought home the chaotic, unsightly reality of the United Kingdom's constitutional and political malaise. As Fintan O'Toole has argued, Brexit is not just another ordinary, cyclical, crisis; it is a 'reckoning', a coming home to roost of all the failures, fudges and fibs of the previous decades.[30] The immense strain placed on both state and people by the COVID-19 outbreak only adds to that sense of reckoning.

The roots of the malaise go much deeper than Brexit. A long string of scandals, abuses of office, bad decisions and bad behaviour has tainted the institutions of state and weakened our trust in them. To list all would take many pages, but some may be called to mind: the Hillsborough tragedy and its cover-up, the handling of the Hutton Inquiry and the Chilcot Report, the 'Black Spider' letters from Prince Charles, the misuse of public money during the 2012 Olympics and the betrayal of the Windrush Generation. To err is human, but this catalogue of misadventures points to a systemic failure of governance. Anthony King and Ivor Crewe, in *The Blunders of Our Governments*, argue that blundering incompetence seems to have become hardwired into the system, under governments of both major parties.[31]

The United Kingdom is also suffering from long-term failures of policy, manifest in social and economic dislocation, widening material inequality, and the return of real economic hardship to millions of households.[32] The state appears increasingly oligarchic, serving rich, especially corporate and financial, vested interests, at the expense of the ordinary people, with monstrous consequences: racism, anti-Semitism, fascism and authoritarian populism have risen from their tombs; want, disease, squalor, ignorance and idleness are again stalking the land.[33] The state's legitimating claim to uphold justice and to serve the common good is revealed as hollow; provoking, instead, public indignation, anger and disgust. Nowhere was this more clearly evident than in the Grenfell Tower fire of June 2017, in which poor Londoners, mostly from immigrant backgrounds, burnt to death trapped in a concrete 'wicker man'; the charred reeking hulk of this ill-designed, poorly maintained tower block still stands as a monument to the crony-capitalist state, with its mantra of deregulation, landlordism and privatization.

Society has fragmented too. Brexit revealed a polarizing separation of worlds between the educated, cosmopolitan 'anywheres' who mostly benefited from the 1980s neoliberal social and economic policies, and the left-behind small town 'somewheres' – communities drained of civic life, and of economic prospects.[34] As full employment and state-led industrial development were abandoned in favour of an economy dominated by retail and financial services, so the stabilizing bonds of place and community – and loyalties to what Edmund Burke called 'little platoons' of mutual interest and support – were weakened. Even the family, although championed by Conservative social rhetoric, was undermined by the policies of neoliberalism. For the educated and middle class, female participation in the paid economy was seen as liberating, fulfilling and equalizing. For many working class women, forced into low-paid service and retail jobs as their husbands' incomes (previously sustained by unionized manufacturing jobs) fell, the burden only increased.[35] Extended families, which were invaluable units of resource sharing and risk pooling among the working class, were strained by longer working hours and increased expectations of geographical mobility.

This may seem a long way from the constitution, but if the teleological aim of the legitimate constitution is to enable the state to discern and promote the common good, then these political, economic and social manifestations of disregard for the common good must be seen as evidence of a constitutional order that is failing to achieve its aim. In the words of Thomas Paine:

> When it shall be said in any country in the world, my poor are happy; neither ignorance nor distress is to be found among them; my jails are empty of prisoners, my streets of beggars; the aged are not in want, the taxes are not oppressive; the rational world is my friend, because I am a friend of its happiness: When these things can be said, then may the country boast of its constitution and its government.[36]

People rarely express dissatisfaction with political ethics or socio-economic outcomes in explicitly constitutional terms, but this does not detract from the constitutional nature of their complaint. The crucial factor is public trust in the integrity, effectiveness and decency of the political system as a whole: the prevailing sense that the state generally, most of the time, more or less, serves the common good. This has been in sustained and precipitous decline.[37]

Writing in 2017, Nick Clegg, the former Liberal Democrat leader, argued that 'Public distrust of politics is at an all-time high – confidence in political, media and commercial elites at an all-time low. British politics is crying out for wholescale renewal. Our unwritten constitution is creaking at the seams.'[38] As Deputy Prime Minister in the coalition from 2010 to 2015, Clegg bears some responsibility for this situation. The reform package promised in the 2010 coalition agreement ground to an early and inconclusive halt. He was, however, able to diagnose the crisis and to understand its inescapably *constitutional* nature. When the debate turns from disagreement with a particular party, or the dislike of a particular leader, to a general rejection of the legitimacy of the political system as whole, the constitution is in crisis.

There is a tendency to use the term 'crisis' too loosely: democracies are perpetually in crisis, bouncing from one to the next as the self-correcting mechanisms kick in.[39] Usually they rescue themselves through the normal operation of democratic institutions. When Neville Chamberlain was deemed unfit to lead the war effort during the 'Norway crisis' of 1940, he was removed and replaced by Winston Churchill. When Anthony Eden mishandled the 'Suez crisis' of 1956 he was duly replaced by Harold Macmillan. These self-correcting mechanisms – enabling the representatives of the public, through political parties, to hold their leaders to account and to change leaders in orderly, peaceful ways – are the secret of democracy's strength and resilience. As long as the political system as a whole works, and those mechanisms are trusted and intact, these little crises are easily weathered. The same can be said for financial or economic crises – a change of government, and a change of policy, is usually sufficient for the country to right itself. Such crises are not constitutional in nature.

A constitutional crisis occurs when these rules do not work – when there is doubt about the content or applicability of the rules, when there is sustained disagreement about who has the authority to interpret and apply the rules, when the rules produce outcomes that seem, in the general court of public opinion, so absurd or unjust as to call the legitimacy or adequacy of the rules themselves into question, or when the rules are under attack.[iv] Brexit has plunged the United Kingdom into a *constitutional* crisis because it has exposed the inability of the existing statutory and conventional rules to perform the most basic functions of a constitution: that is, ensuring that public power is exercised within known limits and in predictable, and legitimate, ways. Andrew Blick and Peter Hennessy, writing in a recent report for *The Constitution Society*, describe the unwritten constitution as 'melting' – the rules are in a 'molten' condition, in which they appear to lose both their form and their effectiveness.[40]

Some of these rules relate to what is sometimes referred to as the 'territorial constitution' – the web of strained understandings and half-agreed bargains governing the relationship between the various constituent parts of the United Kingdom. England and Wales voted to leave the European Union, while Scotland and Northern Ireland

---

[iv] A good example of such a crisis in a Westminster Model democracy occurred in Malta in the 1981 general election, when the Nationalist Party won 50.9 per cent of the vote to the Labour Party's 49.1 per cent, but only 31 seats in Parliament to the Labour Party's 34 seats. In a two-party system based on knife-edge majorities and a consistently majoritarian logic, this was an intolerable result. Not only did the Labour Government formed in consequence of these elections lose legitimacy, but the legitimacy of the electoral system and whole constitutional order was badly shaken. The Nationalist opposition boycotted Parliament, further eroding the legitimacy of Parliament as an institution. Eventually the impasse was broken by interparty negotiations, resulting in a constitutional amendment, to the effect that the party receiving a plurality of votes would, if such circumstances were to repeat themselves, be guaranteed a narrow majority of seats. Constitutional order was restored and faith in the political system, gradually rebuilt. This had all the features of a truly *constitutional* crisis: a breakdown in the constitutional rules leading to the de-legitimation of the constitutional order, which was resolved only by constitutional change. See: W.E. Bulmer (2014) 'Constrained majoritarianism: Westminster constitutionalism in Malta', *Commonwealth & Comparative Politics*, 52, pp 232–53.

voted to remain, yet in its response to the referendum result, the UK government has insisted on a strictly unitary understanding of the state, excluding devolved administrations from any meaningful role in setting Brexit policy and ignoring the 'Sewel convention' (the self-denying rule by which the Westminster Parliament refrained from legislating on devolved matters). The unspoken deal of devolution was broken, and the rules of devolution, whether conventional or statutory, suddenly appeared unfit for purpose; they could be relied upon neither to protect Scottish or Northern Irish interests, nor to facilitate a coherent and inclusive UK-wide approach. While the United Kingdom government under both May and Johnson has responded by doubling-down on an Anglo-centric concept of 'Britishness', many rank-and-file English Conservatives have become indifferent to the Union; outcomes once unthinkable, like Scottish independence and a united Ireland, are now being considered by large numbers of English Conservative party members as acceptable collateral damage in pursuit of Brexit.[41]

The overwrought 'territorial constitution' is only part of the story. The core institutions of the central state – Government and Parliament – are also in this molten condition. On 15 January 2019, the Conservative government led by Theresa May (a minority government dependent upon a 'confidence and supply' deal with the right-wing Democratic Unionist Party) was defeated in the House of Commons on the EU Withdrawal Agreement by 432 votes to 202. This was the flagship policy of the government on the single most important issue of the day. By all established conventions of parliamentary democracy and responsible party government, the response should have been for the government either to resign or to advise the Queen to dissolve Parliament and call a general election. Dissolution was ruled out by the terms of the Fixed Terms Parliament Act 2011, leaving resignation as the only choice. There was no resignation, and the Queen decided not to use the 'nuclear option' of dismissing the Prime Minister. Instead, the government invited the Opposition to submit a motion of no confidence; the Opposition did so, and the motion was defeated. The government received the confidence of the House – the same House which had just defeated the government's most important policy – by 325 votes to 306.

This should not happen. The government is supposed to set the direction of policy and to provide leadership to the House. Parliament in a well-functioning Westminster Model democracy is not supposed to be a mere 'rubber stamp'. It has a vital role in debating policy and scrutinizing legislation, restraining the government and holding it to account. The Opposition and backbenchers can (and sometimes do) influence legislation and policy.[42] However, so long as the government retains the confidence of the House, it should be able to get its major pieces of legislation through. If the government cannot carry the support of the House for its most defining policy, it should no longer be in office. Either a new government should be formed that enjoys the confidence of the House or there should be a general election. This conventional relationship between the House of Commons and the government seems to have broken down.

These events were followed by the introduction of a bill sponsored by Yvette Cooper MP (an Opposition backbencher) to prevent the UK from leaving the European Union without a Withdrawal Agreement in place.[43] The bill was believed to enjoy considerable support on both sides. Pro-Brexit members, fearing that the bill would be passed, reacted by suggesting that the government should advise the Queen to withhold royal assent. The question of whether royal assent could be refused to a bill provoked a flurry of debate from constitutional commentators. There are two good conventional rules here, on which most constitutional scholars are agreed: (i) that the Queen grants assent to legislation passed by Parliament, and (ii) that the Queen acts only on the advice of her responsible ministers. What if these two rules conflict? Which then prevails? Precedents can be martialled on both sides. But the question behind the question goes not only unanswered, but unasked: Why do we not know? Should not these vital rules be clear, unambiguous, written down, enforceable, agreed and legitimate? Rather than trying to discern through arcane historical precedents what the prevailing rule is, could we not decide by some reasonable process what the rule should be and then make that rule applicable?

There are other examples of the disintegration of the unwritten system. It is a long-established convention that Parliament holds a new session each year, beginning with the Queen's Speech – which provides an annual opportunity for the government to prove that it has the confidence of the House. Theresa May decided on a two-year session, to avoid having to face this test of confidence. Minor norms of decency have also been violated. There are usually 'pairing' arrangements in the House of Commons. When an MP from one side of the House cannot be present for an important vote, the whips will agree that an MP on the other side of the House will also abstain, so that the result of the division is unaffected. When the Liberal Democrat (and anti-Brexit) MP Jo Swinson was absent on maternity leave, these arrangements broke down, and the Conservative MP with whom she had been 'paired' voted.[44]

Behind all this Brexit-induced constitutional chaos lies a deeper confusion about the role of the referendum in a parliamentary democracy. Referendums were once regarded as alien to British traditions.[v] That is no longer the case. Several referendums have now been held in various parts of the United Kingdom – in relation to European integration, electoral reform, devolution in Scotland and Wales, and the peace process in Northern Ireland, as well as on local government questions such as the direct election of mayors. In many Westminster Model democracies, referendums are routinely used to approve or reject constitutional amendments. Nevertheless, in the absence of a clear constitutional foundation, confusion over the role and status of the referendum remains, and the tension between parliamentary and popular sovereignty is unresolved.

So the picture builds – a collapse of political ethics, serious and repeated policy failures, the polarization of society, the straining of relations between different parts of the United Kingdom, and the general disintegration of what had been a fairly clear, if rather crude, majoritarian system into a much more complex and confusing system that the existing rules (if, indeed, they can still be described as *existing rules*) are ill equipped to handle. This is a genuinely *constitutional* crisis, not because Theresa May could not get the Withdrawal Agreement through the House of Commons, nor because Boris Johnson attempted unlawfully to prorogue Parliament, but because of the failure of deadlock breaking mechanisms (resignation and dissolution), the breakdown of constitutional understanding between the nations of the UK (violation of the Sewel convention), and blatantly partisan attempts to bring into play arcane but disputed rules (refusal of royal assent, prorogation) while ignoring others (annual sessions of Parliament). There are still, of course, statutes that the courts will enforce, but statutes were never more than the dry bones of the unwritten system; without universally understood, widely accepted and generally enforced conventions to put the flesh of parliamentary democracy on that skeleton, the constitutional order is as good as dead.[45]

The constitutional necrosis goes even deeper, to the heart of our constitutional norms and values. If Britain once had a great political virtue, it was to temper the thrust-and-parry of competitive party

---

[v]   In 1945, when Winston Churchill proposed a referendum to extend the wartime National Government into peacetime, the Labour leader, Clement Attlee, said he 'could not consent to the introduction into our national life of a device so alien to all our traditions as the referendum, which has only too often been the instrument of Nazism and fascism'. Hansard HC Deb. vol. 881, col. 1732, 22 November 1974.

politics with an underlying shared commitment to moderation and civility, and to restrain private motives through a strong sense of public responsibility. As the great Victorian legal reformer James Fitzjames Stephen argued in 1873, these moral foundations were the only stable point of reference, the only guarantee of good governance and public liberty, in a system otherwise predicated upon parliamentary sovereignty:

> The character of our public men is the sheet anchor on which our institutions depend. So long as political life is the chosen occupation of wise and honourable men, who are above jobs and petty personal views, the defects of parliamentary government [i.e. parliamentary sovereignty], however serious, may be endured even where they cannot be remedied or alienated. If, however, the personal character of English politicians should ever be seriously lowered, it is difficult not to feel that the present state of the constitution would give bad and unscrupulous men a power for even hardly equalled in any other part of the world.[46]

It does not do to be too sentimental about this; there are rogues and chancers in every generation and never a pristine golden age. Yet never before in modern British history have we seen such a sudden and precipitous collapse of ethical standards and basic political civility. The old Britain – the Britain in which we could depend upon a general sense of moderation, self-restraint, decency and public duty – is gone, and 'whatever Britain may once have been, it is another country now'.[47] A member of Parliament has been murdered,[48] other members have been too frightened to walk through the streets for fear of mob violence,[49] a major national newspaper published a front page headline accusing the justices of the Supreme Court of being 'enemies of the people',[50] the civil service have been denounced as traitors and saboteurs,[51] and racism of a kind once banished from respectable society is again on the rise.[52]

In a well-constituted polity, the state is a public entity ('*res publica*'), belonging to the public, in which public office is a public trust to be used for public ends, and in which those engaged in public life must be the faithful stewards of the public good. A written constitution is the attempt to give effect to that idea, through the instantiation of certain agreed institutions, procedures, rights and principles; it is the title deed that says the state belongs to the public. In Britain today, as in the last days of the Roman Republic, that concept of the 'publicness of the state' has been lost. We have lost 'political normality', as that normality existed before 2016. In its place, we have something akin to a 'cold civil war', in which one side is the victor – by fair means or foul – and the other side is the vanquished. When this happens, the polity is sundered; politics ceases to be a vocation and becomes a trade for merchant adventurers, struggling for mastery so that wealth and resources can be appropriated for their private gain.

The Conservative victory in the 2019 general election (winning 365 out of 650 seats) ended the deadlock of a hung Parliament and restored single party majority government. It does not, however, mean a return to 'business as usual'. Much damage, in terms of the loss of institutional integrity and the erosion of norms and conventions, has already been done.

The 2019 Conservative manifesto promised to establish a 'Constitution, Democracy and Rights Commission' with a mandate to examine 'the relationship between the government, Parliament and the courts; the functioning of the Royal Prerogative; the role of the House of Lords; and access to justice'. This is not the inclusive constitutional refoundation process we need. It should be seen rather, on the tactical level, as a revenge attack against the institutions – the judiciary, Parliament, the devolved legislatures and civil service – which frustrated, if only temporarily, the hardest of hard Brexits. It is school bully politics of the lowest order. On the strategic level, it marks a consolidation of power, re-making the state in their own image.

There is a very real risk that progress made since 1997 will be rolled back. The result will not, however, be a restoration of the *status quo ante* – that would be impossible. Instead, it might be the creation of a new authoritarian-populist regime. This government has already tried to undermine the judiciary, politicize the civil service, privatize the British Broadcasting Corporation (BBC), and side-line Parliament – all techniques from the play-book of other authoritarian populists.[53] It is as if, having found the old house rotten, they propose not to restore it but to raze it to the ground.

The end of the Hanoverian constitutional settlement

This chapter has traced the decline and fall of the British constitution over the space of 80 years, from its Churchillian triumph, through new challenges it could not meet and reforms that were not equal to the task, to its current Johnsonian catastrophe. A once much-respected and much-emulated constitutional order is now in a state of institutional and moral collapse.

The current constitutional crisis is nothing less than the final unravelling of what might be termed the 'Hanoverian constitutional settlement'. 'Hanoverian' is a bit of a misnomer – much this settlement was in place long before George I, Elector of Hanover, was put upon the throne of Great Britain in 1714. However, it was under the Hanoverian monarchs that this system stuck, put down roots, and became hegemonic in terms of both its red-coated military power and its ideological appeal. Having endured for quarter of a millennium, that settlement defined the constitutional order in which British democracy grew and flourished. It continues to define the assumptions of British constitutional orthodoxy, although with ever-decreasing intellectual vigour and moral credibility. Some residual sense of a constitutional settlement might remain, but it has become so mystical and intangible, so remote from how government actually functions, as to be quite useless as a normative, regulative foundation for the state.

The Hanoverian settlement was a hard-won achievement. From the accession of Charles I in 1625 to the end of the Jacobite wars in 1746, it took more than a century of civil wars, beheadings, rebellions, uprisings, foreign invasions, palace coups, a period of military rule, chronic instability, and the repression of religious minorities, before finally it was possible to reach, by compromise and reconciliation, a constitutional bargain that would work and stick.

Work and stick it did. Although many inequalities, special privileges and corrupt oligarchic practices remained, Hanoverian Whiggery avoided both tyranny and instability. It consolidated parliamentary institutions and established a recognizably modern liberal state. It laid the basis for a complex commercial economy and a flourishing civil society, for naval power and imperial expansion, and for the scientific, agricultural and industrial revolutions.

This settlement was truly constitutional in nature to the extent that it represented a strategic agreement between all then-relevant institutional, political and social groups – between King and Parliament, Lords and Commons, City and Country, Church and State, Anglicans and Dissenters, Tory and Whig, Scotland and England – which answered foundational questions about the nature of the state and the principles and institutions of governance. While it did not produce a written constitution, parts of the constitutional settlement were written down in various legal instruments: the Bill of Rights Act 1689, the Toleration Act 1693, the Act of Settlement 1701, the Treaty of Union 1707, the Septennial Act 1719. Other parts of the settlement were not committed to writing, but were nevertheless generally accepted by all parties – crucially, that the Crown would ultimately yield to the sovereignty of Parliament, that civil war would no longer be an acceptable means of settling disputes, and that peaceful opposition to the policies of the government would be freely permitted, as long as the general terms of the constitutional bargain were respected.

The principles of parliamentary supremacy, peaceful change and loyal opposition enabled the Hanoverian state to evolve incrementally, without fundamental rupture, during the 19th and 20th centuries. Reforming efforts were channelled into specific, piecemeal changes, such as the Catholic Relief Act 1829, the Great Reform Act 1832, the Municipal Corporations Act 1835, and the Parliament Act 1911. At the same time, conventions of cabinet government arose, mostly out of expedience sanctified by precedent, to gradually limit the power of the monarch while increasing that of ministers. This slow transformation of the political system, from the limited monarchy in the early 18th century to parliamentary democracy in the early 20th century, demonstrated both permanence and flexibility.

It was achieved not by re-opening any constitutional discussion about the fundamentals of the constitutional settlement (which might conceivably have led to a new, and possibly written, constitution), but simply by opening access to existing institutions so as to bring previously excluded groups into the original Hanoverian bargain: Catholics in 1829, Jews in 1858, the middle class in 1832, working class men in 1884, and women in 1928. Each group in turn was, in the terminology of the time, 'brought into the constitution'; they became parties to the Hanoverian constitutional settlement, without changing its essential features.

This balance of solid conservatism and pragmatic flexibility was a winning formula. Serene constitutional gradualism became a point of national pride. Other countries might need to write down their constitutional bargains in clear, authoritative documents, but Britain needed no such embellishments, so secure and so celebrated was the historical achievement of the Hanoverian constitutional settlement. Neither was it thought necessary to lay down any formal amendment rule by which the constitutional fundamentals could be renegotiated, because no such renegotiation was envisaged. Even the Chartist movement, the largest mass movement for democracy in the 19th century, while clothing itself in the rhetoric of the Magna Carta, demanded only a bullet-point list of six specific, statutory reforms that would enable them to share in the Hanoverian deal from which they had previously been excluded.[54]

However, the Hanoverian settlement lacked three things common to later constitutional foundations: (a) codification (writing down the rules in one place); (b) supremacy (those rules being superior to other laws); and (c) entrenchment (the rules being harder to change than ordinary law, with a formal mechanism for amendment). Although this allowed for flexibility, it came at a high cost.

Firstly, the lack of codification meant that the actual content of the constitutional settlement was always hard to pin down. What it rejected was clear: royal absolutism and republicanism in the political sphere, Roman Catholicism and Puritanism in the religious sphere. What it embraced – the exact nature of the balance of power between King and Parliament, or the respective status of established Anglicanism and tolerated dissent – was less clear.

Secondly, there was no way to distinguish what might be regarded as constitutional changes from other legislative or policy changes. Each of the long list of reforming statutes, from the Great Reform Act to the Fixed Term Parliament Act, became part of the settlement itself; the very fact that it was enacted was enough to make it part of the revised constitutional settlement. Nothing done could be said to be 'unconstitutional', if the constitution is itself defined in terms of what is done and enacted.

Thirdly, the lack of entrenchment offered no protection against regressive or reactionary change. Parliament retained the constituent power, and never distinguished between its constituent and its ordinary legislative roles. King, Lords and Commons could, by their joint act, revise the terms of the constitutional settlement as easily as they could amend the Dog Fouling of Byways (Supplementary Provisions) Act, or any other trifling piece of legislation.

With the emergence of parliamentary democracy (or 'responsible party government') in the 19th century, the political constitutionalism of the Hanoverian settlement thus gave way to parliamentary absolutism. This was most famously recognized by A.V. Dicey, whose strong doctrine of parliamentary sovereignty rejected any idea of there being fundamental or constitutional laws by which Parliament itself might be bound.[55] In reality, this meant that the government of the day, invariably backed by a loyal, disciplined and well-whipped partisan majority, could change any part of the constitutional settlement unilaterally. No court of law, or other institution, could stop them; although the Opposition could oppose and public opinion could object, ultimately the government was bound only by its own self-restraint and by its calculation of political risk in reshaping what was still called 'the constitution' at will.

The 'constitution' that triumphed during the majoritarian heyday of British democracy was a form of elective parliamentary absolutism tempered by institutional and personal self-restraint. Now that has disintegrated. What remains of the constitution is no longer secure, suitable or sufficient. The very flexibility and imprecision that enabled its growth have also precipitated its decline. It has ceased to provide convincing and broadly acceptable answers to the fundamental constitutional questions that any polity must be able to address: Who are we? What do we stand for? What will we not stand for? How should we govern ourselves? What standards and principles should define our public life? How will these agreements be upheld? What guarantees do we have? How will any future changes to the fundamentals be renegotiated? How do we discern the principles of the common good in our diverse society? What is the point of the British state, and of its institutions built by and for global empire, in an age when the Empire is no more? Why should the United Kingdom continue to exist at all?

These constitutional questions cannot be answered by ordinary party politics. Healthy politics takes place within a public sphere defined and supported by constitutional structures that are broadly agreed and widely accepted. This basic constitutional commonality unites us – despite all differences of party, policy preference or particular interest – in recognition of the same political institutions and processes, without this mutual recognition we are not fellow citizens engaged in argument about alternative visions of what is good for our society and community, as members of one *res publica*, but instead we are enemies, who may co-exist in a fragile and begrudging absence of conflict, but who cannot know the true community, solidarity, peace or fellowship with one another that fellow citizens of a free country ought to possess.[vi]

Neither does piecemeal *ad hoc* tinkering, of the sort experimented with since 1997, offer any solution. As Andrew Blick and Peter Hennessy argue, 'on this occasion muddling through may not be enough. It's time to call upon the best traditions of our constitutional past and the better angels of our nature'.[56] That means consolidating the ground rules and basic principles of our renewed democracy in a written constitution, characterized by codification, supremacy and entrenchment. As the introduction to the draft constitution published by the IPPR in 1991 put it, it is time 'not to change the historical constitution incrementally as been done in the past, but to change the basis of the Constitution', from one based on parliamentary sovereignty to one in which 'fundamental law which is prior to, independent of

---

[vi] On the Friend-Enemy distinction in politics, see C. Schmitt (1932) *The Concept of the Political* (New Jersey: Rutgers).

and the source of authority for the system of government'.[57] This is the cardinal point, without which other reform efforts, however good in themselves, are wasted.

This is not such a novel or far-fetched idea; merely an idea whose time has now come. We are on the verge of a 'constitutional moment' – a liminal time in which the constitutional foundations can be renegotiated, and a new constitutional settlement reached. If we let this moment slip away, the polarization, confusion and corruption, the disregard of all democratic constitutional norms, and the disintegration moral standards in public life so far will continue as to bring us to a state of utter ruin. If, however, this moment is firmly grasped, we might enjoy for generations to come the temporal blessings of good government under a democratic constitution orientated to the common good: peace at home and abroad, justice, freedom, tranquility, an effective administration, decent public services and widely-shared prosperity.

3

Towards a Written Constitution

The constitution and the constitutional order

The question of whether the United Kingdom's 'unwritten constitution' (or, as pedants insist, 'uncodified constitution') is really a constitution at all is ultimately a semantic one. The word constitution means different things to different people. There may be no need to seek final resolution to this semantic dispute, so long as we are clear and consistent about our terms.

One possible definition of a constitution is that suggested by Lord Bolingbroke in 1733: 'the whole assemblage of laws, institutions, traditions, customs and practices that embody how we are governed'.[58] Anthony King refines this as 'the set of the most important rules that regulate the relations among the different parts of the government of a given country and also the relations between the different parts of the government and the people of the country'.[59] According to this definition, every state has some sort of constitution, because even the most absolutist state needs laws, rules and routines that together enable its normal operation.[i]

This definition is, however, inadequate. It might describe what *has* happened, or even what *usually* happens, but such a definition of the word cannot allow the constitution to say much, if anything, about what *will* or *should* happen. It is impossible, under such a definition,

---

[i]   For example, Edward Lane, describing the government of Egypt during the reign of Muhammad Ali in the 1830s, could refer to its 'constitution' in terms of the organization of various institutions of state (the ministers and the council that served as an advisory body to the despot, the judiciary, the institutions of religion, the officials for the regulation of markets and the collection of taxes, the police and the army) even though the state was a despotic one, without any constitutional constraints on the ruler's power.

for any sustained course of action to be unconstitutional. If something else happens, contrary to what 'the constitution' would have predicted, then the constitution is not violated, but changed. The constitution, thus defined, has no normative value, no call upon our loyalties or affections, no authority over and above that of the laws in force at any moment in time.

A second definition looks at the constitution – specifically the British constitution – in terms of the Hanoverian settlement, as altered by subsequent statutes and conventions. If we define the constitution in these terms, it might at least provide some normative foundation for what is, and is not, constitutionally acceptable. The system can mutate, but only to the extent that the various actors – the monarch, the ministers, the House of Commons, the House of Lords, the courts – accept such mutations. If one institution tries to break the bargain in a unilateral way, they might overstep the mark, and do something that the others regard as unacceptable and unconstitutional. If those other institutions can appeal to the notional sense of a constitutional bargain, which has implicit values and norms within it, then the balance might be restored. Of course, since there is no formal way for the bargain to be renegotiated or enforced, this merely changes the nature of the constitution from 'whatever happens' to 'whatever the government of the day can politically, and perhaps morally, get away with'.

The third definition of a constitution is as *a supreme and fundamental law*. This definition has three parts. First, the constitution is a law – not a mere behavioural norm or habit, but an enforceable law. Second, the constitution is supreme – it is the highest law, to which all other laws must conform, and which can only be amended by a special procedure. Third, it is fundamental in content – it concerns things fundamental to the rights of citizens, the nature and purposes of the state, and the institutions of government.

The third definition prevails in most other democracies, including almost all other Commonwealth countries. It implies a written constitution. Indeed, 'written constitution' is little else than a convenient shorthand for a supreme and fundamental law. If the constitution is defined in such terms, an 'unwritten constitution' is either an absurd self-contradiction (a square circle) or something defective and incomplete (a chocolate teapot). If this definition is accepted, the United Kingdom, because it lacks written constitution, has no constitution at all.

A written constitution need not necessarily be contained in one document, although there are good symbolic as well as practical reasons for doing so. There must, however, be a bounded set of such laws, which are distinguished from other laws and whose status as the supreme and fundamental law is known, declared and explicit. In Canada, for example, the constitution includes the Constitution Act 1867, the Constitution Act 1982, and a list of other statutes and orders-in-council specified in a schedule to the 1982 Act.[60]

For clarity, it is helpful to distinguish between 'the constitution' and the 'constitutional order'. The former refers exclusively to a written constitution, as a supreme and fundamental law. The latter refers to a 'larger set of constitutional elements including, but not limited to, the written text'.[61] According to Matthew Palmer's study of New Zealand, the constitutional order (what he calls the 'real constitution'), consists of 'all those factors that significantly affect how public power is exercised'.[62] This includes 'legislation that influences the exercise of public power' and 'other formal instruments of the legislative, executive or judicial branches of government', such as parliamentary standing orders, the Cabinet Manual and international treaties, together with 'judgements in the common law that influence the exercise of public power'.[63] It also includes conventions: the 'observed norms of political behaviour that are generally acknowledged to have attained a significance and status worthy of general acknowledgement'.[64]

Canada is a prime example of a country where the written constitution ('supreme and fundamental law') does not encompass the whole of the unwritten constitution (defined in the first sense, as the most important rules of government). As the Supreme Court of Canada declared in 1998:

> The Constitution is more than a written text. It embraces the entire global system of rules and principles which govern the exercise of constitutional authority. A superficial reading of selected provisions of the written constitutional enactment, without more, may be misleading. It is necessary to make a more profound investigation of the underlying principles animating the whole of the Constitution, including the principles of federalism, democracy, constitutionalism and the rule of law, and respect for minorities.[65]

Nevertheless, Canada does have a written constitution, albeit a messy and patchy one. According to Van Loon and Whittington, the 'conglomeration of British, Canadian and provincial statutes, the British common law, Canadian judicial decisions, and a number of real but invisible conventions, customs, values and assumptions' that make up the Canadian Constitution exist 'all clustering rather loosely and haphazardly around the central kernel of the [Constitution Act 1867] and the more recent modifications in the Constitution Act, 1982'.[66] That 'central kernel', expressed in a set of constitutionally entrenched rules with higher law status and specific amendment formulae, makes all the difference.

Even in more recent Westminster Model constitutions, like those of Barbados or the Solomon Islands, where the main rules of parliamentary democracy are set out in the supreme and fundamental law, it is not possible – or desirable – for the constitution to cover everything.

In any constitutional order, much rightly depends on ordinary laws, parliamentary standing orders, conventions, practices, moral norms, political dynamics and institutional culture. A written constitution does not and should not replace all aspects of the unwritten constitutional order, but rather supports and sustains the constitutional order by giving it shape and strength.

Anatomy and content of a written constitution

Most people in the United Kingdom have never seen a written constitution and have little idea what a written constitution looks like.[ii] Misconceptions abound. Some expect a constitution to be about the size of an old telephone directory and are surprised to discover that most exist in handy pocket-sized printed editions. Even the constitution of a large and complex federation like India is only a little more than 50,000 words, while the constitution of a small, homogenous unitary state like Nauru occupies less than 15,000 words.

A written constitution typically consists of several consecutively numbered sections or articles, usually grouped into parts or chapters. These follow a coherent structure, with specific themes, subjects or institutions being covered in each part or chapter. There might be a preamble prefixed to the constitution, setting out certain values and

---

[ii] A draft constitution for the United Kingdom, incorporating the various reforms and design choices recommended in this book, has been prepared by the author and was originally intended to be included in an annex. This would have provided a 'worked example', demonstrating the practicality of a written constitution, made abstract arguments more tangible, and given readers unfamiliar with written constitutions a realistic idea of what a Westminster Model constitution for the United Kingdom might possibly look like. Regrettably, this draft constitution had to be removed on grounds of space. The intention now is to publish it separately.

aspirations; invocations of historical, democratic or divine authority might also be included. At the end of the constitution, particularly in British-influenced texts, one might find several schedules, dealing in detail with things that would otherwise break up the main body of the constitution.

The content of a written constitution can be summed up by the '7Rs': Recognition, Rights, Representation, Relationships, Regions, Reform and Roadmap. 'Recognition' covers all those things that address the identity of the state, nation and people. It may include recognition of one or more national languages, a dominant religion, or specific recognition for particular minorities. It can also include the general principles or values articulated by the constitution. 'Rights' covers human rights, from basic civil liberties to far-reaching socio-economic promises, limitations on rights (whether in general, or specific limitations in emergencies) and procedures and mechanisms for the judicial and extra-judicial protection of rights. 'Representation' includes the composition of Parliaments, the election or selection of members, terms of office, provisions on referendums, Electoral Commissions and Boundary Commissions, the regulation of parties, and so forth. 'Relationships' includes all the ways in which these institutions of the state interact with one another. Westminster Model constitutions are particularly concerned with these relationships: between the Head of State and Prime Minister, Prime Minister and Cabinet, Cabinet and Parliament, Government and Opposition benches, the front benches and backbenches, Parliament and the Courts, and Parliament and the people – all of which may be constitutionally defined. 'Regions' covers decentralization of power generally, whether to states and provinces, in a federal system, or to local government. 'Reform' concerns the ways in which the constitution can be amended, and 'Roadmap' covers the dynamic parts of the constitution – be that a commitment to certain policy objectives and programmatic goals that are constitutionally mandated, or transitional provisions designed to enable the implementation of the constitution.

These 'seven Rs' will usually be present to some degree in any constitution, but they will be emphasized to different extents in different contexts. A federal constitution, for instance, will typically devote considerably more space to the territorial distribution of power than a unitary constitution. A constitution that sets out to transform society will devote more to 'roadmap' provisions than a constitution that seeks to preserve much of the existing constitutional order.

The case for a written constitution

There are many grounds on which the case for a written constitution can be made. A written constitution can be advanced on liberal principles, as the best way of preserving civil liberties, pluralism and an open society. It can be advanced on federalist principles, as a way of rebalancing power geographically. It can be promoted on democratic grounds, to strengthen the representativeness and responsiveness of the government. A written constitution can be supported on radical social-democratic principles, as a means of redistributing political and therefore economic power away from oligarchs.[67] It can also be advanced on grounds of civic-republicanism, as the best means of promoting an inclusive 'politics of the common good'.[68]

In practical terms, these different justifications for a written constitution complement rather than contradict one another. The differences between them are differences of shade and emphasis, or differences of premise and reasoning but not of conclusion. The nub of them all is the same three simple and self-evident propositions: first, that the substance of our institutions, rights and principles should be clear, declared and explicit; second, that these fundamentals should be capable of being enforced and upheld against the government of the day; third, that they should be protected against hasty, ill-considered, or unilateral change.

As shown in Chapter 2, the indistinctness of the unwritten constitution means that constitutional rules that were once near-universally accepted as authoritative and binding can be forgotten with impunity. The status and applicability of conventions has become less clear. Norms and practices have been mutated, sometimes arbitrarily to suit the government of the day. If the conventions of the constitution cannot hold, the law of the constitution offers no greater reassurance. It is unclear exactly which statutes are regarded as being constitutional in nature. In *Thoburn v Sunderland City Council,* a class of 'constitutional statutes' was judicially discovered and found to be immune from implied repeal.[69] It is impossible, however, to find any two constitutional scholars who can authoritatively agree on which statutes are included in that category.[iii] With a written constitution,

---

[iii] Most would include the Bill of Rights Act, the Act of Settlement, the Parliament Acts, the various Representation of the People Acts, the Human Rights Act, the Scotland Acts, the Government of Wales Acts, the House of Lords Act 1999. Beyond that, the list becomes more porous and disputed.

this distinction between that which is part of the constitution and that which is just ordinary legislation becomes clear. It is possible to put in one document all the most important rules, practices and principles, and to mark them off as being of fundamental importance, of superior legal force, and harder to change.

Dispute over the interpretation of the constitution is a normal part of life under a written constitution. Much of the discipline of constitutional law, in countries with a written constitution, amounts to an attempt to discern what the written constitution *means*. What there is not, in those countries, is a dispute over what the constitution *is*. There is, for instance, no question of whether the Electoral Act 1993 is part of the Constitution of Tuvalu, or whether the Barbados Representation of the People Act 1971 is part of the Constitution of Barbados – there is a distinction between the constitutional order and the constitutional vertebrae that hold it together; in the United Kingdom, in contrast, the constitutional order has no backbone.

It might be argued that the 'case of prorogations' (*R (Miller) v The Prime Minister*) – in which the United Kingdom Supreme Court held that the extended prorogation of Parliament was unlawful and therefore void – shows the health and vitality of the unwritten constitution. As the judgment stated, the United Kingdom has an unwritten constitution 'established over the course of our history by common law, statutes, conventions and practice', containing certain constitutional 'values and principles' that must be upheld by the courts'.[70] Where these values and principles come from – by what authority, and on what basis, they are asserted – is nevertheless precarious. In most Westminster Model democracies, values and principles are derived from the preamble or foundational provisions of the constitution, or from its basic structural rules. We have nothing to rely upon except inferences from history.[iv]

According to the judgment in *R (Miller) v The Prime Minister* the foundation of our constitutional order is representative democracy. The authority of the government depends upon the confidence of the House of Commons, and the House of Commons depends for

---

[iv] The United Kingdom Supreme Court is not alone in distilling implied principles where none are expressly stated. the Supreme Court of Canada identified the core principles of the Canadian constitution as 'federalism, democracy, constitutionalism and the rule of law, and respect for minorities'. But the Canadian court at least had a written constitutional text, with supreme and fundamental law status, containing explicit provisions – such as a division of powers between the federal and provincial Parliaments, regular elections, and human rights, from which such principles could be derived. The United Kingdom has nothing comparable.

its legitimacy on the free suffrage of the people'[71] In a marriage of Dicey and Bagehot, the Supreme Court has joined together the legal concept of parliamentary sovereignty and the political concept of parliamentary government through ministers responsible to, and enjoying the confidence of, the House of Commons. Dicey's classic understanding of parliamentary sovereignty, as the legal supremacy of an Act of Parliament, has been expanded to include the sovereign authority of Parliament *to legislate as it sees fit*. Sovereignty is embodied not only in the laws Parliament has made, but in the right of Parliament to make laws. Parliamentary accountability – the ability of Parliament to hold the government to account, which it must do, if the principle that 'the Government exists because it has the confidence of the House of Commons' is to be effective – is also recognized, on a par with parliamentary sovereignty, as a foundational principle.[v]

This sounds good, but the lack of a solid written constitutional foundation makes it a house built on sand. The unwritten constitution is rendered useless by the very principle of parliamentary sovereignty that defines it. The Supreme Court can apply constitutional principles to limit executive action. It cannot apply such principles to limit legislative action. Parliamentary sovereignty means that those principles are themselves dependent on Acts of Parliament – not on any higher, more fundamental, basis of constitutional law. There is nothing even to prevent Parliament from abolishing the Supreme Court. Within a day of the Supreme Court's decision, some Conservative MPs were publicly clamouring for just such a course of action. The Blair-Brown reforms, because they were merely statutory reforms and not a genuine constitutional re-foundation, could easily be rolled back by a government with a working majority. The Constitutional Reform Act 2005, which established the Supreme Court, can be placed upon the chopping block, alongside the Human Rights Act.

Even those laws that establish a framework of democracy in the first place – the Representation of the People Acts, the Parliament Acts, the Political Parties Elections and Referendums Act – could be amended or repealed at will by a sovereign Parliament. Far from

---

[v]   The House of Lords fits somewhat awkwardly into this scheme (being part, albeit a subordinate part, in Parliament's role as both legislators and the forum of Government accountability, but not being the body to which the Government is held politically responsible), but for now that can be glossed over.

being the great cornerstone of the constitution that the Supreme Court imagines it to be, parliamentary sovereignty is really a sign that we have no constitution at all. Dress it up as one will, sovereign power is unconstitutional power, and parliamentary sovereignty is but a euphemism for the absolute and therefore despotic power of the majority currently in office.

For a long time, the danger inherent in parliamentary sovereignty was remote. During the majoritarian heyday of the British constitution we were always exposed to the potential threat of despotic power, but that threat never materialized. The governing majority, having sovereign powers at its command and being unconstrained by any enforceable constitutional norms, could in principle do unspeakable things, but it chose not to. It stayed its hand. It respected traditional restraints and upheld – with some notable exceptions – a broadly liberal constitutional ethos even though it was not compelled to do so. We were in a condition described by the political theorist Philip Pettit as *domination*, but not *interference*. Pettit likens this to the situation of a slave under a beneficent master: all is well enough, so long as the master remains beneficent – except of course for the nagging fear that whatever liberty one possesses exists by grace-and-favour, and not by constitutional guarantee.[72]

The threat of despotism is perhaps more real than ever before. In part, this is because informal, societal checks and balances have been weakened by four decades of neoliberalism. It is also because we face times of political, economic and climatic turmoil, during which self-restraint, a public-respecting ethos of good government and respect for parliamentary norms will come under great strain. A government backed by about a third of the popular vote could win a solid working majority in the House of Commons and then set about the destruction of whatever remains of our constitutional order: repealing the Human Rights Act and the Freedom of Information Act might only be the start of it; they could rig the electoral rules to their advantage, restrict the freedom of the media, and set aside any of the established practices and conventions of the unwritten constitution that in any way trouble them or aid the opposition. Once upon a time it would have been foolish to imagine such things: self-restraint, fair play and a sense of what is 'not cricket' would have reassured us. Now it would be foolish not to imagine them. The 'good chaps' theory of government has broken down and we have nothing else to fall back on.

Parliamentary democracy and parliamentary sovereignty can easily become mortally opposed principles, if ever control of the parliamentary majority falls into the hands of authoritarian populists. That is the primary inadequacy of an unwritten constitution: it might offer protection against the executive power, but not against the legislative power. It can defend the privileges and freedoms of a sovereign Parliament against the Crown, but not the rights of the people against Parliament.

Despotism, dictatorship and the persecution of minorities are not the only dangers against which a written constitution must guard. A constitution must not only limit power, but also provide certain and predictable rules for its exercise, that enable decisive public action and facilitate good government in the public interest. Constitutional rules allow political actors to know what they can and cannot do – and, above all, what they should and should not be doing. In other words, written constitutions define and establish the state, enable the state to govern the people, and enable the people to constrain and direct the state. They help to ensure that public power is exercised in ways that track and defend the public interest.[73]

Most countries emerging to independence from the British Empire sought to maintain the Westminster Model – a system of democracy that was known to them and admired by them[74] – but to write it down in a supreme and fundamental law. The parliamentary substance was often retained; the unwritten form was almost everywhere rejected. The Colonial Office, well aware of the arguments against a written constitution in a United Kingdom context, never seriously doubted that each newly independent state should have one. Countries that adopted their constitutions after independence, like India and Pakistan, also avoided simple doctrines of parliamentary sovereignty in favour of establishing a supreme and fundamental law.

This development is not surprising, because once all the mysticism is stripped away, a written constitution is simply a practical and useful technology. A 'technology' can be defined as a product of human wisdom and knowledge applied to a practical purpose. A written (supreme and fundamental law) constitution stands in relation to an unwritten constitution as the wheel and axle stands in relation to the rolling log. You can move a heavy stone by using rolling logs, but the invention of the wheel – and later, the pneumatic tyre – makes things easier, safer and more efficient. The new technology completely displaces the old.

The function of a wheel is clear, but what are the functions of a written constitution? The Kenyan constitutional scholar Yash-Pal Ghai, who has had a hand in drafting several Westminster Model constitutions as well as being one of the driving forces behind democratic constitutional change in his own country, articulated a list of such functions.[vi] Ultimately, according to Ghai, the principles and provisions of the written constitution 'ensure the legitimacy of the state and its capacity to deal with disputes between citizens and communities' and 'are necessary to maintain public values, and the fair and impartial exercise of power, enable an orderly and peaceful society, protect the rights of individuals and communities, and promote the proper management of resources and the development of the economy'.[75]

This is a broader set of functions than perhaps generally recognized. In the dominant tradition of liberal constitutional thought, which draws primarily on American constitutional scholarship, the primary function of a constitution is usually understood to be the protection of the rights of minorities and individuals against the tyranny of the majority. A constitution, according to this understanding, exists principally if not exclusively to put limits on power. These limits may be both substantive (what can be done) and procedural (how it may be done).

Protecting human rights is certainly an important function of a written constitution. It would be inconceivable to adopt a democratic constitution today without including at least some basic rights which the constitution seeks to recognize and guarantee. However, the protection of rights is not the only – or even perhaps the most important – function of a written constitution. Rather, the primary purpose of a constitution is to institute legitimate public authority. A constitution con-stitutes ('puts together') the state. It generates public authority by connecting the exercise of political power to some foundational point of principle that is widely accepted as legitimate. In a democratic constitution, this means that it connects the political power of parties, movements, campaigns and social groups to legitimate public authority through rules and procedures of representative and responsible government.

[vi] These are: (a) affirming common values and identities without which there cannot be a political community; (b) prescribing rules to determine membership of that community; (c) promising physical and emotional security by state monopolization, for legitimate purposes, of the use of force; (d) agreeing on the ways in which and the institutions through which state power is to be exercised; (e) providing for the participation of citizens in affairs of the state, particularly through elections, and other forms of social action; (f) protecting rights (which empower citizens as well as limit state action; (g) establishing rules for peaceful changes in government; (h) ensuring predictability of state action and security of private transactions through the legal system; (i) establishing procedures for dispute settlement; and (j) providing clear and consensual procedures for change of these fundamental arrangements. (Ghai, 2010, 'Chimera of Constitutionalism').

The constitution provides the procedural certainty that tells us who at any time is authorized to govern, what powers they are supposed to exercise, how they are supposed to behave, and how they might be removed or held accountable. These are the common ground rules of civic and political life, which help us to avoid the chaos and uncertainty that would otherwise result from unconstituted power. We see the dismal results of unconstituted power in revolutionary situations, where no one knows what the rules are anymore; the absence of shared rules leaves nothing but the jostling of particular persons until either an new constitutional order is arrived at or – more often – a tyranny is established. In a constitutional democracy, the constitution enables the 'abstraction' of power, out of the hands of particular persons and into the hands of stable public authorities.[76] It maintains, through these shared rules and the predictability they create, the 'publicness' of the state – as a *res publica* that is the common property of all its citizens.

A written constitution is an insurance mechanism that helps secure 'losers' consent' to electoral outcomes. Even those who are disappointed in an election result can be satisfied with the legitimacy of the process; they can dislike the Prime Minister, or disagree with government policy, but still recognize the legitimacy of the constitution on which public authority rests. A party can win an election and govern, but because it is bound by a constitution that it cannot unilaterally change, the losers of the election do not need to fear that all is lost. Everyone gets another chance in four or five years. In the meantime, the essence and fundamentals of the political system are safeguarded. No matter who wins an election, they cannot permanently entrench themselves in power. The government in a well-constituted state cannot undermine the civil liberties that a free and democratic society needs. Opposition parties and civil society groups will operate freely, the media will not be muffled, and elections will not be rigged; judges will not be arbitrarily dismissed, the civil service will not be turned into a network of private patronage, and minorities will not be discriminated against. These things are ensured by a written constitution that is out of the reach of ordinary governing majorities. This takes some of the life-and-death conflict out of politics. Everyone can relax a little bit. Election results still matter (this is not an argument for the depoliticization of inherently political policy issues), but the losing side can take comfort in the fact that the winners get only a lease of power, and not the freehold.

In the same way, Westminster Model constitutions typically offer the losers important 'consolation prizes'. These strengthen the legitimacy of the political system as a whole: in a federal system, for example, one party might be out of office at the national level, but still have strongholds of power at the state or provincial level. Most give the Leader of the Opposition certain constitutionally protected powers and privileges. A written constitution can also carve out areas of protection for demographic minorities (whether defined by language, religion, or geography), who could otherwise be permanently outvoted, excluded and even persecuted.

On this latter point, we have looped back to rights, but with an important difference in emphasis from that of liberal theorists. The minority rights being protected are not 'pre-political' rights that must be carved out of the public sphere; they are *citizens' rights* that ensure broader inclusion in, and so promote the legitimacy and effectiveness of, a democratic state.

Finally, it is worth mentioning that written constitutions also vary in their ambitions. Some are relatively 'thin', liberal-procedural frameworks that confine themselves to systems of government and fundamental rights; others proclaim 'thick' covenantal commitments to common values, identities or objectives, with more focus on the nation building, identity-proclaiming, or values-forming, aspects of constitutionalism.[77] Some constitutions promote radical transformation of society, others seek to preserve and protect existing institutions.[78]

The constitution of Burke and Paine

The debate between Edmund Burke and Thomas Paine at the end of the 18th century was both the first sustained critique of the Hanoverian settlement and the first systematic defence of it to be argued out in front of the reading public. Burke's *Reflections on the Revolution in France*, first published in 1790 when he was Member of Parliament for Malton, is an articulate defence of the Hanoverian settlement. The vices of the British system as identified by radical reformers of that time are all turned by Burke's eloquence into virtues: the monarchy, House of Lords, established Church, unreformed electoral system, and of course the lack of a written constitution.

Thomas Paine, in his *Rights of Man* (1791–2), burst through this eloquence with honest plain-speaking. In a still unsurpassed critique of the Hanoverian settlement, Paine developed a democratic theory of constitutionalism, based on a strong notion of popular sovereignty.

Popular sovereignty did not require direct public control over all acts of government, but it did require the people to frame a written (supreme and fundamental law) constitution by which the acts of the public authorities would be authorized and legitimated. The people could act through representation, but had to do so expressly, under the terms of a written constitution that would bind those in power to the terms and conditions set out by the people.

Paine argued that, 'A constitution is not a thing in name only, but in fact. It has not an ideal, but a real existence; and wherever it cannot be produced in a visible form, there is none.'[79] He insisted that the 'constitution is a thing *antecedent* to a government, and a government is only the creature of a constitution'.[80] This led him to conclude that 'though it has been so much talked about, no such thing as a [British] constitution exists, or ever did exist'; 'the whole is merely a form of government without a Constitution, and constituting itself with what powers it pleases'.[81] The absence of such a constitution made the Hanoverian settlement not only defective, but illegitimate, for 'Government without a constitution, is power without a right'.[82]

Paine approved of revolutionary France's democratic root-and-branch approach to constitution-building in the period immediately following the 1789 revolution: electing a constituent assembly in the name of the sovereign people, drafting a constitution in public based on reasoned arguments, and solemnly adopting it as the foundational law of the new regime. Burke, in contrast, was horrified by France's violent overthrow not only of royal absolutism, but also of the aristocracy, the church, provincial and local particularities, and all established laws and institutions. The English had had revolutions in the past – to restore historical rights or to reform a corrupt but ancient form of government; the French had the frightful audacity to go further – to build up a new state, and with it a new social order, upon a new and rational foundations. Burke saw this as a monstrous threat to all that was settled and safe. What terrors might await if such a constituent power were unleashed in Britain?

Paine's arguments sound just as fresh, as radical, and as unsettling to the established order, today as they did in the 1790s. Echoes of Tom Paine's popular constitutionalism have been recently voiced by Professor Jeff King in his 'democratic case' for a written constitution.[83] King's argument is not that constitutions protect rights otherwise at the mercy of parliamentary majorities, or that they provide procedural clarity in place of a pot-mess of conventions, but that they are democratic instruments by which the people can author the rules by which they are governed. No doubt Paine would have approved. The idea of a written constitution based on popular sovereignty has also had some traction in the wider community of Westminster Model democracies; the constitutions of Australia and Ireland, which can only be amended by a direct act of popular sovereignty expressed in a referendum, are close to Paine's ideal. Yet Paine's contribution to both theory and practice remains largely unacknowledged. Like the Levellers who foreshadowed him, he has been relegated in Britain to the minor canon of English political writers.[vii]

Burke, with the whole force of the establishment on his side, won the battle for the public mind. His *Reflections* became a canonical text not only of constitutional conservatism, but of English (and to a much lesser extent, British) constitutional thought across the board. With its scepticism of abstract concepts written on parchment, and a preference for the gradual evolution of historical institutions rooted in the Crown, Parliament and the common law, it continues to shape prevailing English assumptions about the constitutions to this day.[viii]

Burke's arguments could, however, be turned on their head and deployed in favour of a written constitution. If, as Burke asserts, a state is a generation-spanning association of those who were, those who are, and those who are yet to come, then the current parliamentary majority should not be able to make easy or unilateral changes to the fundamentals. The achievements of ages should not depend on the outcome of one election, nor on the goodwill of the government of the day. Parliamentary sovereignty allows the incumbent majority to change all constitutional laws, destroy all institutions, and uproot all rights, according to the arbitrary, fleeting, capricious will of those currently in power. It leaves nothing settled but throws everything into perpetual doubt and precariousness. A written constitution – with a more or less rigid amending formula – is therefore to be accepted as a means of protecting historically achieved liberties and evolved institutions from wayward governing majorities.

This 'neo-Burkean' argument for a written constitution therefore confronts head-on the main argument against a written constitution advanced by contemporary theorists of parliamentary sovereignty such as Richard Bellamy.[84] Bellamy argues from the abstract political equality of each individual citizen that the *status quo* should not be privileged over any alternative proposal. Constitutional entrenchment means minorities may restrain the power of the majority, and the decisions of the past may procedurally constrain those of the present.

[vii] Paine is still sometimes portrayed as a mere 'pamphleteer', rather than as one of the finest constitutional theorists of the 18th century, just because he wrote for a popular audience.

[viii] In 2002, Professor Neil MacCormick argued that support for a written constitution had become 'part of the common stock of constitutional thought in Scotland today'. W.E. Bulmer (2011) 'An Analysis of the Scottish National Party's Draft Constitution for Scotland', *Parliamentary Affairs*, 64(4), pp 674–93.

This, so it is argued, gives the vote or opinion of the one who is in the majority less weight than the one who is in the minority (living or dead). Bellamy insists that the only way in which such formal political equality can be maintained is to allow everything to be decided by ordinary Acts of Parliament. Jeff King accepts much of the premise of Bellamy's argument, even while altering the conclusion. He frames his proposed amendment rule (which relies on majoritarian decisions in a referendum, without minority vetoes or any kind of super-majority mechanism) and his provision on the periodic renovation of the constitution on the principle that the current majority, not historical legacy, is the basis of legitimacy.[85]

A neo-Burkean case for a written constitution would be suspicious of such an abstract understanding of political equality. Much more important is the protection of the essentials and fundamentals from manipulation and abuse by those currently in power. This does not mean political equality is rejected, but it is reframed as the equal right of all to a share in their common inheritance of constitutional rights as members of the polity. From this perspective, a relatively rigid written constitution is necessary to prevent the valuable deposit of freedom, democracy and good government, built up over centuries of experience, from being despoiled by braying populist authoritarians.

The neo-Burkean case for a written constitution is not an argument for utopian constitution-making, speculative experimentation or stylistic modernizing. It is specifically an argument for a Westminster Model constitution that is in accordance with British (although not perhaps narrowly or insularly British) constitutional traditions. Westminster Model constitutions owe little or nothing to French revolutionary thought. They are not blueprints for an imagined society; rather, they are practical and pragmatic documents, which attempt to give expression, in a particular context, to well-proven institutions and principles. This makes them very different creatures from the highly innovative French Constitution of 1791 to which Burke objected. If Burke had been aware of the Westminster Model constitutions of the middle decades of the 20th century, he might well have praised them, in the language of his famous speech on reconciliation with the American colonies, as being 'devoted not only devoted to liberty, but to liberty according to English ideas and on English principles'.[86]

In so far as Burke recognized the need for a state to change in order to conserve, a neo-Burkean justification for a written constitution need not be limited to merely codifying and entrenching existing practices. Reform of the electoral system, reform of the second chamber, a bill of rights, and other ameliorative reforms, which have already been applied in other Westminster Model constitutions, and which are tried and tested, are compatible with a neo-Burkean approach. To adopt a Westminster Model written constitution is to restore, reaffirm and retain all that is best in our constitutional heritage through a reformative refoundation.

The purpose of the foregoing is to advocate neither for the conservatism of Burke nor the radicalism of Paine. It is rather to show that these two giants are not, perhaps, as mutually opposed as they might at first appear. One can support a written constitution on the grounds of Tom Paine – that on point of democratic principle the people should be the authors of the overarching rules by which they are governed. One can also support a written constitution on the grounds of Edmund Burke – that some things are just too import, too fundamental and too valuable to be placed at the delicate mercies of an ordinary parliamentary majority. There may be differences of emphasis, which may give rise to some different preferences in terms of the content of the constitution, but in practical terms both views can elide into one unifying position: that the essentials should be written in a supreme and fundamental law so that they are not dependent on the whims of an ordinary majority in a sovereign Parliament.

4

Some Objections Answered

Failure of constitutional regimes

It is sometimes still argued, against written constitutions, that they are neither a necessary nor a sufficient constitution for a flourishing democratic state. This argument points to the many cases where seemingly well-intentioned democratic written constitutions have failed, being unable to contain or withstand the forces of oligarchy, reaction or authoritarian populism.

The most notorious example of such a failed constitution is the German Constitution of 1919, which ultimately could not save the Weimar Republic from Hitler and Nazi tyranny. Moreover, inter-war Germany was not an isolated example of constitutional failure. Many of the European constitutions of that era suffered a similar fate. The Polish Constitution of 1921 – a parliamentary constitution modelled on that of the French Third Republic – failed to provide a stable foundation for democracy and was replaced in 1935 by an authoritarian constitution concentrating power in the hands of the President.[87] Romania's Constitution of 1923, a liberal-democratic constitution on Belgian lines, suffered a similar fate. After a relatively good beginning, it was unilaterally abrogated by a palace coup in 1938 and replaced with a reactionary authoritarian constitution.[88]

The record of written constitutions in the developing world after decolonization was also patchy. Carefully drafted and decently democratic Westminster Model constitutions in Burma, Ghana, the Gambia, Kenya, Malawi, Nigeria, Sierra Leone, and many other developing nations were either undermined by authoritarian amendments that gutted them of their checks and balances (as in Kenya during the period from 1963 to 1967) or swept aside in military coups (as in Burma in 1962 and Nigeria in 1966). As Yash-Pal Ghai, put it:

The record of these new constitutions is uneven, but on the whole not encouraging. They have not significantly changed state practices, corruption continues unabated and unpunished, political mobilisation and voting are still based on ethnicity, robust judiciaries or independent prosecutorial policies have not emerged. The rich get richer and poor, poorer. Armed forces defy public accountability, and do the bidding of the executive. In general, as we know, a constitution is not a self-operating or self-executing instrument.[89]

It would be easy for a British scholar writing in the 1960s, to conclude that 'paper constitutions' are either irrelevant pieces of confetti that can be easily ignored or pernicious fraudulent charades.

However, this interpretation misses out important parts of the story. Firstly, it ignores those cases where a constitution did succeed, directly or indirectly, in restraining abuses of political power, maintaining the regularity of competitive elections, and preserving institutional stability. Some Commonwealth countries – like Jamaica and Malta – had bitterly divided and polarized politics which, in the absence of the undergirding common framework of a written constitution, could easily have resulted in a breakdown in democracy. In Malta, the crisis – which had resulted in disturbances, an opposition boycott of Parliament, and outbreaks of political violence including the burning down of newspaper offices – was ultimately solved by amending the constitution. Because the amendment required a two-thirds majority in Parliament, it had to be the result of negotiated compromise between the two main parties. Because the constitution was the supreme and fundamental law, and could not be overturned by ordinary legislation, both sides knew that the other would be bound by the bargain. Parliamentary sovereignty in its simple form, which could have seen any decision reversed by the next government, could not do this.

Much the same could be said of India during and after the Emergency of 1975 to 1977. Its constitution, and in particular the willingness of the Supreme Court to defend the 'basic structure' of the constitution against wrecking amendments,[90] ultimately saved Indian democracy. Mere parliamentary sovereignty could not have done so.

When trust is low, and fellow-feeling weak, a shared commitment to common rules, even if it is merely a matter of mutual convenience (that is, each side has more to lose by suspending the rules than it has to gain), can help a country to maintain its institutional integrity, and to get out of the crisis without a complete democratic breakdown. The fact that liberal-democracy sometimes fails despite the presence of a seemingly adequate written constitution does not negate the case for having such a constitution – no more than the fact that cars sometimes crash negates the need for brakes.

Secondly, the story ignores *how* written constitutions prevent authoritarianism. The naïve view that mere words on the page will protect liberty is of course inadequate. It is not the words as such, but the deep consensus that those words represent, and the legitimacy with which that consensus is invested, that gives the constitutions their potency. Constitutions are worthy of respect because they embody the *quod semper, quod ubique, quod ab omnibus* of the polity: that which is most broadly accepted as the result of an inclusive constitution-building process or hallowed by general acceptance over time. For a government to violate or suspend a written constitution is therefore to place itself in a very vulnerable position, where even its supporters may question the legitimacy of the government's actions. The fact that it is written down and plain to see raises the stakes. It becomes harder to push the margins when those margins are hard, not soft (as they would be, if the constitution consisted merely of statutes and conventions, with no written supreme and fundamental law). To violate a written constitution is a highly visible, contentious act: it is a point of no-return for a would-be authoritarian regime. It crosses the Rubicon in a way that the incremental change of statutory powers or conventions does not.

The constitution also provides a common point of reference and a focal point of legitimacy around which opposition to authoritarianism can unite. Defence of the constitution is a powerful rallying cry. A written constitution ensures that the legal-political foundation of the government's authority to govern and the foundation of the right of opposition parties to organize, criticize, present alternatives and contest elections are one and the same. If a government tries to undo those protections, it not only unites all the opposition against it, but also undermines the source of its own legitimacy.

Changing (as opposed to violating, abrogating or suspending) a written constitution is also an intentionally complex process that contains checks on the power of the ruling majority. These may be popular checks (referendum, intervening general election) or counter-majoritarian checks (approval by super-majorities, sub-national legislatures), but either way they prevent the winners of one election from using their temporary majority status to change the fundamental rules. Incipient authoritarian rulers must do more than win a bare majority once. They must build a more or less broad and sustained majority if they are to change the constitution, and this gives the people an opportunity to vote them out, or to mobilize to thwart authoritarian ambitions before irreparable harm is done. It is true that this might not ultimately protect against deliberate, wilful, concerted attempts to destroy democracy – but it might, nevertheless, make these less likely to succeed, while protecting effectively against accidental, reckless, opportunist attacks.

Authoritarian constitutions

A second, and related criticism, is that written constitutions are found in authoritarian and even totalitarian regimes, as well as democratic ones. Sometimes, the constitution is unambiguously and unashamedly opposed to democratic norms. The current Fundamental Law of Saudi Arabia establishes an Islamic monarchy with no pretence of democracy. The constitution of Iraq during the Ba'ath regime established authoritarian rule by the President, who was leader of the Ba'ath party and chairman of the Revolutionary Command Council. The 1966 Constitution of Burundi created a one-party state and put all powers in the hands of the President, who was the leader the official party and 'elected' by the party congress.

Elsewhere, the constitution of an authoritarian or totalitarian state may look superficially democratic. The 1936 Constitution of the Soviet Union established a Parliament (the 'Supreme Soviet') consisting of two Houses, both popularly elected; these elected the 'presidium' (a sort of collective presidency) and a 'Council of People's Commissars' (or Cabinet) which was nominally responsible to the Supreme Soviet. It also boasted a catalogue of fundamental rights, including extensive social and economic rights. None of this prevented a concentration of power in Stalin's totalitarian regime of terror, nor did it stop brutal purges, show trials, the Ukrainian famine, or the inhuman horrors of the gulag system. Aside from the blatant violations of the rule of law and the use of the party, alongside the state, as a blunt instrument of power, the devil was in the details: there were 'free' elections, but only the Communist Party and affiliated organizations could nominate candidates; rights granted by the Soviet Constitution could be used only 'in conformity with the interests of the working people, and in order to strengthen the socialist system' (article 125), as defined by the Party.

Even in non-democratic regimes, however, constitutions perform a number of important functions. They might not reliably protect rights, but in so far as they establish formal rules for the allocation and transfer of powers, non-democratic constitutions are something more than just window-dressing.[91] Authoritarian regimes that wish to establish, legitimate and stabilize their powers may find a written constitution particularly beneficial: in Spain under Franco a set of 'Fundamental Laws' having a constitutional character was established, while in Chile a constitution was specifically drafted to reinforce the Pinochet regime.[92]

The point here is not that written constitutions are bad because authoritarians abuse them, or tailor them to their own needs. The same might be said for elections, bureaucracies, judiciaries, political parties, or indeed any other political institution. Rather, the conclusion to be drawn is that far from being mere pieces of confetti, constitutions actually matter. They matter enough, in practical legal ways as well as in symbolic-rhetorical ways, that even non-democrats want to be seen as having them for the legitimacy and practical benefits that they confer – just as they often want to be seen to have elections. The answer to non-democratic abuses of elections is not to reject elections as irrelevant, but to take steps to ensure they are free and fair. So likewise, the answer to non-democratic abuses of written constitutions is not to reject written constitutions, but to ensure these are properly and resiliently democratic in nature. It is not that a written constitution – regardless of its content – will automatically produce a better democracy, but the content of a written constitution matters.

Excessive rigidity and inability to adapt

Another frequently recited objection to a written constitution is that it precludes future changes. This can be framed as a matter of democratic legitimacy and intergenerational rights: What right have we to bind future generations – and what legitimacy does a constitution have when all those who voted for it or supported it at the time of its adoption have died, and those alive today have merely inherited it? Aside from these normative or theoretical arguments, the responsiveness and flexibility of unwritten constitutions are praised. The constitution, it is argued, should not lock in the wisdom, values or mores of today, while excluding those of tomorrow. At the same time, it should not undermine the ability of institutions to respond to new and unpredictable challenges.

Some Westminster Model constitutions do contain provisions prohibiting the amendment of certain parts of the constitution. As noted earlier, the Indian Supreme Court has developed the 'basic structure doctrine', prohibiting the amendment of the 'basic structure' of the constitution, as a form of constitutional defence against destructive changes. This principle has been ingrafted to the Constitution of

Bangladesh, which declares (article 7B) that provisions on fundamental principles and rights, as well as the 'basic structures of the Constitution', cannot be amended. Such prohibitions on amendment do give rise to the aforementioned difficulties of long-term democratic legitimacy, responsiveness and flexibility. These are not, however, an essential, or usual, feature of constitutions in general or of Westminster Model constitutionalism in particular.

With the exception of such 'eternity' or 'basic structure' provisions in a minority of cases, written constitutions are not set in stone. They are deliberately harder to change than ordinary laws, so that they cannot be easily, hurriedly or unilaterally amended by the government of the day or by an ordinary working parliamentary majority, but they are not impossible for future generations to amend, nor to adapt to changing circumstances. The constitutional amendment rules serve only to ensure that any changes are properly considered and broadly agreed.

In fact, constitutional amendment is relatively common in Westminster Model constitutions. The Indian Constitution is up to its 103rd amendment in 69 years, or on average just shy of one and a half amendments per year (in practice, amendments tend to come in batches). The Irish constitution has been amended 38 times in 82 years, or a rough average of one amendment every two years. Even the Australian Constitution – which is notoriously hard to change, has been amended eight times in 120 years.

It is the practice of some countries with written constitutions to undertake systematic reviews of its functioning, with a view to making recommendations for reform. Structured in general along the lines of a Royal Commission, these bodies take evidence, consider options and offer proposals for constitutional change. Examples include the Constitution Commission ('Wooding Commission') in Trinidad & Tobago (1971–74),[93] the Barbados Constitution Review Commission (1996–98),[94] and the Constitutional Review Group in Ireland (1995–96).[95]

While defending the amendability of written constitutions, it is necessary to push back a little against the prevailing assumption that openness to future change is a good thing. It is true that needs and times change – and a state must be able to change with them – but there are no grounds for belief that future generations will be wiser or better than past generations. Innovations can be bad as well as good, and new errors are as likely to arise as old ones are to be corrected. Moreover, just as in every generation there are reformers who seek to bring about changes for the public good, so there are people in every generation who would trample on the public good and reduce the *res publica* to a private fiefdom for the satisfaction of their own greed and ambition. Part of the duty of a written constitution is to 'hold fast to that which is good' and to secure our heritage against the incursions of charlatans, chancers and Caesars.

Judicial powers and the exclusion of democratic politics

Some scholars have criticized written constitutions for restricting the space for, and downgrading the importance of, democratic deliberation and contestation.[96] Written constitutions, according to this argument, seek to limit the scope and substance of democratic politics, excluding certain topics from democratic deliberation. Instead, they give that power to the courts. The democratic expression of the public opinion through Parliament is thereby subordinated to the judicial power and the opinions of judges who are unelected, unrepresentative and unaccountable.[97] It is argued on democratic grounds that decisions over the limits of rights ought not to be decided by judges, but by ordinary democratic politics.

This view misunderstands the role of the judiciary under a written constitution. It is of course true that an Act of Parliament that is contrary to a written (supreme and fundamental law) constitution, and that has not been passed in accordance with the rules for a constitutional amendment, is void, and that the duty of annulling it falls squarely on the courts. It would be a mistake, however, to see this as a threat to democracy. On the contrary, enforcement of these foundational rules by an impartial arbiter is a buttress to democracy. It ensures that no government can easily undermine the foundations of the democratic system.

Besides, authority lies not in the court, but in the constitutional rules themselves, of which the court is merely the implementer and enforcer. It would make as much sense to oppose a written constitution on the grounds of empowering the courts over parliamentary majorities as it would to oppose the Laws of Cricket for empowering umpires and not team captains. This is not to deny the discretion that apex courts have to exercise in their task of constitutional adjudication, but their decisions are not those of mere opinion or political will; they are the application of legal reasoning to particular cases that are brought before them for decision. Judges exercise such legal reasoning all the time in the interpretation and application of statutes; it is no great leap of the imagination to do the same in relation to a written constitution.

Faced with an apparent conflict or incompatibility between an ordinary Act of Parliament and the Constitution, the Constitution would prevail. In other words, the authority of the whole community of the realm, expressed through the Constitution, which represents the settled will of the people, prevails over the authority of Parliament expressed through an Act of Parliament that represents the decision of an ordinary majority. That which is enduring prevails over that which is ephemeral, and that which is general prevails over that which is particular. Democracy is not reduced to a series of life-or-death knife-edge decisions made by an unlimited and unconstrained sovereign power; it is, rather, a system of government resting on constitutional rules that are legitimated by the breadth and depth of public support.

Constitutions do not exclude these difficult or divisive moral issues from politics (that would be the case only if the constitution were immune from all change, which as we have seen is not the case). On the contrary, constitutional amendment procedures can require these issues to be given exactly the sort of democratic deliberation they require. Decisions that call for major constitutional change cannot be rammed through by narrow parliamentary majorities. They need a broader consensus to be built, which in turn requires the argument to be made in more open and inclusive forums: not merely between a minister and a group of senior civil servants, or between a handful of ministers in a cabinet committee, as is the case with ordinary policies, but in cross-party working groups, in constitutional review committees that include non-partisan experts and members of civil society, in public meetings, and in some cases by means of a citizens' assembly or referendum. The Constitution of Ireland's prohibitions on same-sex marriage, abortion and divorce, for example, did not prevent these issues from being publicly debated; they ensured extensive, and open, public debate, leading over time to a shift from a conservative Catholic consensus to a liberal secular one. These changes could not be imposed at will by any one party of government. They could only come about through a very open decision-making process with much wider public participation.

The rights constitutionally protected in Westminster Model constitutions – personal liberty, right to a fair trial, freedom of expression, freedom of association and assembly, freedom of religion, freedom from discrimination, freedom from slavery and freedom from torture – are the product of historical experience and of a particular tradition of liberty with its roots in the Magna Carta.[98] They should not be seen as abstract 'pre-political' rights existing in some imaginary natural state, but as broadly accepted foundations for a civil community in which citizens can pursue and discern the common good through democratic politics.

Crucially, these rights extend to all, including those who might not be able to make themselves effectively heard in democratic politics. Courts are not flawless by any means, but they do provide an additional forum in which those who have been ignored, excluded or discriminated against can find justice. To protect these rights, for minorities who might fall foul of majority prejudice, is to strengthen democracy by making it more egalitarian and more inclusive. In a democracy everyone, not just the popular majority, should have their say.

Moreover, while courts have an important role, they are not the only interpreters or enforcers of written constitutions. They are a complement to, not a substitute for, democratic legislatures in the protection of a free and decent society. When legislating on rights issues, parliamentarians may refer to the constitution and can apply their own interpretation to it. Having a written constitution, rather than a vague, nebulous unwritten one, empowers Parliament – and particularly Opposition parties and backbench members – to perform this role of ensuring constitutional compliance. Likewise, ministers can be required to perform a pre-legislative check, and to satisfy themselves that a bill is compatible with the constitution before introducing it. The court serves as an additional defence for the constitution and for the fundamental rights that it protects. If the apex court disagrees with Parliament's interpretation of the constitution, then that of the court prevails. However, this does not end the dialogue between the courts and Parliament. If a judicial decision is contrary to the broad consensus of public opinion, then Parliament can, following the correct procedures, and with the necessary super-majority, make amendments to the constitution.

An example of this dialogic relationship between the courts and Parliament is provided by the debate on the death penalty in the Commonwealth Caribbean. Most of the Commonwealth Caribbean countries adopted on independence written constitutions with bills of rights based on the European Convention, which in its original form did not expressly forbid the death penalty, but did prohibit 'torture or inhuman or degrading punishment or other such treatment'. This had consequences for the application of the death penalty. In the landmark case of *Pratt & Morgan v AG for Jamaica* [1993] the Judicial Committee of the Privy Council, Jamaica's highest appellate court, interpreted this as prohibiting long delays on death row. In 2002, the Judicial Committee of the Privy Council went further, holding in a series of three cases from several Commonwealth Caribbean countries that the death penalty was itself unconstitutional.[99] This decision represented a gulf, in the interpretation of constitutional rights, between the ethical assumptions of the judges (who happened to be in London) and the people of Jamaica – where according to a 2002 report by Amnesty International, the death penalty remained a popular and democratically legitimate, if constitutionally doubtful, form of punishment.[100] Seven years later, the Jamaican constitution was amended to overturn these decisions. The revised Jamaican Charter of Fundament Rights and Freedoms expanded a number of rights, but it specifically endorsed the death penalty as one that could lawfully be imposed. This revised Charter was proposed by a Constitutional Commission that had been established by Parliament and that had consulted with the public before making its recommendations. Those recommendations had been considered by a joint select committee of both Houses, before being passed by a constitutional amendment formula requiring a two-thirds majority vote in both Houses. Ultimately, the Judicial Committee of the Privy Council did not thwart democracy, nor did it in the end decide policy. It merely required a delicate question of rights to be settled by broader deliberation at the constitutional level.

Jamaica's experience also demonstrates the value of specificity. If the constitutional rules are tightly drafted – as they have been in Jamaica, with regard to the death penalty, since the 2011 amendments – then there is less scope for judicial interpretation. If we are concerned about the democratic legitimacy of allowing the judges to determine controversial issues like the death penalty (or abortion, euthanasia, same-sex marriage) then the constitution can be drafted to explicitly address those issues. This means either coming down on one side or the other of an issue, where there is a sufficient consensus to do so, or else, where there is no such consensus, expressly leaving it for Parliament to decide. No such consensus could be reached, in relation to the death penalty, in the drafting of the South African constitution, which did ultimately rely on a judicial decision to prohibit the death penalty. Nevertheless, it is to be hoped and expected that in the United Kingdom a consensus for prohibition of the death penalty – in accordance with Protocols No. 6 and 13 of the European Convention on Human Rights – could be reached.

In any case, more powerful judiciaries are in practice the least of our worries. The threat to freedom, democracy and human rights comes not from activism on the judicial bench, but from authoritarian leaders who would promote a pastiche version of democracy – a crass populism that claims to speak for the majority while ignoring due process and checks and balances.[101] The theoretical arguments advanced by 'political constitutionalists' against judicial power fall in the face of this reality. Courts can and do protect democracy, which is why would-be authoritarians invariably aim to undermine them in the pursuit of power.

One recent Commonwealth example is provided by Sri Lanka, where on 26 October 2018 President Sirisena arbitrarily dismissed Prime Minister Ranil Wickremesinghe and appointed Mahinda Rajapaksa instead, contrary to the normal rules of parliamentary democracy. When Parliament refused to give Rajapaksa a vote of confidence, Sirisena dissolved Parliament. The Centre for Policy Alternatives, a pro-democracy civil society organization, brought challenge to the Supreme Court of Sri Lanka. On 13 December, the Supreme Court ruled that Sirisena's actions were unconstitutional. In this case, the Supreme Court defended constitutional democracy, not by protecting human rights, but by upholding the correct democratic process, and not on its own, but in concert with Parliament and civil society.[102]

As the Sri Lankan example shows, strong judiciaries enforcing written constitutions can actually enhance, not diminish, democratic processes and participation. The 'legal constitution' is not supposed to be in opposition to, or be a replacement for, the 'political constitution'. Many of the arguments of the 'political constitutionalists', in so far as they seek to promote the importance of democratic politics and not keep constitutions shut up in the private world of lawyers and judges, are valid. They are simply mistaken in seeing a written constitution as an impediment to, rather than as the foundation and guarantee, for such democratic politics.

Practical objections need not worry us either. British judges at the highest levels have long experience in the interpretation and enforcement of written constitutions. The Judicial Committee of the Privy Council, which consists for the most part of senior British judges and sits in London, was the final court of appeal throughout the Empire and Commonwealth, and remains the apex court for many independent Commonwealth countries. Why is it that it is perfectly possible for the same judge to apply a written constitution in Grenada, Jamaica, Trinidad & Tobago, or any number of other countries that have or had appeals to the Privy Council, but then to be incapable of applying a written constitution for the United Kingdom? There is no reason in theory or practice why it should be acceptable for British judges to have this power in relation to Saint Lucia or Tuvalu, but not in relation to England and Wales.

Protecting bourgeois interests

There is a school of thought that criticizes written constitutions as bourgeois instruments for the protection of private property. Written constitutions, so it is claimed, limit the extent to which democracy is able to restrict private capital and stop political democracy from bringing about social and economic democracy. This argument is not without justification. There are written constitutions that do, indeed, protect plutocratic interests. This criticism has long been levelled – and fairly so – against the United States constitution, which according to Charles Beard's 1913 book *An Economic Interpretation of the Constitution of the United States*, was devised by oligarchic property-owners and creditors seeking to protect their economic interests.[103] In more recent times, the 1980 Constitution of Chile was put in place by the Pinochet regime to constitutionally ring-fence Chicago School neoliberal policies from democratic challenge.[104]

That is, however, far from the whole story. Roberto Gargarella identifies, in addition to the dominant liberal-conservative strains of constitutionalism, a radical constitutionalism that seeks to use the constitution to transform social and economic relations though the power of a democratic state.[105] Soviet-influenced constitutions are fascinating in this regard: the 1947 Constitution of Bulgaria, to cite one typical example, made a constitutional commitment to a planned socialist economy.[i]

Most Westminster Model constitutions, past and present, are effectively neutral on social and economic questions. Their founders took the view that the role of the constitution is not to prescribe outcomes or constrain policy decisions, but only to ensure that decisions are made within a democratically inclusive and accountable framework. Such constitutions have enabled left-leaning Prime Ministers (like Michael Mannley in Jamaica and Dom Mintoff in Malta) to pursue their economic and domestic policies within a constitutional framework. Right-leaning governments have done likewise.

On the other hand, some modern Westminster Model constitutions include socio-economic rights, directive principles, or references to

---

[i] 'All state, co-operative, and private economic activity is directed by the State by means of a general economic plan with a view to the most rational development of the country's national economy and the promotion of the public welfare.' Constitution of the People's Republic of Bulgaria, 1947, Article 12.

the public provision of certain social goods. This will be discussed further in Chapter 6, but the examples of Australia, Ireland and Fiji will illustrate the present point. Australian's constitution was amended in 1946 to give the federal Parliament authority to legislate for 'provision of maternity allowances, widows' pensions, child endowment, unemployment, pharmaceutical, sickness and hospital benefits, medical and dental services, benefits to students and family allowances'. This does not create a *right* to any such provision, but it does establish a constitutional and political *expectation* that the federal government will act in these areas. The Constitution of Ireland – albeit in a non-enforceable Directive Principle – requires the state to direct its policy to ensuring 'That the ownership and control of the material resources of the community may be so distributed among private individuals and the various classes as best to subserve the common good.' The Constitution of Fiji (sections 33 to 38) obliges the state to 'take reasonable measures within its available resources to achieve the progressive realization of the right' to a just minimum wage, public transport, housing and sanitation, food and water, social security and healthcare.

One may argue about the effectiveness of such provisions, but there can be no doubt that constitutions such as these envisage an active state, able to intervene in the economy and to promote the common good. It is not therefore a question of having a written constitution or not, but of what goes into the constitution. There are neoliberal oligarchic constitutions, just as there are autocratic constitutions, but a constitution of that type is not being proposed.

Incompleteness of a written constitution

It is said that no written constitution can provide for everything and that there will always be a gap between the 'constitutional order' and the 'constitutional text' to be filled by custom and convention. This point may readily be conceded. What cannot be conceded, however, is the argument that incompleteness renders the task of constitutional codification pointless.

One might point to the early dominion constitutions, whose authors were reluctant for reasons of deference to state the operating rules of parliamentary democracy in unambiguous terms, and see they make no mention of the office of Prime Minister, votes of no confidence, or the extent (if any) of the reserve power of the Governor-General in relation to matters such as dissolution of Parliament and the granting of royal assent. Comparativists for whom these constitutions are the only point of reference might therefore argue that a written constitution will not provide the greater clarity we seek.

That argument becomes substantially less convincing, however, when one examines the constitutions adopted after the Second World War. As will be discussed in Chapters 5 and 7, these 'second generation' constitutions do typically codify the main conventions of the constitution and seek to enact these as binding constitutional law. Even if gaps remain, they will be smaller and fewer than if no attempt at codification was made. Besides, it is not necessary for written constitutions to contain everything, so long as they contain those things that are essential and fundamental.

The Canadian constitutional scholar Philippe Lagassé classifies different elements of the constitutional order in Westminster Model constitutions, distinguishing 'conventions', 'practices', 'customs' and 'norms'.[106] According to Lagassé's definitions, a convention refers to 'what must be done, constitutionally'. An example of a convention is that the government should command the confidence of the elected House. A practice refers to 'what is currently being done'. An example of a practice is the Commons holding authorizing votes on military deployments, as happened in the invasion of Iraq in 2003 and attacks on Syria in 2013. This practice has arguably not hardened into a convention yet. A custom refers to 'what is traditionally done', such as the Crown not entering the House of Commons. Finally, norms refer to 'what one should do, morally' – for example, that ministers should act for the public interest and not for their own private benefit.

In Lagassé's terms, modern Westminster Model constitutions codify the conventions, and perhaps some of the most important practices of the constitution. Customs and norms may also be incorporated, but not normally to the same extent. Many Westminster Model Parliaments have a 'Black Rod' and a parliamentary mace, for example, but these details are rarely if ever constitutionally specified. Some constitutions, such as those of the Solomon Islands and Papua New Guinea, express norms about acting in the public interest, in the form of a 'Leadership Code', but many constitutions do not – leaving such things to ordinary laws, standing orders, codes of conduct, and the unwritten norms of civility, decency and integrity.

In any case, it should not be thought that a written constitution negates the need for custom, tradition, or other norms, whether written or unwritten. The purpose of the written constitution is not to supplant these things but to solidify and reinforce them, where they exist in a healthy condition, and to encourage their restoration where they have fallen into neglect.

Post-liberal and moral communitarian arguments

One strand of thinking particularly hostile to written constitutions, in an English (but rarely Scottish) context, is that advanced by the 'post-liberal' movement. Inspired by Anglo-Catholic and Radical Orthodox forms of Christian political theology, this movement rejects both the amoral individualism of the free market neoliberals and the amoral permissiveness of liberal social and sexual ethics. It joins the economic and fiscal policies of the old left with the social and cultural policies of the old right. While few in number, post-liberal thinkers have had an influence beyond their numbers, being associated – in 'Red Tory' and 'Blue Labour' guises – with both the main political parties.

The Red Tories might best be seen as English Jacobites, or as the intellectual, spiritual and aesthetic descendants of the Royalists and Cavaliers of the Civil Wars. Nostalgic utopians, they yearn back to a romanticized depiction of the English (not British) system of government as it stood at the Restoration. Their political 'beatific vision' is of a perpetual Oak Apple Day fete in a bustling Wessex village, with cakes and ale in the church hall under the kindly supervision of the Anglican priest and the Tory squire, who together exert a gentle, paternal rule, guarding the folkways of a merry, devout and deferential people. Naturally loyal to the Queen, the aristocracy, and the Church of England, the Red Tories admire all that is ancient, arcane and decorous about our institutions. They attach great importance to the notion that we live not in anything so vulgar as a 'democracy', but under a medieval 'mixed constitution' – governed not by representatives responsible to the people, but by the Estates of the Realm under God. In this timeless 'Village Green Preservation Society' ideal of England, there is no need for a written constitution. They put their trust instead in Magna Carta, the common law, the ancient traditions of Parliament, the parish vestry, and the Coronation Oath of a God-anointed monarch.[107]

Blue Labour also cherish a nostalgic ideal, but it is of post-war Britain. Their vision is of trestle tables, bedecked with bunting and union flags, in the middle of a street of terraced houses with well-scrubbed doorsteps. It is a scene of working class solidarity and moderate contentment. The institutions of the British state, with the Crown-in-Parliament at their apex, are an unquestioned source of loyalty, unity, national cohesion and social stability. Those same institutions, democratized by the Representation of the People Acts and Parliament Acts, are the instruments through which the people – under the leadership of a Labour government assisted by a competent civil service – can build their New Jerusalem: a Britain made great by the National Health Service, the National Coal Board, and plates of coronation chicken.

Both these versions of moral communitarianism are opposed to a written constitution. For Blue Labour a written constitution is an encumbrance, a betrayal and a distraction. It is an encumbrance, because they fear that a written constitution would bind and tie the hands of a Labour government in its plans for social and economic reform: 'Atlee could never have done what he did,' they say, 'if he'd had to govern under a written constitution'. It is a betrayal, because working people did not fight for the right to vote only to give their power away to unelected (and upper class) judges. It is a distraction, because constitutional change is seen as an issue that only motivates metropolitan liberals, in which ordinary working people are presumed to have little interest. Better, they say, to concentrate on bread-and-butter policies.

The first two of these Blue Labour objections have been dealt with in previous sections of this chapter; that they are still regularly circulated shows a simplistic, outdated and totally unrealistic understanding of how modern written constitutions actually work. On the third point, there are waiters in Kenya and taxi drivers in Fiji who have a very clear idea of what a written constitution is and does. They understand why the constitution matters and have a lot of passion for getting the constitution right. Working people fully understand that letting the people in charge make up the rules as they go along seldom has good results.

Red Tory hostility to written constitutions is ideological. Since the French revolution, there has been a latent but persistent fear among 'Crown and Church' High Tories that a written constitution must be based solely on godless Enlightenment ideas. Such a diabolical thing must lead, sooner or later, to the triumph of secular ideologies such as rationalism, logical positivism and utilitarianism, the sacking of the churches and a return to heathenism.

This need not be the case. Constitutional government is fully consistent with Christian political thought. Even during the Middle Ages, Christendom contained self-governing city-republics with elaborate constitutional systems, as well as kingdoms whose representative assemblies and fundamental rights were anchored in constitutional charters. The first article of the Magna Carta declares, 'the English Church shall be free, and shall have its rights undiminished, and its liberties unimpaired'.[108] The tradition of constitutionalism is older, and much more Christian, than Enlightenment liberalism would sometimes have us imagine.[ii]

From the perspective of Red Tory or Blue Labour cultural conservatives afraid of the twin assault on Christian civilization by extreme secularism and the rise of militant Islam, a written constitution might be welcomed as a protector of the rights of Christians – alongside everyone else – to live in freedom. Indeed, Christians above all – although not exclusively – should appreciate the ability of written constitutions to protect those who might otherwise be abandoned by majoritarian democratic politics: the poor, refugees, people with disabilities, ethnic minorities, prisoners and others who lack political clout. If there is concern that a progressive judiciary may turn ancient rights into instruments with which to attack the church or undermine Christian values, this may be prevented by careful drafting; specific exceptions or limitations may be provided, for example, to ensure that there is nothing in the constitution to prevent the public funding of church schools. The constitution could even – as discussed in Chapter 6 – retain some form of religious establishment, or at least a recognition of Christian values and ideals in its preamble.

The wider point is that it is possible to take seriously moral communitarian critiques of neoliberalism, in economic and social matters, without rejecting the principle of a written constitution. The objections raised to written constitutions can be inverted to make the case for a Westminster Model constitution. Such a constitution would not be an alien imposition, nor a product of French revolutionary thinking, nor a charter of amoral liberal individualism. It could express and reaffirm shared identities. It could uphold common moral standards and ethical norms, especially in respect of the behaviour of those in public office. It could protect historically hard-won rights from being eroded and encroached upon. It could even protect those things moral communitarians hold dear – not only in church–state relations, but also in the rights of the family, local autonomy, and a strong and capable, but responsible, executive. This might be regarded, if not as a Red Tory or Blue Labour position, then as Purple Whiggery.

[ii]   As Tom Holland has argued quite convincingly in *Dominion* (2019), the humane, democratic values that we regard as 'universal', and that are contained in such documents as the United Nations Universal Declaration on Human Rights, the European Convention of Human Rights, and the Commonwealth Charter, are, at the root and in essence, Christian values; the idea that they are universal is itself a product of a distinctly Christian form of universalism.

Impossibility of adopting a written constitution

The final argument against a written constitution is that it would be impossible to adopt. The argument goes something like this: the British Parliament is so sovereign that it cannot limit its own sovereignty. A constitution could only be adopted by an Act of Parliament, but, as a mere statute, it could be repealed or amended by any subsequent Act of Parliament.[109]

This argument has been challenged on at least two grounds. The first is that the sovereignty of Parliament may be limited through the use of so-called 'manner and form' provisions. The principle is that Parliament is sovereign but only exercises its sovereignty through Acts of Parliament; the requirements to enact an Act of Parliament are prescribed, or may at any rate by altered, by statute – as was done with the Parliament Acts 1911 and 1946. So one Parliament can by law determine the manner and form in which any future Parliament may enact laws.

These 'manner and form provisions' are most notably found in Australian state constitutions, where the ability of the state Parliament to enact certain types of constitutionally entrenched laws is constrained by the need for a super-majority in Parliament or a confirmatory referendum. A bill that is not passed in the appropriate manner and form (for example, passed by an ordinary majority when a super-majority is required) cannot receive royal assent, and so is no Act of Parliament at all.[110] In a British context, a Constitution Act passed by Parliament may require that any future amendment to that Act be passed in a specified manner (for example, by a two-thirds majority in both houses) and form (for example, being designated as an Constitutional Amendment in its title), and a bill not passed in that way could not be submitted for royal assent.

The other example of the British Parliament limiting its own sovereignty is in passing the various Independence Acts, by which it is declared that a territory either 'ceases to be part of Her Majesty's dominions' or that Her Majesty's government 'ceases to be responsible' for the government of that territory. Either of these formulations will be accompanied by a transfer of legislative power, providing that future Acts of the British Parliament would not apply to the territory (or, in the case of old dominions under the Statute of Westminster, that they would not apply without the consent of the dominion Parliament). In theory, the Westminster Parliament could repeal, for example, the Barbados Independence Act 1966, or, contrary to the provisions of that Act, attempt to legislate for Barbados. A British court would probably recognize that Act.[111] No Barbados court, however – presumably not even the Judicial Committee of the Privy Council in London, which for those purposes would apply the law of Barbados – would recognize the validity of such an Act. By granting independence, the former colonial constitutional order in which the Westminster Parliament could legislate for Barbados was extinguished. A new constitutional order, in which only the Parliament of Barbados can legislate for Barbados, and only to the extent permitted by the Constitution of Barbados, has come into being. There is no going back from that.[112]

Both 'manner and form' principles and the idea that 'sovereignty extinguished cannot be revived' could be applied to the adoption and entrenchment of a written constitution for the United Kingdom. Of the two, however, the idea of extinguished sovereignty is stronger, and perhaps the better analogy. The sovereignty of Parliament is a feature only of the current constitutional order. Once a written constitution is adopted as a supreme and fundamental law, Parliament ceases to be sovereign in the new constitutional order. It becomes what almost every other Parliament in the world – including most Westminster Model democracies – is: a legislature operating under, and constrained by, the higher law of the Constitution.

If the Parliament elected following the adoption of a written Constitution attempted to assert sovereign power, the courts would immediately restrain it. In case of any incompatibility between an Act of Parliament and the Constitution, the latter would prevail. In other words, the Constitutional Transition Act providing for the adoption of a written Constitution would be the final act of parliamentary sovereignty, by which parliamentary sovereignty is itself extinguished when a new constitutional order comes into effect. It is hard to imagine that the courts would have any difficulty in recognizing this change from one constitutional order to another.

5

The Westminster Model as a Constitutional Archetype

Defining the Westminster Model

Defining the Westminster Model is not easy. There is 'no rigid and idealised Westminster Model'; its 'malleable nature', 'ambiguous tenets', 'ever-present exceptions' and 'numerous mutations' make attempts to pin it down very difficult.[113] Part of the difficulty therefore lies in distinguishing the 'essential elements', defining the nature, character and identity of the Westminster Model, from the particular aspects of any national constitution at a given time.[114]

Arend Lijphart attempted to define the Westminster Model in terms of macro-level institutional design choices, such as the type of electoral system used, whether there is a strong second chamber, whether the state is federal or unitary, or whether there is a constitutionally entrenched and judicially enforceable set of fundamental rights.[115] In other words, he equates the Westminster system with a majoritarian understanding of democracy.

Lijphart's approach, while it might be useful for political scientists, is unhelpful for comparative constitutional scholars. Table 5.1 contrasts six constitutional systems – Australia, Barbados, Canada, India, Malta and New Zealand. As can be seen, there is considerable variety of design choice between them on issues such whether or not there is a written constitution, whether the state structure is federal or unity, the strength of judicial review, the electoral system, and bicameralism. None of these countries would be regarded as an unambiguously 'Westminster' system by Lijphart (Barbados, and New Zealand before the 1996 electoral reforms, are closest). Yet any useful definition of the Westminster Model as a global-imperial family of constitutional systems would have to include all of these countries.

Table 5.1: Examples of constitutional design variance in 'Westminster Model' systems

	Australia	Barbados	Canada	India	Malta	New Zealand
Head of State	Monarchy	Monarchy	Monarchy	Republic	Republic	Monarchy
Written (entrenched) constitution	Yes	Yes	Yes	Yes	Yes	No / Partial
State structure	Federal	Unitary	Federal	Federal	Unitary	Unitary
Judicially enforced bill of rights	No	Yes	Yes (with exceptions)	Yes	Yes	No
Electoral system (Lower / only house)	AV	FPTP	FPTP	FPTP	STV	MMP
Bicameralism	Strong	Weak	Weak	Medium	None	None

To avoid confusion, this book defines the Westminster Model as 'a parliamentary democracy in the British-imperial constitutional tradition'. This definition has two criteria, both of which must be satisfied for a country's political system to be regarded as belonging to the Westminster Model. First, it must be a parliamentary democracy. Second, it must belong to, or have been profoundly influenced by, the British-imperial constitutional tradition.

At the core of parliamentary democracy is a complex, multi-faceted relationship between the Head of State, the Prime Minister and Cabinet, the parliamentary majority, the Opposition, and the voting public. It is known as a 'parliamentary democracy' because the executive is politically responsible to Parliament, and Parliament has the final say both in legislation and government. It could, with no less accuracy, be described as system of 'cabinet government', because the Cabinet (subject to the ultimate control and sanction of Parliament) is the main centre of decision-making authority. It is also a system of 'responsible party government' because ministers are responsible for political decisions to Parliament, and through Parliament to the people, with political parties being the main instrument through which this relationship is mediated. These three ways of describing the Westminster Model, emphasizing the roles of Parliament, Cabinet and party respectively, capture the essential features of this system. In a summary of these arrangements, S.A. de Smith characterized the Westminster Model as:

a constitutional system in which the head of state is not the effective head of government; in which the effective head of government is a Prime Minister presiding over a cabinet composed of Ministers over whose appointment and removal he has at least a substantial measure of control; in which the effective executive branch of government is parliamentary in as much as Ministers must be members of the legislature; and in which Ministers are collectively and individually responsible to a freely elected and representative legislature.[116]

The second criterion is more nebulous. The British-imperial constitutional tradition, from a historical-institutional perspective, can be characterized by the 'norms, values and meanings' given to institutions and practices within that tradition; these are sustained by 'the legitimating expectations and historical customs that embody those political traditions and shape political behaviour'.[117] Some of these expectations, customs and traditions are, in more recent Westminster Model systems, expressed in constitutional form – for example, by the codification of the conventions of ministerial responsibility, or by the establishment of a public service commission to ensure the neutrality of the civil service. Other elements may be embodied in convention or practice, or in sub-constitutional rules such as Acts of Parliament, parliamentary standing orders, a Cabinet Manual, or codes of conduct.[118] It is this common cultural heritage, within wide but bounded institutional forms, that gives the Westminster Model its unity-in-diversity. Westminster Model constitutions around the world 'have developed and are developing independently in different ways', yet nevertheless 'share a British heritage' which continues to create expectations and to 'guide and justify behaviour'.[119]

The norms, traditions, values and practices that characterize the Westminster Model are those relating only to the political, legal and administrative institutions, not necessarily those prevailing in the wider society. As long as those official and institutional elements are maintained, the Westminster Model can take hold in a wide variety of religious, ethnic and linguistic contexts. In adapting to the circumstances of creed, culture and climate, 'the practices of Westminster systems have shown remarkable resilience'.[120] Common British institutional ancestry ensures that these systems 'retain a certain familial resemblance' while '[adapting] to the evolutionary pressures of different political and cultural environments'.[121]

Almost every democratic constitution in the world has been influenced by the British example to some extent or other, whether directly or indirectly. As Leslie Wolf-Philips noted, it is hard to be the world's leading maritime, commercial, technological, industrial and imperial power, for most of the period during which democratic institutions took root in the Western world, without a little of the reflected glory rubbing off on a country's political institutions.[122] However, not all British-influenced constitutions conform to the Westminster Model, failing either on the 'parliamentary democracy' test or the 'institutional culture' test.

The most notable example of a British-influenced constitution not part of the Westminster Model family is that of the United States of America. However, it is an oddity. It became independent from Great Britain while the British Empire was still in its infancy, and before parliamentary democracy had developed. There are, however, other examples of constitutions that have had more recent and more direct British-imperial influence, but which cannot be regarded as Westminster Model constitutions because they are not parliamentary in nature. The Donoughmore Constitution of Ceylon (1931 to 1947) was British-derived but was not a Westminster Model constitution because it lacked responsible cabinet government. Likewise, Kenya's institutional culture has undoubtedly been influenced by British models – its Parliament looks like something from Nairobi-on-Thames – but it soon abandoned the Westminster Model constitution under which it won independence and now has an unambiguously presidential system that owes far more to Washington than Westminster.

On the other hand, British influence spread further than the bounds of Empire. After the defeat of Napoleon at Waterloo, moderate sentiment in continental Europe looked for ways in which to build a new institutional stability that would preserve the gains of the French revolution (abolition of feudalism, restriction of church privileges, improved legal codes) while creating the conditions for an open, civil, commercial society (freedom of religion, expression, assembly and association). The British system seemed to offer a way of avoiding both reaction and revolution by combining monarchy with liberal parliamentary government. These ideas were embodied in the constitutions of France (1814, 1830), the Netherlands (1814, 1848), Portugal (1822, 1826), Belgium (1831), Spain (1837, 1845), and Piedmont-Sardinia (1848).[123]

Despite such imitation of British institutions, these continental European examples should not be regarded as Westminster Model constitutions; their Napoleonic legal, judicial and administrative institutions give them a character of their own. No Westminster Model constitution has anything quite answering to the French *conseil d'état* or the *préfet*, nor does any Westminster system expect members to leave their places and mount a tribune to address the House. These differences are revealed also in styles of constitutional drafting, which in turn reflect different starting assumptions: in countries once ruled by Napoleon, constitutions are based on abstract juristic principles; in those once ruled by Queen Victoria, they are based on historically evolved legal and political institutions.[124]

The development of Westminster Model constitutions

While the roots of what became the 'British constitution' go back to the Hanoverian settlement and further into medieval English history, the 'Westminster Model' is far newer. We can only really speak of Westminster Model constitutions appearing in the latter half of the 19th century, once parliamentary democracy began to flourish. 1867 – the year of the British North America Act, which sought to provide Canada with a 'constitution similar in principle to that of the United Kingdom' – is an obvious starting point, although 'responsible government' had already been granted to (pre-confederation) Canada in 1840 and to New Zealand in 1852. Even these 19th century examples are the exceptions. The majority of Westminster Model constitutions were adopted in the three decades after the Second World War.

Like other legal-political institutions, the Westminster Model has evolved to meet the needs of time and place. The process of constitutional transmission, borrowing and adaptation was not all one way. From the earliest days, the pupil has become the master. Very often, new 'constitutional technologies' (innovative constitutional rules, mechanisms or devices) that arose in a particular context to meet immediate political needs were thereafter adopted on their merits by other countries. Payment of Members of Parliament, for example – a demand of the Chartists designed to enable people without private incomes to enter Parliament – was first instituted in New South Wales in 1889, 22 years before the United Kingdom.[125]

Two countries stand out as particularly influential constitutional innovators: Ireland and India. Ireland, tentatively in 1922 and more fully in the constitution of 1937, combined the Westminster Model with judicially enforced fundamental rights. Ireland was also an early pioneer of directive principles, proportional representation, grafting an elected non-executive President to the parliamentary system, and the referendum. India adopted and adapted the British system, but it took it secondhand, via Dublin, nor directly from the source. From India, the Westminster Model was enhanced by new modes of flexibly centralized federalism and minority guarantees that were later adapted in Malaysia, Nigeria and elsewhere. We call it the Westminster Model, but the 'Dublin-Delhi Model' would probably be a fairer name.

In mapping this development, R.A.W. Rhodes and Patrick Weller distinguish between *transplanted* and *implanted* variants. Transplanted Westminster systems are those occurring in 'settler societies without prior local traditions other than indigenous cultures' – such as Australia, Canada and New Zealand; implanted Westminster systems occur where 'former colonies inherited British constitutional arrangements as part of decolonisation and winning independence' – such as India, Pakistan, Malaysia, Fiji and Papua New Guinea.[126] Similarly, Harshan Kumarasingham makes a distinction between 'New Westminsters', found in the old dominions, and 'Eastminsters' – found in the Indian subcontinent, where British-trained elites adapted British-derived institutions to different social, religious and cultural contexts.[127]

In terms of constitutional design, rather than socio–cultural context, the key differences are between 'first generation' and 'second generation' constitutions. If there must be a line to divide what was in reality a gradual evolution, perhaps the constitution of Ceylon (1947), or more decisively that of India (1950), is the point at which it should most properly be drawn.

First generation Westminster Model constitutions relied on what Glover and Hazell call 'political constitutionalism', with deference to Parliament and to convention.[128] They were characterized by the lack of judicially enforced fundamental rights, limited constitutional entrenchment (Australia is the notable exception), and a reluctance to codify the conventions of parliamentary government. As de Smith, noted, they continued to shroud parliamentary democracy in polite circumlocutions and deferential silences, since 'To bring strict law into accord with political reality, to make it plain that the Governor-General, like the Queen, has only a narrow range of limited discretions, to mention the Cabinet, the Prime Minister and other conventional institutions, would be un-conventional, indecorous, unacceptable.'[129]

Second generation constitutions are different in all these respects. They typically rely more on what Glover and Hazell call 'legal constitutionalism':[130] including judicially enforced fundamental rights, rigid rules for the amendment of the constitution, explicit codification of parliamentary conventions. Each of them 'has a written constitution, the more important provisions of which cannot be altered except by a special procedure requiring more than a bare legislative majority vote'.[131] They include 'a constitutionally entrenched bill of rights fortifying the basic rights and freedoms of the individual'.[132] The courts are empowered to conduct the judicial review of the constitutionality of legislation.[133]

Second generation Westminster Model constitutions typically codify the conventions of parliamentary democracy.[134] Codification was an innovation, in drafting technique if not in substance.[i] Dismissing the obfuscation of the older constitutions, de Smith was adamant about 'the advantages of being explicit'.[135] He favoured a clear statement of the rules. Given a choice between flexibility and certainty, certainty should prevail. Exact specification of the political rules in the constitution would avoid 'uncertainty not only as to what rules should be applied but also how in any particular case they should be applied'.[136] In writing down the conventions, the newer Westminster Model constitutions also adapted and refined them, making them different in some minor respects from the British archetype. The extent of this will become clearer in subsequent chapters, as the rules on government formation, dissolution of Parliament, royal assent, and so forth, are considered. Even so, de Smith argued that these rules were usually 'consonant with the principles of the British constitution' and many of them 'would be strong candidates for inclusion in a written constitution for Britain'.[137]

In particular, the role of the head of state or Governor-General was narrowly defined in these second-generation constitutions. De Smith supported this, arguing that 'residuary discretions which become exercisable in an atmosphere of political crisis inevitably expose the person who exercises them to partisan criticism'.[138] The danger of imprecision lay on both sides. On the one hand, 'the absence of definition may prevent an over-careful Governor-General from acting when he should'; on the other hand, 'it may enable an imprudent or over-zealous Governor-General to act where no reasonable ground for intervention exists'.[139]

---

[i]   The Status of the Union Act (South Africa) 1934 was an interesting missing link in the process of constitutional codification. This provided that the executive power was to be vested in the King acting through the Governor-General on the advice of his South African ministers, but it specifically marked out certain reserve powers (concerning the appointment and dismissal of the Prime Minister and the dissolution of Parliament) that the Act allowed to be exercised in at the Governor-General's discretion in accordance with constitutional conventions, but without stating explicitly what those conventions were. A similar approach was taken by the 1947 Constitution of Ceylon (S.4(2)).

Another feature of second-generation Westminster Model constitutions was greater reliance on independent 'neutral guardian' institutions.[140] As de Smith noted:

> Attempts may be made to screen sensitive areas of public administration from political control – the delimitation of electoral constituencies, the conduct of elections, the administration of justice, the process of prosecution, the civil service and the police, the audit of public accounts. The methods used for this purpose all involve the imposition of restrictions on legislative and executive competence.[141]

This was not entirely an innovation. As early as 1909, the South Africa Act provided for an Auditor-General, a Commission for the Delimitation of Electoral Divisions, and a Public Service Commission. Nevertheless, these institutions expanded from the post-war era, with New Commonwealth constitutions frequently including a Judicial Service Commission, Police Service Commission, and Electoral Commission. All these were intended to protect the proper and impartial functioning of the core democratic apparatus at arm's length from the government.

Various efforts were made, in second generation constitutions, to make the electoral system more inclusive of the diversity of society, and to ensure the adequate representation of minorities.[142] Occasionally – as in Ireland, Malta and Guyana – this meant abandoning First Past the Post in favour of proportional representation. Often the approach was more subtle. In Ceylon, Sir Ivor Jennings attempted to over-represent the Tamils by massaging the size and boundaries of constituencies.[143] In India, seats were reserved for Scheduled Castes and Tribes. In Mauritius, an ingenious system of ethnic balance was developed, with extra parliamentary seats being allocated to under-represented ethnic groups. As de Smith notes, 'Such contrivances are not necessarily incompatible with outright majority rule.'[144] The majority can still ultimately decide, but not without having heard and considered the minority.

Aside from its general functions in improving the quality of debate and the scrutiny of legislation, a second chamber might provide both an additional safeguard for minorities and opportunities for broader representation. The Caribbean Senates frequently reserve a share of seats for the Opposition, which (either alone or in combination with the independent 'cross bench' Senators) is able to block constitutional amendments. This veto power might also be extended to other types of legislation affecting the interests of particular communities. In the 1970 Constitution of Fiji, for example, one-third of the Senate seats were reserved for nominees of the Great Council of Chiefs, who had a power of veto over legislation concerning customary law and traditional land rights. Several other countries, besides Fiji, sought to represent traditional leaders in the legislature. In the Gambian constitution of 1965 constitution (Section 33), for example, four Members of Parliament were elected by chiefs.

While the old dominions acknowledged the Leader of the Opposition in parliamentary practice, the second generation constitutions – starting with Jamaica in 1962 – typically acknowledged '[t]he legitimacy of organised dissent' through the formal constitutional recognition of the Leader of the Opposition and entrusted the Leader of the Opposition with specific constitutional functions.[145]

Some second-generation Westminster Model constitutions were adopted in small and homogenous countries suited to unitary government. Many, however, have been adopted in large, diverse countries, in which demands for the constitutional decentralization of power have made themselves felt. A characteristic of such constitutions is therefore that, 'There may be a division of legislative and executive powers between central and regional authorities, each having an exclusive field of constitutional competence.'[146] In contrast to the primitive constitutional architecture of federalism in Australia and Canada, later examples – such as India, Malaya and Nigeria – developed more complex, nuanced and flexible federal systems.

A further distinction can be made between 'Westminster Export' and 'Westminster Influenced' constitutions. The Westminster Export constitutions are those formally adopted either by an Act of the British Parliament or by a British Order-in-Council. Their essential characteristic is that they were adopted before independence was granted, and indeed were often the instrument by which independence was attained; they were ultimately dependent upon the formal, and sometimes more than merely formal, approval of British authorities. 'Westminster Influenced' constitutions, by contrast, are adopted after independence. These were shaped, consciously and perhaps unconsciously, by the fact that national elites had an affinity and familiarity with British parliamentary, legal and administrative institutions, but they did not require formal legal sanction or political agreement from the British authorities.[ii]

[ii] By these definitions, some countries had 'Westminster Export' constitutions in the past, and now have 'Westminster Influenced' constitutions (having re-written their constitutions after independence in the pursuit of greater autochthony or to resolve issues that have arisen). One might regard, for example, the 1970 Constitution of Fiji as a 'Westminster-export' constitution, while the 2013 Constitution of Fiji is a 'Westminster-influenced' constitution.

Table 5.2: Typology of Westminster Model constitution

	Westminster Model constitutions			
	Westminster Export constitutions			Westminster Influenced constitutions
	Commonwealth			Non-Commonwealth
	Old Dominions (Transplanted)	New Commonwealth (Implanted)		
Extant	Canada (1867–) Australia (1901–)	Jamaica (1962–) Malta (1964–) Dominica (1982–) Fiji (1970–1987)	India (1950–) Pakistan (1956–) Bangladesh (1972–) Fiji (2013–)	Ireland (1937–)
Defunct	New Zealand (1852–1986) Union of South Africa (1909–61) Irish Free State (1921–37)	Ceylon (1947–72) Kenya (1963–67)	Sri Lanka (1972–78)	Burma (1947–61) Republic of South Africa (1961–83) Rhodesia (1965 70)

These typologies are shown in Table 5.2, with examples of extant and defunct constitutions in each category.

A Westminster Model constitution for today

As the previous sections have shown, the Westminster Model is capable – without sacrificing its general principles and practices – of being expressed in different ways, through different institutional forms, in different settings, responding to different needs. Far from being a fixed, static or hidebound system, the Westminster Model is able to incorporate major constitutional reforms. An unavoidable conclusion is that the system of government in the United Kingdom today is no longer a normal, standard, typical example of the Westminster Model. In the great family of Westminster Model democracies, Britain has become the oddball and the outlier.

There is an unfortunate tendency in British constitutional debates (in so far as they have any comparative dimension at all) to look mostly at the constitutions of the old dominions, with their first-generation constitutional technologies. This leads to some false conclusions about the possibilities of constitutional design for the United Kingdom, particularly when it comes to the codification of the conventions of parliamentarism.[iii] However, just as no one today would design a car by copying a Model T Ford – because technology has moved on – so no one today would design a British constitution by exclusive reference to first generation examples. The old dominion constitutions were important milestones in the development of the Westminster Model, and particular lessons might still be derived from them, but they cannot be regarded as examples of the Westminster Model in its mature form. When it comes to adopting a new constitution for the United Kingdom, we must look principally to the New Commonwealth, or second generation, examples.

Constitutional conservatives are therefore wrong to insist that the particular institutions and practices now found at Westminster have to be preserved in aspic. Their fear that any constitutional change – beyond the lightest tinkering – would undermine the principles and foundations of the Westminster system, and would lead us into an abyss of constitutional uncertainty, is misplaced. Radicals are equally misguided, if they insist that the Westminster Model must be thrown away, in favour of a continental import, or new-fangled and untried invention. A middle course is possible. The Westminster Model can be democratized and reformed – and, crucially, written down in codified supreme and fundamental law – without losing its essential character. To do just that – by the adoption of a second generation Westminster Model constitution – may be the only thing that can reinvigorate parliamentary democracy in the United Kingdom in the future.

Why limit ourselves to the Westminster Model?

Some may argue that the Westminster Model should not limit our constitutional imagination. Britain is, after all, a Northern European

---

[iii]   In a recent exchange with a respected professor of constitutional law at an English university, I was boldly told that a written constitution would do nothing to address uncertainties around the refusal of royal assent (then a live concern in relation to Yvette Cooper's bill to prevent a 'No Deal' Brexit) because 'Canada has a written Constitution and yet matters of royal assent are there still regulated by political conventions, which alone have rendered the provisions on reservation and disallowance inoperative'. In relation to Canada, this is of course true, but Canada does not have the last word in constitutional design. Had the professor been aware of the rules in the constitutions of Dominica (s.49(2)), Fiji (s.48), Malta (art.72(2)), the Solomon Islands (s.59(2)), or Saint Lucia (s.47(2)), he might have reached a different conclusion about the extent to which Westminster Model constitutions can – and actually do – provide clear and explicit codification.

country. Perhaps we should look as much to Norway, Sweden or the Netherlands, as to the Commonwealth. In the abstract, there might be some truth in that. Westminster Model democracies do not have a monopoly on good constitutional ideas. There is plenty to be learned from European countries. To give two small examples, the German mechanism of electing and removing the Chancellor by means of a 'constructive vote of no confidence', and the Dutch practice of requiring an intervening general election before passing a constitutional amendment, are worthy of study and – perhaps – emulation.

It is also fair to acknowledge that the development of the Westminster Model owes something to continental European innovations: Directive Principles were introduced into the Westminster Model tradition through Ireland and India, but ultimately have Spanish origins. German constructive votes of no confidence have made their way into the 2013 Constitution of Fiji. The workings of the Scottish Parliament, in particular in the expanded role of committees to initiate as well as scrutinize legislation, derive from Scandinavian practices.[147]

The aspect of the Westminster Model most open to justifiable criticism is its adversarial nature. The government is supposed to govern, and the Opposition is supposed to oppose. To use a cricketing analogy, only the government can make runs, but it is the Opposition's duty, by strong fielding, to put the minister at the crease under pressure, to stop the government hitting easy sixes, and occasionally to take a wicket in a dramatic parliamentary defeat. This way of doing politics encourages competition and confrontation over compromise, consensus and cooperation. Such thinking is nonsense to sensible nations like the Dutch and Swedes, who would rather sit down around the table work out a sensible solution to problems; they see politics as a dull but serious business, not as a sporting event, and all the circumstantial evidence seems to suggest they are better governed for it. One would not wish to remove the adversarial element completely – there is something to be said for giving the government the power to act with responsibility while the Opposition has the tools to hold them accountable – but there is a strong case for mitigating it, chiefly through proportional representation.[iv]

[iv] New Zealand, which adopted the Mixed Member Proportional electoral system in 1996, has found a good balance – mitigating the worst effects of adversarial politics without compromising effective government. It is worth considering that effectiveness should not be understood simply as the ability of the government to enforce *its* policy, but the ability of the state as a whole to deliver *good* policy.

Despite these concerns, drawing exclusively on Westminster Model constitutions for our examples and inspiration has a number of advantages. First, it challenges the assumption that adopting a written constitution in the United Kingdom would be technically difficult. It is not so often heard as it once was, but there are still some who take the view that the British system of government is just too wondrously complex, and its genius too nuanced and subtle, ever to be reduced to writing. Such views cannot survive the first encounter with the constitutions of the Bahamas or Barbados. It is in these constitutional texts – and many others like them – that one finds the Westminster Model in its essence, and in its mature form, codified in a single constitutional document. Any student wishing to better understand the Westminster Model is well advised to begin his or her studies by reading these constitutions. There is nothing mysterious to it. Whatever the political obstacles might be, from a legal-technical point of view there is, in Milton's words, a '*Readie and Easie Way*' clearly marked out.

Second, drawing on Westminster Model examples takes away much of the burden of having to invent. There is no shame in copying whole chunks of text from constitutions (indeed, many Westminster Model constitutions do just that), if what is being copied is sound. Unlike borrowing from foreign sources, these Westminster Model constitutions share not only similar underlying ideas and institutional arrangements, but also similar 'terms of art' and conventions of drafting, based on similar approaches to statutory interpretation. The United Kingdom would be what is sometimes known as a 'late adopter' of constitutional technology. We need not take leaps in the dark. The path, so long as we do not wander off it, is safe.

From the experience of the many other Westminster Model democracies that have already adopted written constitutions, many useful lessons can be learned, both in relation to the process of constitution-making and in terms of deciding upon the specific questions of constitutional design. With so many adaptations and variations of the Westminster Model around the world, we can find patterns, precedents, models, examples, inspirations and cautionary tales available to guide us through just about any proposed constitutional reform. S.A. de Smith noted that Commonwealth constitutions 'offer an impressive array of material to anyone who wishes to analyze the transplantation and adaptation of British institutions overseas', including such details as provisions governing the office of Speaker, parliamentary financial procedures, a novel rule in India, Malaysia and Nigeria giving ministers the right of audience in both Houses, and the Indian rule that prorogation does not cause Bills to lapse.[148]

In the same way, if we propose adopting a system of proportional representation for the House of Commons, we can look to Ireland, Malta, Fiji and New Zealand. For federalism, we can look to Australia, Canada, India and Malaysia for various models and examples. For a reformed second chamber, we can look to direct popular election in Australia, indirect election in India, Pakistan and South Africa, and nomination in Canada, Jamaica and Barbados. For an elected Head of State, we can look to Ireland, India, or Trinidad & Tobago. For limitations on the Crown prerogative and the transference of parliamentary conventions into clear constitutional rules, we can look to the Commonwealth Caribbean states or South Pacific countries like the Solomon Islands. For transformative socio-economic provisions we can look to the relatively weak 'Directive Principles' of India, Ireland and Malta or the stronger socio-economic rights found in the Constitution of Fiji. There are many permutations and possibilities. Decisions that might otherwise have to be made in a vacuum can be made, without reinventing the wheel, by drawing upon a stock of established constitutional designs.

Third, the Westminster Model is a guarantee of compatibility. An accepted wisdom of constitution-building is that each country's constitution must be an expression of its own history, needs and experience: a constitution must 'fit' – culturally, historically, ideologically, sociologically, and symbolically – the people for whom it is intended. There is what political scientists call a 'path dependency' behind most constitutional changes, whereby the range of future options is constrained by past choices. This is not to say that constitutions are fixed in time, that change is not possible, or that countries cannot learn from each other's experiences; only that things work better when they go with, not against, the historical and cultural grain.

Usually, this path dependency and sensitivity to context is interpreted to mean that we should avoid so-called 'boilerplate' constitutions with *prêt-à-porter* designs. Westminster Model constitutions have been criticized for attempting 'to reproduce, as closely as seemed expedient or possible' British institutions 'without sufficient regard for differences in the environment and in the functions which it is intended to perform'.[149] However, the same principle could also be applied the other way around. The record of Westminster Model constitutions, where they are willingly adopted and faithfully applied, is remarkably good, in part because they adhere to a shared constitutional tradition. The family resemblance between Westminster Model constitutions is close enough that they still, to a very large extent, form a coherent and mutually intelligible whole. There is an epistemic community of practice that enables people from Vancouver to Sydney, and from Port of Spain to Port Moresby, to literally speak the same constitutional, legal-political and institutional language. In a United Kingdom context, borrowing only from within the Westminster Model family would be the safest course of action. It would help us to ensure that the various parts of the constitution fit together, and avoid the culture shocks otherwise likely to result from constitutional reform.

Fourth, to seek a constitutional re-foundation within the framework of the Westminster Model is to embrace practical and pragmatic constitution-making, avoiding all that is utopian, speculative, unproven or outlandish. There is nothing pie-in-the-sky or 'Alice in Wonderland' about a Westminster Model constitution. It appeals to those who prefer practical to idealistic solutions. This does not rule out major institutional reforms (as we have seen, there are many Westminster Model constitutions around the world with all sorts of institutional adaptations and improvements grafted into the stem) but it does encase those reforms in a constitutional ethos that has a strongly practical and pragmatic orientation. Those who dismiss written constitutions as exercises in rhetoric and fancy will be disappointed when they encounter a typical Westminster Model constitution. Abstract ideas and high-blown phrases are notably absent. Except perhaps for a few heart-stirring sentiments in the preamble, they are full of dull practical, important stuff: how members of an Electoral Commission are to be appointed, the procedure by which judges can be removed, the mechanisms for delimiting parliamentary constituency boundaries, the rules governing the exercise of discretion by the Head of State in refusing dissolution to a Prime Minister who has lost the confidence of the House, the schedule of powers to be exercised by provincial legislatures.

Fifth, constitutions need broad public support across party lines. Support for a constitutional change, at least until recently, has been confined to the Whiggish-Radical centre-left of British politics. This includes the Liberal Democrats, the SNP and Plaid Cymru, the Green Party, and some parts (but rarely the bulk) of the Labour Party, as well as campaigning organizations such as Charter 88, Open Democracy, Democratic Audit, the Electoral Reform Society, and the IPPR. These are the ideological descendants of Roundheads, Levellers, Chartists and Suffragettes. They represent a democratic undercurrent in English (and later British) politics, which has never prevailed over the dominant Tory constitutional orthodoxy, but never been silenced by it either.

By focusing on the Westminster Model, we can see what a constitution looks like when devised according to British democratic principles, drafted by British civil service lawyers, and operated by those steeped in the best of British parliamentary, administrative and judicial practices. Adopting a Westminster Model constitution means that it is possible to have a modern written constitution, rooted in British historical experience, expressed in familiar legal and political idioms, and related to our own culture, identity and sense of nationhood. This might enable constitutional refoundation to go beyond its base of 'Guardian reading liberals' and to build a broader coalition of support that includes moderate conservatives. This is not just a tactical ploy. Constitutional change imposed without sufficient consensus is unlikely to endure, and can set up further problems for the future. By sticking to a Westminster Model constitution, there is hope that we can build a constitution that will both work and last.

6

Foundations, Principles, Rights and Religion

Principles and values

As prosaic and practical as a written constitution might be, it is still as much a moral document as a legal one. As well as being a charter of self-government, a constitution is a covenantal statement of identity, purpose and values. It proclaims the highest aspirations and deepest sentiments of the community, and affirms the common things that unite us as a *res publica* despite our many differences of party, ideology or interest.[150] The constitution reflects, in the words of Hassen Ebrahim, 'the soul of a nation'.[1]

Most Westminster Model constitutions are somewhat reticent about expressing these covenantal features. They maintain what Hannah Lerner describes as a 'liberal-procedural' constitutional order based upon democratic procedures, fundamental rights and guarantees to minorities.[151] They have little rhetorical or emotive content and do not make detailed commitments to any particular policy outcomes. Nevertheless, even the most prosaic liberal-procedural constitutions articulate some shared values, even if – in the absence of agreement about ultimate ends – these are 'thin' values, limited to a commitment to democratic process, to an open and pluralistic society, to basic universal human rights. These commitments may be implicit in the institutional structure; in the rules for the delimitation of constituencies, the constitution signals the value of equal representation; in the

---

[1] Hassen Ebrahim was a constitutional negotiator for the African National Congress in South Africa and chief executive officer of the Constitutional Assembly (1994–96). *The Soul of a Nation* is the title of his 1998 book.

composition of the Public Service Commission, it signals the value of a professional and non-partisan bureaucracy; in the rules for the appointment and tenure of judges, it signals the value attached to the rule of law.

Covenantal commitments can also be explicit. Many Westminster Model constitutions *declare* the country to be a democracy. This is usually dealt with either in the preamble or in the first section or article of the Constitution. For example, the Constitution of Antigua & Barbuda opens with the words, 'Antigua and Barbuda shall be a unitary sovereign democratic State' (Section 1). The Bahamas (Section 1) declares itself to be 'a sovereign democratic State'. Belize (Section 1) 'shall be a sovereign democratic State of Central America in the Caribbean region'. The Solomon Islands (Section 1), likewise 'shall be a sovereign democratic State'.

The preamble to the Constitution of Barbados refers to the country's history and its long parliamentary traditions going back to 1639. It celebrates the historic rights of Barbados and claims that Barbadians have 'not only successfully resisted any attempt to impugn or diminish those rights and privileges so confirmed, but have consistently enlarged and extended them'. The people of Barbados, through the preamble to their constitution, 'proclaim that they are a sovereign nation'. They 'acknowledge the supremacy of God' and 'the dignity of the human person'. They affirm 'their unshakeable faith in fundamental human rights and freedoms', insist upon their belief that 'freedom is founded upon respect for moral and spiritual values and the rule of law' and 'declare their intention to establish and maintain a society in which all persons may, to the full extent of their capacity, play a due part in the institutions of the national life'. They further 'resolve that the operation of the economic system shall promote the general welfare by the equitable distribution of the material resources of the community, by the human conditions under which all men shall labour'.

The preamble of the Constitution of the Solomon Islands sets out the basics of democratic governance in explicit terms, declaring that, 'all power in Solomon islands belongs to its people and is exercised on their behalf by the legislature, the executive and the judiciary established by this Constitution'. It commits the state to a system of government 'based on democratic principles of universal suffrage and the responsibility of executive authorities to elected assemblies'. In terms that are expressly covenantal, the people 'agree and pledge' to 'uphold the principles of equality, social justice, and the equitable distribution of incomes', to 'respect and enhance human dignity', to 'build on our communal solidarity', to 'cherish and promote the different cultural traditions within the Solomon Islands', and to 'ensure the participation of our people in the governance of their affairs'.

Some Westminster Model constitutions – like those of Ireland, India and Tuvalu – go beyond these 'thin' commitments, asserting a 'thicker' commitment to a particular vision of the good life. The Irish constitution, while faithful to the Westminster Model in many of its institutional processes, is deeply infused with Catholic social teaching and a particular form of republican nationalism.[152] The preamble to the Irish constitution invokes 'the Name of the Most Holy Trinity', humbly acknowledges 'all our obligations to our Divine Lord, Jesus Christ', gratefully remembers the 'heroic and unremitting struggle' of 'our fathers through centuries of trial' who sought to 'regain the rightful independence of our nation'. It declares the intention to 'promote the common good, with due observance of Prudence, Justice and Charity', with the aim that the 'dignity and freedom of the individual may be assured, true social order attained, the unity of our country restored, and concord established with other nations'.

The Indian constitution, in contrast, is a testament to Nehru's vision of a secular, social democratic order which the power of the modern democratic state would transform society and break the bonds of tradition, village and caste.[153] The preamble to the Indian constitution originally declared India to be a 'sovereign, democratic republic'.[ii] The preamble was adopted by the Indian Constituent Assembly after the rest of the constitution had been passed, and it was intended as a sort of explanatory gloss on its principles.[154] It commits India to the principles of 'Justice – social, economic and political', 'liberty of thought, expression, belief, faith and worship', 'equality of status and opportunity', and to promoting 'fraternity assuring the dignity of the individual and the unity and integrity of the nation'. Article 38 of the Indian constitution encapsulates this covenantal commitment to a common vision and common purpose:

> The State shall strive to promote the welfare of the people by securing and protecting as effectively as it may a social order in which justice, social, economic and political, shall inform all the institutions of the national life. The State shall, in particular, strive to minimise the inequalities in income, and endeavour to eliminate inequalities in status,

---

[ii] The words 'socialist and secular' were added by the controversial 42nd Amendment in 1976.

facilities and opportunities, not only amongst individuals
but also amongst groups of people residing in different areas
or engaged in different vocations.

In India, the structure of flexible federalism also reflects a covenantal
commitment to shared national development goals: the central
government is given powers to overcome poverty through economic
development achieved principally through infrastructure projects. Thus,
there is a connection between Article 38 cited earlier and Article 249,
which enables the Union Parliament in certain conditions to legislate
on state matter in the national interest.[iii]

The Constitution of Tuvalu was originally (1978) made relatively
'thin' – or in any case generic – commitments in its preamble to 'a
free and democratic sovereign nation' based on 'Christian principles,
the Rule of Law, and Tuvaluan custom and tradition'. The preamble
was amended in 1986 to include a set of seven principles, mostly re-
affirming a commitment to maintaining the traditional communal way
of life. Sections 15 and 29 of the constitution allow certain rights, and
limitations on rights, to be interpreted in the light of these principles.

The re-constitution of the United Kingdom is not simply matter
of institutional reform. It is also a matter of reclaiming values and of
restoring principles, so as to reaffirm a common sense of political
morality. Having clear constitutional principles is an integral and
necessary part of that project. The examples considered in this section –
from Barbados and the Solomon Islands to Ireland, India and Tuvalu –
do not provide an exhaustive list of possibilities, but they do illustrate
the range of different approaches.

There is a case for both compromise and self-restraint. A written
constitution, even as it tries to pin down the fundamentals we have
in common, must still leave plenty of room for ordinary politics and
for the ebb and flow of elected parliamentary majorities. In a country
of divergent views and contested identities, too firm a commitment
to a particular ideology or set of policy goals may be divisive. The
constitution cannot be a wish-list of policy ideas that would be more
suited to a partisan election manifesto. Nevertheless, we might well
find, in the process of constitution-building, that we have more in
common than we think. We might argue, during the constitution-
making process, about the depth and breadth of our covenantal
undertakings on issues like socio-economic rights, but an explicit

---

[iii] For more on Article 249 of the Indian constitution see Chapter 10.

commitment to democracy, human rights, the rule of law and good government ought to be universally welcomed. The aim is not to determine outcomes or prescribe policies, but to define the terms on which we agree – at a constitutional level – to live together as fellow citizens of a self-governing polity.

One source of potential consensus may lie in the Commonwealth Charter of 2013, which commits members of the Commonwealth to the principles of democracy, human rights, international peace and security, tolerance, respect and understanding, freedom of expression, separation of powers and the rule of law, good governance, sustainable development, protecting the environment, access to health, education, food and shelter, gender equality, and recognizing the contribution of youth and civil society.[155] These are as decent and inclusive a statement of meta-constitutional principles as any – and they have the advantage of having been signed by the Queen and endorsed by a former Conservative British Prime Minister (David Cameron), so can hardly be dismissed as a left-wing manifesto.

Simply declaring that a country is a democracy, or that it respects human rights, does not, of course, make it so; the purpose of these provisions is not to conjure democracy out of thin air, but to provide a coherent moral foundation for the constitutional rules through which the principles of parliamentary democracy are given effect. Declaratory provisions might, in some situations, help the courts to interpret the constitution – as in India, where the Supreme Court has held that the preamble 'is of extreme importance' and that 'the Constitution should be read and interpreted in the light of the grand and noble vision expressed in the preamble'.[156] The courts, however, are not the primary audience of declaratory or preambular provisions. Their importance lies chiefly in their symbolic presence and their rhetorical influence on public discourse and the political culture. They help a country to live up to its best image of itself, to remember its founding principles and values, especially in times of crisis or confusion when we are otherwise apt to jettison them. They provide something solid and good to cling to when all else seems to have gone awry.

Citizenship

Many Westminster Model constitutions contain provisions regulating citizenship. Often these provisions, established at the time of transition to independence, are relatively detailed: the rules on citizenship by marriage, and the naturalization of aliens, is in many cases prescribed by the constitution, and not by ordinary law. Provisions such as those in the Constitution of Bangladesh (article 6), simply stating that 'The citizenship of Bangladesh shall be determined and regulated by law', are the exception. The Constitution of the Bahamas, in devoting more than 2,000 words to the specifics of citizenship law, is more typical.

The constitutional regulation of citizenship can have an identity-defining purpose. The Constitution of Fiji (article 5), for example, declares that, 'All citizens of Fiji shall be known as Fijians'. Previously, the term 'Fijian' was reserved for indigenous Fijians, while the descendants of Indian migrants or European settlers were hyphenated as Indo-Fijians or European-Fijians. The declaration that all Fijian citizens are 'Fijians' in an attempt to overcome racial tensions and promote a unified sense of national identity. This is another example of how, beyond its function as a basic rulebook for politics, the constitution can have a nation-forming, unifying potential. In a United Kingdom transformed by decades of immigration, a strong constitutional commitment to inclusive citizenship might send a powerful message that belonging – being one of us – is not dependent on colour, religion, ancestry, or whether you eat traditional British foods like onion bhajis or exotic Eastern European dishes like fish deep fried in batter,[iv] but on the membership of a democratic polity defined by its constitution. Only a civic, constitutional, democratic, and inclusive nationalism can maintain social solidarity and prevent society from slipping either into an amoral individualism which ends in anarchy or into authoritarian forms of ethnic nationalism.

Even if it is not necessary or desirable to prescribe all the details of citizenship law in a constitution for the United Kingdom, the right not to be arbitrarily deprived of citizenship ought to be constitutionally protected. The citizenship is perhaps the most important of all rights. Without it, one is outside the political community – someone who might have the right to dwell in a particular territory but does not truly belong to it. The fact that in several cases British citizens have been stripped of citizenship by executive decision, without due process and without having being convicted of any crime, is – or ought to be – unacceptable, even in the case of persons accused of terrorism. This is a wrong which the constitution should put right.

[iv] According to a report by *The Times of Israel*, the classic British 'fish and chips' was introduced to Britain by Eastern European Jews in the 1800s (Sue Surkes, 14 March 2017).

Fundamental rights and freedoms

The old dominion constitutions displayed a wariness of including justiciable fundamental rights. The protection of civil liberties was supposed to rest on parliamentary sovereignty mitigated by a vigorous Opposition, the common law, a vigilant public and free press, and shared reverence for the historical tradition of Anglosphere liberty.

Some rights were expressly protected by these early constitutions – the language and religious rights of the French-speaking Catholic minority in Quebec, and the equal language rights of Dutch and English-speaking whites in South Africa – but these owed more to a nascent attempt at intercommunal accommodation than to a strongly developed sense of human rights and civil liberties that should be constitutionally prescribed. The Australian Constitution of 1901 included a commitment to freedom of religion and separation of church and state (Section 116) and a weak protection for trial by jury (Section 80). The Irish Free State's constitution contained a short bill of rights (articles 6 to 9) designed to protect and reassure the Protestant minority.[v] But that was it.

After the Second World War, however, judicially enforced bills of rights became an increasingly standard feature of Westminster Model constitutions. The story of how that came to be so has been aptly told by Charles Parkinson and it is not necessary to repeat it in detail here.[157] Two points, however, are worthy of note. Firstly, when adopted in divided, multi-cultural societies, where voting was determined in part along ethnic or religious lines, bills of rights were seen as a means of safeguarding the minority and promoting intercommunal harmony. Even Sir Ivor Jennings, no supporter of bills of rights in principle, allowed specific restrictions on religious or communal discrimination to be inserted into the Ceylon constitution of 1947. Secondly, these bills of rights, of which British officials were initially sceptical, came in time to be insisted on by the British out of fear that the traditional, informal protections of civil liberty – including property rights – would not be sufficiently robust in post-colonial contexts. It was necessary to distil that tradition, to take its essence and its principles, and translate it into an enforceable form.

---

[v] The Irish Free State constitution could be amended, in principle, only by referendum. There was a transitional period, however, in which the Parliament could amend the constitution by ordinary legislation – this breach in the constitutional armour enabled the government, which was to be fair in the midst of civil war, to insert a provision effectively neutering these rights.

In other words, low levels of trust in the goodwill and self-restraint of political leaders pushed aside any previous theoretical reservations about the relationship between legislative supremacy and judicial constraints on power. In both senses, bills of rights were an insurance mechanism, intended to protect election losers from election winners. Winners could govern, but only with respect for the rights of others.

By the 1960s a standard, generic bill of rights was being included in new Commonwealth constitutions around the world. These were closely modelled on the European Convention on Human Rights, which was itself a British-influenced statement of those fundamental basic rights essential to a free, open and democratic society. As such, the bills of rights were limited in scope to civil, legal and political rights, sometimes known as 'first generation rights'.[vi] They also allowed for various limitations to be placed on certain rights by law to the extent 'reasonably justifiable in a democratic society'. The aim was not to unduly restrict the discretion of the state, but simply to protect the baselines of a liberal-democratic order against the most egregious abuses of power.

Not all countries have followed this model. Canada (under the Charter of Rights and Freedoms adopted in 1982), India, Ireland, Jamaica (following amendments adopted in 2011), Trinidad & Tobago and Vanuatu have slightly different approaches to the way in which their Bills of Rights are framed. Nevertheless, the norm is for most Westminster Model constitutions to have a Bill of Rights that is based on the European Convention.

The Human Rights Act 1998, which incorporated the European Convention on Human Rights into domestic law, has had a profound and mostly beneficial impact on the protection of rights. As well as its direct legal effects, in making it easier to challenge the lawfulness of public acts against human rights law, the Human Rights Act has contributed to a new awareness of human rights by citizens, advocacy groups and public authorities alike. It is, however, a poor substitute for the proper Bills of Rights found in most Westminster Model constitutions.

Human Rights Act is deficient in two respects. Firstly, it lacks effective bite. If the courts find an Act of Parliament incompatible

---

[vi] The usual practice is to make a clear distinction between what are called 'first generation' rights (such as freedom from arbitrary arrest and detention, the right to a fair trial, freedom of speech and expression, freedom of assembly and association, and freedom of religion) and 'second generation' socio-economic rights (discussed in the following section).

with European Convention rights, they can only issue a Declaration of Incompatibility, which opens up a fast-track procedure for Parliament to amend the incompatible Act. The incompatible Act itself is not annulled. Secondly, the Human Rights Act is an ordinary statute, which is neither procedurally entrenched nor superior to other laws. Many Eurosceptic Conservatives oppose it and seek to repeal it.[vii] This means it fails as an 'insurance mechanism'. We can never know whether the next government will use its majority to repeal the Human Rights Act and so do away even the scant and partial protection that it offers.

It has been argued that the United Kingdom's Human Rights Act points towards a 'new Commonwealth model of constitutionalism', in which legislatures rather than courts have the last word.[158] New Zealand, the only other Commonwealth country to lack a written constitution, and Canada (where the legislature can, in certain circumstances, enact legislation that is declared to be valid notwithstanding the Canadian Charter of Rights and Freedoms) are the other examples. However, rather than pointing to a 'Commonwealth model of constitutionalism' that is trusting of legislatures and shy of judiciaries, these examples are in fact the outliers. Most Commonwealth countries have judicially enforced bills of rights as part of their written constitutions – and the United Kingdom can and should do likewise.

The argument for a justifiable bill of rights usually depends on the question of whether it would, in practice, improve the protection of the rights and liberties of individuals or minorities, or how it might alter the balance of power between the executive, legislature and judiciary. The question is rarely addressed from the perspective of national identity and civic-constitutional unity. Yet bills of rights are expressions of identity, unity and purpose. They are above all moral documents. Adherence to a set of constitutional rights can be seen as a way of giving public recognition to the set of values and principles that those rights embody.

The Canadian Charter of Rights and Freedoms, for example, was in part intended to strengthen national unity by enabling a thin, procedural agreement, in a highly diverse country, around a set of basic rights. These rights would enable different groups and individuals to pursue their own objectives within a loosely-fitting Canadian whole; yet they would also give everyone a stake in the constitutional order, regardless

---

[vii]   In so doing they are not spurning a continental Napoleonic abstraction, as they might imagine; they are going against the democratic heritage of Britain and the Commonwealth and are turning their backs on the accumulated tradition of Anglo-Saxon liberty going back to the Magna Carta.

of ethno-cultural background, and thus replace a politics of divided identity with a politics of rights that would be inclusive and integrative. To be a member of the nation, in that case, is to be a member of a body-politic in which freedom of religion, speech, assembly and association are guaranteed within well-established constitutional limits, and where basic rule of law freedoms (right to a fair trial, due process) are protected.

In a United Kingdom context, a constitutional bill of rights is not only, therefore, about protecting our inherited and hard-won rights and liberties against the encroachment of arbitrary power. It is also about re-creating, in a state that has become plagued by division, distrust and disenchantment, a new sense of a moral community in which we are bound together by certain shared standards and norms. It says what we stand for, and what we will not stand for. Perhaps once upon a time these things could have gone unsaid. No more. If we wish to reclaim and restore our values, we must be bold about declaring them in a new Magna Carta that can be a touchstone of both liberty and unity.

It remains to consider the restriction of rights in emergencies. Westminster Model constitutions recognize that the balance between civil liberties and the public interest is a dynamic one, which must respond to changing circumstances and events. Restrictions that would be a dangerous threat to liberty in times of peace and safety, may be necessary, proportionate and reasonably justifiable in a democratic society in times of war, natural disaster or pandemic.[159]

Usually a state of emergency can be declared by the head of state or Governor-General acting on the advice of the Prime Minister but can only remain in effect for a limited period. In the constitutions of St Christopher & Nevis (Section 19) and St Vincent & the Grenadines (Section 17), that period is seven days – unless Parliament is not sitting at the time, in which case it is 21 days. In the constitutions of Barbados (Section 25), Belize (Section 18) and India (article 352), it is one month.

A state of emergency may in each case be extended beyond this initial period by a parliamentary resolution, usually for up to six months (as in Barbados and India) or twelve months (Belize and St Christopher & Nevis) at a time. The precise rules vary. In India, both Houses of Parliament must approve the extension. In the other cases under consideration, the consent of the lower House alone is sufficient (the Parliament of St Christopher & Nevis is unicameral). Sometimes a special majority is required: in Barbados and India, an absolute majority of the total membership of the House is necessary; in Belize and St Christopher & Nevis, a two-thirds majority is needed.

In a United Kingdom constitution, it would be wise to err on the side of caution in granting extraordinary powers to the government, and to design the rules in such a way as to enable the proper use of such powers, without facilitating their improper abuse. That means: (a) restricting to one week – or two if Parliament is not in session, to allow for time for it to be recalled – the time during which the government can act on its own without parliamentary approval; (b) limiting the period for which initial approval can be granted by Parliament to six months at the most, after which it must be renewed if necessary by another parliamentary vote; and (c) structuring the rules in such a way as to prevent the government, with a working majority in Parliament, from being able to extend emergency powers beyond that initial period without political consensus, for example by a super-majority vote in both Houses.

The South African constitution (Section 37) requires the first extension of a state of emergency to be approved by absolute majority in the National Assembly, but any subsequent extension to be approved by a three-fifths majority. Under most expected circumstances in the United Kingdom, this rule would enable the governing party to deal with the initial emergency situation on its own responsibility, but not allow any subsequent extension unless the Opposition agrees – a neat and nice balance.

Not all rights can be suspended or restricted during an emergency. Legislation restricting rights may still be subject to judicial review. Under international law, some rights are non-derogable, which means they apply at all times and in all situations. The government cannot use war, unrest, or epidemic as an excuse to impose slavery, allow torture, or deny the due process of law. Even in the toughest times – especially in the toughest times – we must hold on to the principles of a decent and civilized people.

Socio-economic rights and directive principles

Some Westminster Model constitutions go further than the minimal bill of civil, legal and political rights as discussed in the preceding section. They also assert various social, economic and cultural commitments, such as the right to a living wage, the right to decent and humane working conditions, the right to leisure through days of rest and paid holiday, the right to education, the right to healthcare, and the right to housing and sanitation.

These socio-economic provisions, articulated at the constitutional level, represent a covenantal commitment to pursue economic justice, human flourishing, and the common good. They are integral to the realization of the 'good life in common' which according to Aristotle is the aim of a just constitution.[160] After all, civic and political life is unavoidably incarnational: without a body that is fed, clothed, housed and healthy, one cannot take advantage of the civil and political rights that enable one to engage in public life.

In some Westminster Model constitutions these socio-economic provisions are stated as 'Directive Principles', which are morally and politically – but not legally – binding on the Government and Parliament. The Irish and Indian constitutions, which were pioneers in developing the concept of Directive Principles and grafting them into the Westminster tradition, provide examples of typical formulations, in terms of the status and effect of such provisions:

> The principles of social policy set forth in this Article are intended for the general guidance of the Oireachtas [Parliament]. The application of those principles in the making of laws shall be the care of the Oireachtas exclusively, and shall not be cognisable by any Court under any of the provisions of this Constitution. (Constitution of Ireland, Art. 45).

> The provisions contained in this Part [Directive Principles of State Policy] shall not be enforceable by any court, but the principles therein laid down are nevertheless fundamental in the governance of the country and it shall be the duty of the State to apply these principles in making laws. (Constitution of India, Art. 37).

The reason for these socio-economic matters to be dealt with by Directive Principles rather than directly enforceable rights stems not from unimportance, but principally from difficulties of enforceability. It is argued that enforcing these socio-economic rights creates greater burdens on the state – financial, administrative and regulatory duties and responsibilities. The constitution may, as a civic covenant and expression of values, purposes and principles, declare those duties and responsibilities, and enjoin the institutions of the state to fulfil them. It can, likewise, keep these duties and responsibilities constantly before the eyes of the voting public, as a signpost and a reminder that they are not to forget them, and are to consider them when voting.

According to supporters of the Directive Principles approach, we cannot rely on the courts to decide whether these duties and responsibilities have been adequately fulfilled, or to grant any kind of relief against the government if they are not. This may be argued on simple grounds of capacity – that the courts are not very good at determining difficult questions like whether enough has been spent on public education, and if so whether that funding has been used wisely. But it can also be argued on the grounds of democracy. Deciding how to deliver on these state obligations, how to prioritize between different projects and programmes, and how to allocate scarce resources between them, is inherently a political function. Political parties may differ on how they view these obligations – one might prioritize old age pensions, other improvements in affordable housing – both may be constitutionally recognized directives, but choices have to be made between them. The ballot box, not the courtroom, is, according to this view, the proper place to ensure accountability for the performance of these duties and the proper discharge of these responsibilities by the state.

Despite these difficulties, some Westminster Model constitutions do contain justiciable socio-economic rights. These are framed as positive constitutional obligations on the state. The 2013 Constitution of Fiji, for example, obliges the state to take steps in order to progressively realize, in accordance with its resources, the right to education, the right to 'economic participation', the right to 'a just minimum wage', the right of 'reasonable access to transportation', the right to housing and sanitation, the right to 'adequate food and water', the right to social security ('including the right to such support from public resources if they are unable to support themselves and their dependents'), the right to 'the conditions and facilities necessary to good health, and to health care services', freedom from arbitrary eviction, and the right 'to a clean and healthy environment'. If the public authorities claim they do not have the resources to implement these rights, it is the responsibility of the state to show that the resources are not available. Similar provisions committing the public authorities to the progressive realization of socio-economic rights in South Africa have had mixed results, with the courts interpreting these rights as creating an obligation on the state to act, rather than an entitlement of the individual to a guaranteed outcome. The constitutional right to housing, for example, requires the state to have a credible social housing policy, but it does not ensure than any particular person will get a house.[161]

The difference between socio-economic rights framed in this way and Directive Principles might therefore be narrower that it at first seems. The aim in both cases is ultimately to maintain a focus on certain objectives, without unduly limiting the flexibility of the government in deciding how to meet those priorities. Nevertheless, constitution-makers in the United Kingdom would have to find a compromise position, and it might be that socio-economic rights framed in the manner of South Africa or Fiji would be a step too far, both for legal traditionalists afraid of judicial power and for political conservatives opposed to radical policies. A set of non-justiciable Directive Principles would then be the best compromise.

Religion–state relations

The Hanoverian constitutional settlement was as much a religious settlement as a political one. The compromise reached was complex: established Anglicanism in England, Wales and Ireland, established Presbyterianism in Scotland, institutional anti-Catholicism, and a limited toleration of Protestant dissenters. During the 19th century this gave way to a general religious freedom in a pluralist society – although there are still established churches in both England and Scotland, and a lingering identification of state institutions with Christianity.

However, the particular mode of religion–state relations that evolved in the United Kingdom is not a necessary part of the Westminster Model. In a modern Westminster Model constitution, there is a baseline of liberty to be maintained: freedom of religion, expression and association, and a general principle of non-discrimination. Beyond this, Westminster Model constitutions have existed, and continue to exist, in a wide variety of religious environments, with just about every conceivable form of religion–state relations.[viii]

Some Westminster Model constitutions have an unambiguously religious identity. The 1986 Constitution of Tuvalu declares the state to be 'based on Christian principles'.[162] The Constitution of Samoa, as amended in 2016, proclaims that 'Samoa is a Christian nation founded on God the Father, the Son and the Holy Spirit'. The preamble to the Constitution of the Bahamas refers to 'an abiding respect for Christian values'.

It is perhaps ironic, for a constitutional system so closely associated with Protestantism, that it is in the Roman Catholic-majority countries of Ireland and Malta that the Westminster Model (outside

---

[viii] It may surprise some to learn that from 1964, when Malta became independent, to 1974, when it became a Republic, the Queen – as Queen of Malta – was head of state of a country in which Roman Catholicism was the constitutionally established religion. From 1947 to 1956, as Queen of Pakistan, she was Queen of a nation that had defined itself in terms of its Muslim identity.

the United Kingdom) makes the fullest constitutional commitment to religious identity. The Irish Constitution of 1937, while stopping short of making Roman Catholicism the religion of the state, originally recognized 'the special position of the Holy Catholic Apostolic and Roman Church as the guardian of the Faith professed by the great majority of the citizens'.[163] This provision was removed in 1973, but the preamble to the Irish constitution continues to invoke 'our Divine Lord, Jesus Christ'.[164] The Constitution of Malta goes further, claiming that, 'The religion of Malta is the Roman Catholic Apostolic Religion' and that 'The authorities of the Roman Catholic Apostolic Church have the duty and the right to teach which principles are right and which are wrong.' This is about as strong and clear a provision on religious establishment as it is possible for a constitution to have, while still maintaining – through its freedom of religion, freedom of expression, freedom of association and non-discrimination clauses – a liberal-democratic nature.

Non-Christian religions may also have constitutionally recognized or privileged status in Westminster Model constitutions. The Constitution of Malaysia, while guaranteeing that 'other religious may be practiced in peace and harmony', declares that 'Islam is the religion of the Federation', and that the Ruler of each of the Malay States is 'the Head of the Religion of Islam in his State in the manner and to the extent acknowledged and declared by the Constitution of that State'.[165] The 1972 Constitution of Sri Lanka recognized the 'foremost place' of Buddhism and acknowledged the 'duty of the state to protest and foster Buddhism', while assuring to all the rights to freedom of thought, conscience and religion.[166]

Other Westminster Model constitutions are explicitly secular. The Constitution of Australia, for example, states – in terms not accidentally similar to those of the US Constitution – that 'The Commonwealth shall not make any law for establishing any religion, or for imposing any religious observance, or for prohibiting the free exercise of any religion, and no religious test shall be required as a qualification for any office or public trust under the Commonwealth.' The 2013 Constitution of Fiji declares, in a provision entitled 'Secular State' that 'Religion and the State are separate, which means the State and all persons holding public office must treat all religions equally' and that 'the State and all persons holding public office must not prefer or advance, by any means, any particular religion, religious denomination, religious belief, or religious practice over another, or over any non-religious belief'.[167] India, since the 42nd Amendment to the constitution in 1976, has also defined itself as a 'secular' republic – although secularism in India takes a rather softer and more pluralistic form, according to which the state, although not favouring or endorsing any particular religion, does recognize and accommodate religious groups in various ways, most notably perhaps in the retention of separate personal legal codes for Hindus and Muslims.[168]

A third set of Westminster Model constitutions refrain from formally establishing any religion, but at the same time they do not go so far as to declare themselves explicitly secular. Some of these include a general invocation of God. The Canadian Constitution Act 1982, for example, refers to Canada being 'founded on principles that recognize the supremacy of God'.[169] Other constitutions are simply silent about the issue of the state's religious orientation, or lack thereof. The picture here is somewhat muddied by history; for it was once standard (if not universal) colonial practice that a territory, on coming under the sovereignty of the Crown, became subject to English laws and, with it, the Church of England. Residual, vestigial, elements of religious establishment may remain in some Canadian provinces.[170]

In Barbados, for example, the Church of England was established before independence. The independence Constitution of 1962 made no mention of the established church – neither confirming its continued status, nor seeking to abolish it. At independence, Barbados could be said to have a statutory (as opposed to constitutional) establishment: the Church was established as a matter of policy and law, but not as a matter of constitutional identity. Once a written, supreme and fundamental law constitution is adopted, it becomes possible – as it is for the moment impossible in the United Kingdom – to distinguish between these two things. Barbados later disestablished the church, by means of the Anglican Church Act 1969, without a constitutional amendment.

Tuvalu's constitutional adherence to 'Christian principles' has already been mentioned, but it is worth noting that Tuvalu also has a statutory establishment of one particular denomination – the *Ekalesia Kelisiano Tuvalu*, a reformed Congregationalist church founded by missionaries from the London Missionary Society, is recognized as the 'State Church' by virtue of the State Church (Declaration) Act 1993, and as such has certain ceremonial privileges – including the right to perform services at public events – not extended to the other churches.

A constitutional refoundation of the United Kingdom might, if so desired, disestablish the Church of England while still preserving the Westminster Model and all that is best in the British institutional, political and legal traditions. The fact that disestablishment has already occurred in two of the four parts of the current United Kingdom (Wales and Northern Ireland) only confirms this argument. The very different sort of establishment prevailing in Scotland also shows that establishment need not take only one form. Two potential compromises are possible. The first is to build a consensus around 'recognition without establishment'; that is, to separate the Church of England from the state in terms of its governance and institutional links, while recognizing – through preambular or declaratory provisions – the 'foremost place' or 'special position' of Christianity in our culture and society. The second is to follow the route of Barbados, and to adopt a constitution that leaves the current church–state relationship undisturbed but does not constitutionally entrench it. This would leave the way open, if so desired, to disestablishment by ordinary Act of the English Parliament in due course (we must assume, in a federal union of four equal states, that ecclesiastical law would be a state matter). These are not entirely mutually exclusive. A preambular constitutional commitment at the Union level to Christian principles and values might be combined with a differentiated, state-specific, statutory approach to establishment. It might even be necessary, as a pragmatic step, to provide in the Constitution that, while the distinct forms of establishment in England and Scotland can continue until changed by state law, the Northern Ireland Parliament and the Welsh Parliament cannot – for reasons of peace and community relations – establish a religion.

The composition of a reformed second chamber is discussed in Chapter 8, but it must be added for clarity that a second chamber with at least a partially appointed element, chosen on a non-partisan basis represent experience, expertise and the various interests of society, might as a matter of practice continue to include a number of Anglican bishops, as well as representatives of other religions and denominations, without a specific reservation of seats for Lords Spiritual. Disestablishment need not therefore mean the exclusion of bishops, or other faith leaders, from the second chamber – the two issues can be handled separately.

7

The Crown, Prime Minister and Government

Republic or monarchy

The earliest Westminster Model constitutions – those of Australia, Canada, New Zealand and South Africa – took unambiguously monarchical forms. Executive power was vested in the Crown, which was also an integral part of the legislature. Even in the post-war era, many former colonies, on becoming independent from the British Empire, did not cease to be part of 'Her Majesty's dominions'.[171] They continued as 'Commonwealth realms', with the functions of the Head of State being performed by a Governor-General nominally appointed by the Queen.

The Irish Free State was a more difficult case to classify. The characteristic 'dominion-style' provisions of the 1922 constitution, which were included to satisfy the terms of the Anglo-Irish treaty, were whittled away by successive amendments. The new Irish constitution adopted in 1937 established a popularly elected president as *de facto* Head of State. Yet it formally retained at least a vestigial link to the Crown, through the Executive Authority (External Relations) Act 1936; this strange arrangement persisted until 1949, when the Republic of Ireland Act 1948 came into effect.[172]

Although the powers and privileges of the Crown could be determined by each dominion through its own constitutional processes, Commonwealth membership at the time entailed a common allegiance to the Crown. By becoming a republic and ceasing to be part of His Majesty's dominions, Ireland – like Burma two years earlier – thereby ceased to be part of the Commonwealth.

Despite this change in status, both Ireland and Burma retained Westminster Model constitutions in republican guise, with a ceremonial figurehead president taking over the functions that elsewhere would normally be performed by a Governor-General. The separation between what Walter Bagehot called the 'dignified' (ceremonial) and 'efficient' (governing) parts of the constitution, and the relegation of the Head of State to primarily symbolic and civic functions, makes the identity of the Head of State a secondary matter.

In April 1949 – too late for Ireland – the rule binding Commonwealth membership to allegiance to the Crown was relaxed, by means of the London Declaration. The purpose of this was to enable India to remain in the Commonwealth despite its decision to adopt a republican constitution. It was agreed that allegiance to the monarch *as head of the Commonwealth*, and not necessarily as the Head of State of each Commonwealth country, would henceforth be sufficient.

Today, only 16 of the 53 members still keep the Queen as Head of State. Current examples of Westminster Model republics include Bangladesh, Dominica, India, Ireland, Malta, Samoa and Trinidad & Tobago. Malta and Trinidad & Tobago, was well as Ireland, first became independent under the Crown and later became republics, swapping the Governor-General for a figurehead President by means of a constitutional amendment.

In Ireland, the President is directly elected by the people – albeit from a small pool of candidates nominated by Members of Parliament. In all other cases, the President is chosen indirectly – either elected by Parliament (or, in India's case, by an electoral college of Union and State parliamentarians) or nominated by a resolution of the House. Such indirect selection is intended to prevent the President from having a personal legitimacy that might challenge that of the government. Bi-partisan appointment mechanisms, in which the Prime Minister and Leader of the Opposition co-nominate a candidate for President (used in Dominica, and proposed in 1999 for Australia, if Australia were to become a republic) are intended to ensure that the President has cross-party appeal and can, in principle, be a symbol of unity.

It would be perfectly possible, therefore, without deviating from the core principles of the Westminster Model, to replace the Queen with a non-partisan, indirectly elected Head of State, who could smile and wave, host diplomatic dinners, pin medals on chests, cut ribbons, and wear silly hats like the best of them. Such a person – probably a retired ambassador or senior judge, or perhaps a former minister who has been out of office for a decent amount of time and well respected across party lines – could also be trusted with the few 'reserve' powers that the Head of State in a Westminster Model democracy is occasionally called upon to exercise. If we wanted a republic, we could have one.

The fact that a British Republic is constitutionally possible does not necessarily make it desirable. A working, practical constitution must unite, not divide. The monarchy remains the one institution that might, at a symbolic and ceremonial level, provide a focus of unity and continuity for an otherwise divided people in the midst of unsettling change. Keeping the Queen and her 'heirs and successors according to law' as a fixed point of historical-traditional legitimacy is still likely to be necessary if the new constitutional settlement is to enjoy broad public acceptance. It connects the previous constitutional settlement to the new. It reassures socio-cultural conservatives that they and their values will continue to have a place in the refounded democratic constitutional order.

At the same time, however, the monarchy can be reinvented, through the constitution, in ways that make it more democratically legitimate. Some Commonwealth realms, especially those of the South Pacific, expressly derive the Crown's authority from the people through the constitution. The Constitution of the Solomon Islands, for example, declares (Section 1) that 'Solomon Islands shall be a sovereign democratic state. Her Majesty shall be the Head of State of Solomon Islands'. The Tuvaluan Constitution (Section 48) declares that 'Her Majesty Queen Elizabeth II … having at the request of the people of Tuvalu graciously consented, is the Sovereign of Tuvalu and, in accordance with this Constitution, the Head of State'. That of Papua New Guinea (Section 82) declares a contractual, constitutionally mediated relationship between the Crown and people:

> Her Majesty the Queen having been requested by the people of Papua New Guinea, through their Constituent Assembly, to become the Queen and Head of State of Papua New Guinea; and having graciously consented so to become, is the Queen and Head of State of Papua New Guinea.

The personal union that unites the legally distinct Crowns of the Commonwealth realms in the physical person of one monarch means that there is no mention, in most of these constitutions, of matters such as regencies, abdication, the age of majority of the monarch, the coronation oath, the religion of the monarch, or the civil list. Where the order of succession is mentioned, it is only by reference to the United Kingdom. For example, the Constitution of the Solomon Islands (Section 144) specifies that, 'The provisions referring to Her Majesty shall extend to Her Majesty's Heirs and Successors in the sovereignty of the United Kingdom of Great Britain and Northern Ireland.' Such arrangements, while perhaps sufficient for other parts of Her Majesty's dominions, would be incomplete if applied to the United Kingdom. Those countries of the Commonwealth that have their own monarchs – such as Lesotho, Tonga, and Malaysia – do deal with such matters in their constitutions, as do European constitutional monarchies.

Perhaps the best course of action is for the constitution of the United Kingdom to incorporate the essentials of existing law and practice, in terms of succession to the Crown and regencies, while also incorporating some reform (for example, changing the coronation oath to include a duty to obey and uphold the Constitution). This would marry the institution of the monarchy revered by Burke to the principles of democratic constitutionalism of Paine.

All this assumes, of course, that the Queen and royal family behave themselves well, as the figureheads of a free people under a democratic constitution. If the monarch or royal family were ever to collude in actions harmful to a democratic constitutional order, the House of Windsor could suffer the same fate as that which befell the House of Savoy, which colluded with Mussolini in 1923 only to find itself rejected by the Italian people in 1946.[173]

Powers and functions of the monarch

Keeping the monarchy does not mean that the powers and functions of the monarch have to remain as broad, or as vaguely defined, as they are at present. The constitutional powers of the Queen, or of the Governor-General as her official representative, vary considerably between the Commonwealth realms. The Queen of Canada does not have the same powers, on paper or in practice, as the Queen of the Bahamas, whose powers are in turn quite different, in many small but important matters of constitutional detail, from those of the Queen of Tuvalu or the Solomon Islands. The Westminster Model is sufficiently flexible that, within a broad shared understanding of the role of the Head of State, constitutional powers and functions can be tailored to need.

Most modern Westminster Model constitutions define the powers of the Head of State quite narrowly. Codifying the conventions of parliamentary democracy and cabinet government leaves only a little room for the exercise, in rare and exceptional cases, of the Head of State's personal discretion. The Head of State has plenty to *do*, and can be kept quite busy with ceremonial and civic duties, but ordinarily has very little to *decide*. What is important, though, is that in those extraordinary situations where the Head of State does have to exercise discretionary power, it is possible to do so in accordance with clear constitutional rules that legitimate the Head of State's action and prevent, as far as possible, any question of political bias or favouritism from arising.

The key to this separation between the roles and functions of the monarch as Head of State on the one hand, and those of the Prime Minister as Head of government on the other, is the principle of 'acting on advice'. Executive power is said to be 'vested in' Her Majesty (or, in republics, the President) but is normally exercised only in accordance with the advice of the Prime Minister, the Cabinet, or a minister acting under the general authority of the Cabinet. This advice is not mere 'consultation'. It is binding advice. The one who advises is the one who takes the decision and bears responsibility for it; the Head of State's role is purely formal.

Benjamin Constant, a 19th century theorist of constitutional monarchy and a great admirer of the British parliamentary system, made an important conceptual distinction between what he called 'executive' and 'moderating' functions. Executive functions, which concern everyday acts of policy, governance and administration, are the exclusive domain of the ministers; in these matters, the monarch must act only in accordance with ministerial advice and on ministerial responsibility. Moderating functions, according to Constant, are those in which the Head of State might occasionally have to exercise their personal discretion, as sort of a constitutional umpire.[174]

Constant's terms have never been accepted into the Westminster constitutional lexicon;[i] instead we speak of 'reserve' or 'discretionary' powers.[ii] The boundaries of the reserve or discretionary powers are not always clear, especially in first generation Westminster Model constitutions, where they are determined only by convention. In general, we may say that the scope of reserve powers seems to have narrowed over time, if only because in cases of doubt acting on the Prime Minister's advice usually seems like the least controversial – if not always the most correct – course of action.

---

[i] An expressly designated royal 'moderating power' was for some time in the 19th century a feature of constitutions in the Lusophone tradition, both in European Portugal and Brazil.

[ii] 'Reserve' and 'discretionary' in this context are interchangeable, except that 'reserve power' is more often used in some countries (Australia, Canada) and 'discretionary' in others (Ireland).

In second generation Westminster Model constitutions, in contrast, the scope of reserve powers is normally tightly and specifically stated in the constitution. It is made very clear, in the texts of these constitutions, that the Head of State (or Governor-General) normally acts only on ministerial advice. This rule applies to all ordinary executive functions: policy is determined, and decisions made, by ministers who are responsible to Parliament. The rule of acting on binding ministerial advice is waived only in certain specific circumstances which are expressly stated in the constitution.

The Constitution of Jamaica expresses the principle in what has become the standard way, and a detailed examination of that constitution will illustrate the point. Section 68 states that 'The executive authority of Jamaica is vested in Her Majesty. Subject to the provisions of this Constitution, the executive authority of Jamaica may be exercised on behalf of Her Majesty by the Governor-General either directly or through officers subordinate to him.' The Governor-General, according to Section 38, 'shall act in accordance with the advice of the Cabinet or a Minister acting under the general authority of the Cabinet in the exercise of his functions'. This is because, under Section 69, 'The Cabinet shall be the principal instrument of policy and shall be charged with the general direction and control of the Government of Jamaica and shall be collectively responsible therefor to Parliament.' In other words, executive authority is vested in the Queen, exercised by the Governor-General, acting on the advice of ministers who are responsible to Parliament. That neatly echoes S.A. de Smith's definition of the Westminster Model referenced in Chapter 5.[iii]

Although acting on ministerial advice is the norm, Section 38 of the Jamaican Constitution also states that this does not apply to 'any function which is expressed (in whatever terms) to be exercisable by [the Governor-General] on or in accordance with the recommendation or advice of, or with the concurrence of, or after consultation with, any person or authority other than the Cabinet' or in relation to 'any function which is expressed (in whatever terms) to be exercisable by [the Governor-General] in his discretion'. This

---

[iii] To save flicking back: 'a constitutional system in which the head of state is not the effective head of government; in which the effective head of government is a Prime Minister presiding over a cabinet composed of Ministers over whose appointment and removal he has at least a substantial measure of control; in which the effective executive branch of government is parliamentary in as much as Ministers must be members of the legislature; and in which Ministers are collectively and individually responsible to a freely elected and representative legislature.'

means that exceptions to the rule of ministerial advice therefore fall into two categories. Firstly, there are those where the Governor-General takes advice, or acts after consultation with, another person or authority. Secondly, there are those where the Governor-General is able to act with personal discretion.

The Governor-General of Jamaica acts on the advice of the Public Service Commission in the appointment of public officers (Section 125) and the Director of Public Prosecutions (Section 96). The Governor-General acts on the advice of the Judicial Service Commission in the appointment of judges (except for the Chief Justice and the President of the Court of Appeal) (Section 98 and Section 112), and on the advice of the Chief Justice in the appointment of a special tribunal that may be appointed to investigate the removal from office of the Auditor-General (Section 121). Police officers are appointed by the Governor-General acting on the advice of the Police Service Commission. All these powers are exercised, in principle, independently of the government. They are deliberately designed to exclude the Prime Minister and Cabinet, or at least keep them at arm's length. The reason is that these powers are those that maintain the proper functioning of the independent institutions of the state – the civil service, the judiciary, the police force, the prosecutions service, the auditing of accounts – rather than those that are concerned with policy making and partisan politics. In addition, the Governor-General exercises the power of pardon and mercy on the recommendation of the Privy Council (Section 90 and Section 91). The power to appoint Opposition Senators (amounting to just over a third of the total number of Senators) is vested in the Governor-General acting on the advice of the Leader of the Opposition (Section 35 and Section 45). This rule is intended to give the Opposition a veto over amendments to entrenched provisions of the constitution, which require a two-thirds majority in both Houses.

There are several powers that the Governor-General of Jamaica can exercise at their own personal discretion. Under Section 70, the Governor-General, 'acting in his discretion' is required to appoint as Prime Minister that member of the House of Representatives who, 'is best able to command the confidence of a majority of the members of that House'. This is interesting because it shows that a discretionary power is not an unfettered power. The Governor-General has discretion but is not without constraint. The Governor-General cannot appoint whoever they like to be the Prime Minister, but only that person who, in their deliberate judgement, is best able to fulfil that role, in terms of commanding the confidence of the House. The Governor-General's function is not to select a government of their own choosing, but to identity the government that the House will support. Similarly, under Section 71, the Governor-General may in their personal discretion remove a Prime Minister when a new Prime Minister able to command the confidence of the House is to be appointed. So, for example, if a government were defeated in a general election and the Prime Minister refused to resign, the Governor-General would be acting within their constitutional powers to remove the Prime Minister so that a new Prime Minister, who is 'best able to command the confidence of a majority' of the members of the newly elected House, could be appointed. Again, this may, in certain circumstances, call for careful judgment, but the constitution only allows the Governor-General to read and express the sentiments of the House, not to impose a view or policy of their own.

Under Section 34, the Governor-General of Jamaica has the discretionary power to appoint members of their own personal staff. Under Section 72, the Governor-General is empowered to designate another minister to perform the functions of the Prime Minister in situations where the Prime Minister is incapacitated or absent. If the circumstances of the Prime Minister's illness or absence are such that the Prime Minister is unable to advise the Governor-General in the designation of a deputy, the Governor-General may exercise discretion in order to ensure continuity of government. Section 80 allows the Governor-General to exercise discretion in the appointment and the removal of the Leader of the Opposition. However, as in the case of the appointment of the Prime Minister, this discretionary judgement is not a license to make a free choice. The Governor-General is only to appoint as Leader of the Opposition

> the member of the House of Representatives who, in [the Governor-General's] judgment, is best able to command the support of a majority of those members who do not support the government, or, if there is no such person, the member of that House who, in his judgment, commands the support of the largest single group of such members who are prepared to support one leader.

The Governor-General under Section 88 may summon the Privy Council of Jamaica on their own discretion. The members of the Privy Council are appointed (under Section 82) by the Governor-General after consultation with (not on the advice of) the Prime Minister – so that, too, is a matter ultimately for the Governor-General's discretion. The Privy Council in Jamaica, as in some of the other Commonwealth Caribbean countries, is mainly concerned with the prerogative of mercy and the granting of pardons – powers which are exercisable by the Governor-General on the recommendation of the Privy Council. This is potentially a not-insignificant power, and it is one that is exercised, at least in principle, independently of the government.

This deep dive into the Jamaican constitution show the sorts of powers that the Governor-General as the representative of the Queen typically exercises in a modern Westminster Model constitution. There are many variations. The Governor-General of the Bahamas, in a rule typical of other Westminster Model constitutions but strangely absent from that of Jamaica, is permitted to act according to their own personal discretion in dissolving Parliament 'if the office of Prime Minister is vacant and the Governor-General considers that there is no prospect of his being able within a reasonable time to appoint to that office a person who can command the confidence of a majority of the members of the House of Assembly' (Section 66). The Governor-General of Belize – again in a provision typical of many Westminster Model constitutions – may refuse to dissolve Parliament on the advice of the Prime Minister if 'the Governor-General, acting in his own deliberate judgment, considers that the Government of Belize can be carried on without a dissolution and that a dissolution would not be in the interests of Belize' (Section 84). These further examples illustrate the same general point: that the exceptions to the rule of acting on the advice of the Prime Minister, or the Cabinet, or a minister acting under the general authority of the Cabinet, apply to the 'moderating' functions of the Head of State, either as an impartial constitutional umpire in situations such as the dissolution of Parliament, or as a guardian of the institutional integrity of the permanent administrative and judicial structures of the state.

So it should be in a written constitution for the United Kingdom. Using quite standard, well-proven formulae found in these and similar Westminster Model constitutions, the Head of State should be formally, explicitly and unequivocally bound to act on ministerial advice, except in relation to a limited range of powers and functions where the Head of State must act on the advice of another person or authority, or is expressly permitted to exercise a limited personal discretion.

It is proposed that the following discretionary powers – and no others – should be allowed to the Head of State in a new constitution for the United Kingdom. Firstly, the Queen should be permitted to refuse the Prime Minister's request for a dissolution in cases where the government has been defeated in a vote of no confidence, or if the government could be carried on without a dissolution and a dissolution would not be in the public interest. Secondly, the Queen should be permitted to dissolve Parliament if the office of Prime Minister is vacant and the Head of State 'considers that there is no prospect of the House of Commons being able within a reasonable time to nominate a Prime Minister'. Thirdly, if the House of Commons passes a vote of no confidence and the Prime Minister does not within a short stated interval either resign or advise a dissolution, the Queen should be able to resolve the crisis by deciding to dissolve Parliament or dismiss the Prime Minister. Fourthly, the Queen should be able to appoint members of her own household staff (such as the Queen's Private Secretary). Fifthly, she should be able to award those honours that are by law or custom in the personal gift of the monarch (such as membership of the Royal Victorian Order). Finally, for as long as the monarch remains the Supreme Governor of the Church of England, there is a case for her being permitted to exercise certain ecclesiastical functions without ministerial advice, ending the anomaly that the Prime Minister is involved (even nominally) in the appointment of bishops. These limited discretionary powers, and no more, would be entirely in keeping with the principles of parliamentary democracy in the Westminster tradition.

The constitutional restrictions that limit and define the Head of State's powers would also legitimate the exercise of those powers in the exceptional cases where they are needed – to dismiss a Prime Minister who loses a vote of no confidence but refuses to go quietly, or to break the deadlock by forcing new elections when a hung Parliament cannot choose a Prime Minister. These are delicate functions. They are never needed, except in fraught times of high political drama. Just as it is vital in a parliamentary democracy to keep the Head of State above and beyond the fray of day-to-day politics, so it is equal vital that the Head of State be able to intervene, decisively and legitimate, in situation where normal politics has stalled. For this to be possible, the rules must be explicit.

According to Walter Bagehot, Queen Victoria retained in relation to the ordinary powers governance three powers: to be consulted, to encourage and to warn.[175] Anne Twomey notes that at the time this formulation was devised, it understated – and perhaps continues to understate – the vast potential behind the scenes influence of the monarch.[176] After all, a person who can meet regularly in private with the Prime Minister, whose formal approval is required for almost every significant act of government, who is head of a church, colonel-in-chief of many regiments, joined by ties of blood and history to all the most powerful aristocratic families in the country, entitled to deal directly with the heads of the military and the security services, has worldwide fame and media influence, and is herself one of the richest people in the land, can hardly be powerless. The full extent of this influence and its effect on policy might never be known. This is not to say that the Queen dictates policy. The Head of State must, in the end, yield to formal advice – or else the whole edifice of parliamentary democracy and cabinet government comes crashing down. Before that formal advice is tendered, however, the informal personal influence of the Head of State may be brought to bear. It is not impossible to imagine that the private meetings between the Prime Minister and the Queen do occasionally result, if not in changes of policy, at least in moments of reflection and reconsideration. Some Westminster Model constitutions attempt to replicate this relationship between the Head of State and the Prime Minister. The Constitution of India (Section 74), for example, allows the President of India 'to require the Council of Ministers to reconsider' advice given; but demands that 'the President shall act in accordance with the advice tendered after such reconsideration'. In other words, the President can bounce something back once, and must then act on ministerial advice after reconsideration. The Constitution of Samoa (Section 40) similarly allows the Head of State to return a decision to the Cabinet for reconsideration, after which the Head of State must act in accordance with the reconsidered advice. These provisions are, however, exceptions. The standard formula used in most Westminster Model constitutions simply recognizes that the Prime Minister must keep the Head of State (or Governor-General) informed. Once again, the Constitution of Jamaica (Section 76) provides a typical example, stating that the Prime Minister must 'keep the Governor-General informed concerning the general conduct of the government' and 'furnish the Governor-General with such information as he may request with respect to any particular matter relating to the government of Jamaica'. In a United Kingdom context, it seems unnecessary and undemocratic to recognize the power to be consulted, to encourage and to warn in the constitution, or to allow the monarch to refer advice back for reconsideration. It is sufficient that the monarch be informed, and that an open channel of confidential communication between the Head of State and the Prime Minister be maintained. If the Head of State, with the supposed advantages of experience, permanence and non-partisanship, has wise and beneficial counsel to give, that open channel of confidential communication is all that is needed for it to be heard.

Finally, something must be said about the Privy Council. William Blackstone described the Privy Council as 'the principal council belonging to the king'.[177] When the monarch was the head of government, the Privy Council acted very much as a modern cabinet – a body made up of the principal officers of state and a number of trusted counsellors to the monarch, to discuss, decide and supervise the implementation of policy. With the Hanoverian constitutional settlement and the emergence of conventions of ministerial responsibility, the Privy Council ceased to be an active decision-making body. It not only became too large and unwieldy to discuss policy questions, but also fell out of step with the rise of responsible party government: the Privy Council includes people from across the political spectrum, including those of the Opposition. The usual practice was therefore to summon only the members of the Ministry – the Prime Minister's colleagues – to meetings of the Privy Council. In this way the modern Cabinet, as a board of senior ministers united under the leadership of the Prime Minister, was created. This transformation in the nature of the Privy Council is reflected in Westminster Model constitutions. The Canadian Constitution Act 1867 (Section 11) establishes 'the Queen's Privy Council for Canada', which remains the formal executive body, of which the Canadian Cabinet is technically a committee. By the time the Constitution of Jamaica was drafted, nearly a century later, the Privy Council and the Cabinet had become distinct, with the Privy Council for Jamaica acting as an advisory body to the Governor-General, particularly in relation to the prerogative of mercy.

Yet in the United Kingdom the Cabinet remains, in principle, a sort of executive committee of the Privy Council. The Privy Council is the body through which, formally at least, much of the workaday business of government is transacted. Policy decisions are taken in Cabinet, which then might have to be turned into formal instruments of governance through the Privy Council. In a refounded constitution for the United Kingdom, it seems wise to maintain the Privy Council as a wider body, including people of great eminence from across the political spectrum. It provides, in particular, a mechanism for communication between the Prime Minister and the Leader of the Opposition on sensitive subjects of great national importance, on which a bi-partisan approach may be valued. The real work of the Privy Council, though, would be done only by the ministers.

Cabinet government I: government formation and removal

The government in a Westminster Model democracy is directed by the Cabinet, a council of senior ministers headed by the Prime Minister. The ministers in principle take decisions collectively and are collectively responsible for them to Parliament. The government holds office in this system only by virtue of enjoying the confidence of a parliamentary majority. The first duty of Parliament, therefore, is to give its confidence to a government that can govern in accordance with the wishes of the parliamentary majority, and to withdraw that confidence if the government cannot govern or insists on governing in ways that are contrary to the wishes of the parliamentary majority. The government is, according to the famous 19th century political analyst Walter Bagehot, an 'executive committee' of Parliament, consisting of those who command the confidence of the parliamentary majority and are responsible to Parliament for the administration of public affairs; Parliament, in this scheme, is primarily an 'electoral college' that chooses and removes the government.[178]

When parliamentary democracy works well, there is a reciprocal relationship of mutual trust between the government and Parliament. The parliamentary majority can be said to act through the government, since the government is trusted to lead, take the initiative, formulate policy, propose legislation, and direct the administration, on behalf of the parliamentary majority; in so doing, the government gives effect to the majority's political programme as laid out in its manifesto – or, in the case of a coalition, as laid out in the coalition agreement. At the same time, the government can be said to act through Parliament, since Parliament is usually willing, so long as the relationship of confidence continues, to defer to the government's leadership, to pass the government's proposed budget, and to support – at least in broad and general terms – the government's legislative agenda. If Parliament withdraws its confidence from the government – either by a formal vote of no confidence, or by rejecting the budget or the Queen's Speech – then in most Westminster Model constitutions one of two things must happen: either the government must resign, enabling the formation of a new government that does enjoy the confidence of Parliament, or Parliament else must be dissolved, allowing the people to give their verdict in a new general election.

In principle, this system of government is both effective and responsible. It is effective because the government can set out a coherent policy programme to give effect to its manifesto commitments with reasonable expectation of being able to get most of their legislation through Parliament – not without challenge, scrutiny, some backbench amendments, and perhaps even concessions to the Opposition, but mostly intact. It is responsible because the government can only lead in the direction, and to the extent, that the parliamentary majority is willing to be led. If the government fails to lead, or tries to lead where Parliament is unable to follow, then the 'vote of no confidence' rule and the power of dissolution provide ways of resetting the system. The sort of prolonged impasse that occurs in the United States, where the President and congressional majority are of different parties, and can neither agree on policy nor pass a budget, should never happen in a Westminster Model democracy – or, if it does happen, should be swiftly resolved.

In recent years, the conventional rules and practices that once governed this relationship of confidence and mutual dependency between the government and the parliamentary majority have become increasingly strained. Theresa May and Boris Johnson have both clung on to office despite suffering the sort of devastating defeats in the House of Commons that would have forced any of their predecessors either to resign or request a dissolution. Once again, we see conventions and practices that were relatively clear, fairly well enforced, and functioned tolerably well, during the majoritarian heyday, have been pulled apart. Often, this takes the form of tension between two conventions or practices, both of which might be valid, and which used to work in sync, but which in today's unprecedented political situation create confusing, unpredictable ambiguities. For example, it is an established practice that if a general election results in a hung Parliament, the incumbent Prime Minister can remain in office and try to put together a working government that can pass a Queen's Speech. It is also a recognized principle, reflecting a democratic norm, that following such a general election the leader of the largest party should have precedence in the formation of a government. In 2010, the second of these practices seemed to have prevailed. Despite Prime Minister Gordon Brown attempting to hold on to power and to make use of the incumbency advantage to shore-up his majority by doing a deal with the Liberal Democrats in the days after the election, it very quickly became apparent that the initiative lay with David Cameron, whose Conservatives had won the most seats, and who were therefore seen as the more legitimate coalition partner. To some extent, the question of whether the incumbent or plurality winner should have priority in the government formation process is a secondary issue. The most important thing is that there be some rule, and that the rule be clear and enforced. We can drive on the left or drive on the right, as long as we have a clear and enforced rule so that we all drive on the same side – and can realistically expect others to do likewise. There should be no chance, in the midst of a high-pressure, high-stakes political drama, for uncertainty about the basic rules.

The deficiency of unwritten rules has long been recognized. As mentioned in Chapter 4, S.A. de Smith identified the advantages of explicitly codifying the conventions and practices of the Westminster Model in the text of New Commonwealth constitutions in the 1960s. The countries with older constitutions, without such explicit codification, have been forced to play catch up. After the constitutional crisis of 1975, when the Governor-General dismissed the Prime Minister, Australia attempted to write down – albeit in a merely declaratory, non-enforceable form – the key conventions and practices of parliamentary democracy and cabinet government.[179] In New Zealand and the United Kingdom – the Cabinet Manual performs a similar function, also in non-binding declaratory form.[180] Such arrangements can be useful. They may provide some much-needed authoritative guidance. They may help those seeking to act within the spirit of the constitution to do so with greater certainty. However, they are inferior substitute for proper, explicit treatment of the matter in the text of a written constitution. Being expressed only in non-binding and sub-constitutional texts, they are easier to ignore, change or violate, when politically expedient to do so. This is why, in most Westminster Model constitutions today, the basic principles of parliamentary democracy and cabinet government, including the rules on government formation and removal have been carefully inscribed in the constitution. The process of writing them down forced constitution drafters to decide between various competing interpretations of the conventions and practices. In the process, some decided to improve on those rules. This led to variations in practice between Westminster Model constitutions, in the details of the rules, if not in their general principles.

In terms of government formation, there are three main approaches. The first is to allow the Head of State (or Governor-General) to appoint the Prime Minister in accordance with his or her own discretion, based on a personal judgement of who is 'best able to command the confidence of a majority' in the elected House. For example, the Constitution of Barbados (Section 65) states that 'Whenever the Governor-General has occasion to appoint a Prime Minister he shall, acting in his discretion, appoint the member of the House of Assembly who, in his judgment, is best able to command the confidence of a majority of the members of that House.' The Constitution of Jamaica uses almost identical wording (Section 70). The Constitution of Malaysia (Section 43) provides that the Head of State is to appoint as Prime Minister 'a member of the House of Representatives who in [the Head of State's] judgment is likely to command the confidence of the majority of the members of that House'. The differences between 'most likely to command', 'best able to command' and other similar formulations are discussed by S.A. de Smith, who argues that 'best able to command' most accurately captures the essence of the conventional rules.[181]

The second approach is to explicitly recognize the practice that, in normal conditions, the leader of the majority party in the elected House will become Prime Minister. When there is a majority party, the leader of that party in the House has a constitutional expectation, perhaps a right, to be appointed as Prime Minister. Of course, if there is no such person (either because no party has an overall majority in the House, or because the party with an overall majority does not have a recognized leader), it becomes necessary to fall back on some other method of selection. In Antigua & Barbuda (Section 69), Belize (Section 37) and Trinidad & Tobago (Section 76), the fallback position is that the Head of State (or Governor-General) must exercise discretion in deciding who best commands the confidence of the House. The relevant provisions are as follows:

> Whenever there is occasion for the appointment of a Prime Minister, the Governor-General shall appoint as Prime Minister: a member of the House who is the leader in the House of the political party that commands the support of the majority of members of the House; or where it appears to him that such party does not have an undisputed leader in the House or that no party commands the support of such a majority, the member of the House who in his judgement is most likely to command the support of the majority of members of the House, and is willing to accept the office of Prime Minister. (Constitution of Antigua & Barbuda, Section 69).

> Whenever the Governor-General has occasion to appoint a Prime Minister he shall appoint a member of the House of Representatives who is the leader of the political party which commands the support of the majority of the members of that House; and if no political party has an

overall majority, he shall appoint a member of that House who appears to him likely to command the support of the majority of the members of that House. (Constitution of Belize, Section 37).

Where there is occasion for the appointment of a Prime Minister, the President shall appoint as Prime Minister – a member of the House of Representatives who is the Leader in that House of the party which commands the support of the majority of members of that House; or where it appears to him that that party does not have an undisputed leader in that House or that no party commands the support of such a majority, the member of the House of Representatives who, in his judgment, is most likely to command the support of the majority of members of that House; and who is willing to accept the office of Prime Minister. (Constitution of Trinidad & Tobago, Section 76).

The third approach is to enable the House to designate a Prime Minister by a formal vote. This approach is used in Ireland, where under article 13 of the Constitution, the President is required to appoint the Taoiseach (Prime Minister) on a resolution of the House. It is also used in Tuvalu and the Solomon Islands, where the Prime Minister is formally elected by a vote of MPs. The distinction between nomination by a resolution of the House and formal election by the House can be a blurred one, especially where there is only a single candidate proposed, whom members of the House vote for or against. Regardless of the details of the electoral or nominations process, the common feature of this approach is that it makes the office of Prime Minister depend on the express vote of the House. This has three advantages. Firstly, it increases the democratic legitimacy of the Prime Minister. They cannot sneak in by the back door. They have to submit to, and win, a vote in the elected chamber of people's representatives. Secondly, it keeps the Head of State out of the picture, with no need to exercise discretionary judgement as to who is best able to command the confidence of a majority. Thirdly, it is unambiguous. The result of the vote speaks for itself, and there can be no dispute as to whether the Prime Minister does or does not have the necessary parliamentary support. These three advantages may not be so significant if the electoral system and party system are such that single party majority governments are the norm. Under such conditions, there is not much room for discretion or dispute. In the context of multiparty politics, and in a proportionally elected House, these advantages become much more important.

Perhaps the best solution is a mixture of the second and third approaches. If there is a majority party or coalition, then its leader in the House of Commons would be appointed as Prime Minister. If there is no majority party or coalition, or if the majority party or coalition does not have a recognized leader in the House of Commons, then the House would nominate a Prime Minister by resolution. This can be seen either as the Trinidad & Tobago model, with nomination by Parliament as a fallback position if there is no party or coalition with an overall majority, or as the Irish model, but with nomination by formal vote dispensed with when the result would be a foregone conclusion because one party or coalition has an overall majority. The most important things are that the Head of State be removed from the process of government formation and that, in cases where there is any doubt, the government be legitimated by a formal parliamentary vote.

This combination is similar to that in the Constitution of Fiji (article 93). The difference is that the Fijian rules do not allow for the formation of minority governments: if after three attempts no Prime Minister has been elected by an overall majority of the Members of Parliament, Parliament is automatically dissolved and a new general election held. This is unduly restrictive and inflexible. Notwithstanding the deadlock of British politics, hamstrung by Brexit after the 2017 general election, minority governments can work. If ministers are willing to make certain concessions to the Opposition or to minor parties, they can get their legislative agenda through Parliament, and they are subject to more effective scrutiny. The advantage of nomination by a resolution of the House, over a formal majoritarian election, is that it enables the formation of a minority government if the House so desires. This is especially important as under these proposed rules, the formal nomination by the House would only take place in situations where no party or coalition has an overall majority. The practical effect of the resolution would, in many cases, therefore, be to authorize, by declaring the House's acceptance, the formation of a minority government.

A similar variation is evident in relation to the removal of the government. In some of the Westminster Model constitutions, a vote of no confidence removes the government from office (for example, Tuvalu, Solomon Islands). In others, a vote of no confidence results in the dissolution of Parliament and a new general election (for example, Barbados, Jamaica). In most, a vote of no confidence forces a situation in which the Prime Minister has a choice either to resign or request a dissolution of Parliament, and if a dissolution is requested the head of state or Governor-General then has a choice between granting that request and calling a general election, or refusing it and appointing another Prime Minister (for example, Malta, Ireland). This is discussed more fully in the section on the dissolution of Parliament. For now, it is sufficient to note that the two halves of the equation have to be balanced. The rules on the formation and removal of governments and the rules on dissolution have to be harmonized. There was a harmony in the old conventional rules. There are different types of harmony in the rules found in modern Westminster Model constitutions. The Fixed Term Parliaments Act 2011, by attempting to regulate only one-half of this equation, has introduced a disharmony, and contributed to exactly the sort of impasse that should not occur.

Cabinet government II: ministers and civil servants

Westminster Model constitutions provide for the appointment of ministers other than the Prime Minister by the Head of State (or Governor-General) on the advice of the Prime Minister. In Ireland, approval by the House is necessary, but this is a unique exception. Elsewhere, the binding advice of the Prime Minister suffices. A typical example is provided by the Constitution of Grenada (Section 58), which provides that

> Appointments to the office of Minister, other than the office of Prime Minister, shall be made by the Governor-General, acting in accordance with the advice of the Prime Minister, from among the Senators and the members of the House of Representatives.

It is a longstanding convention in the United Kingdom that ministers must be appointed from among the members of the two Houses of Parliament. Since the Prime Minister can make appointments to the House of Lords, there is always a way in which a non-MP can, if so desired, be appointed to ministerial office. Gordon Brown made use of this power when he appointed the former First Sea Lord, Alan West, and the entrepreneur Alan Sugar to the House of Lords in order that they might, despite lacking any previous parliamentary experience, hold ministerial office. A similar loophole exists in those countries where the Prime Minister can appoint members of the Senate – as in most of the Commonwealth Caribbean. Elsewhere, a requirement for ministers to be Members of Parliament is a more stringent restriction on the Prime Minister's choice. This is the case both in countries with unicameral Parliaments – like Malta and the Solomon Islands – and in countries where all members of the upper House are elected, like Australia and Pakistan.

In the 19th century, it was by no means unusual for a Prime Minister to sit in the House of Lords. By the middle of the 20th century this had become unacceptable. The new convention, that the Prime Minister must be a member of the House of Commons, was solidified in 1963, when Lord Home, on becoming Prime Minister, had to renounce his peerage and seek election to the House of Commons as Sir Alec Douglas-Home. This convention spread to other Commonwealth realms, even to Australia where the Senate is popularly elected: in 1968, when Senator John Gorton became leader of the governing Australian Liberal Party and thereby Prime Minister, he resigned from the Senate and was elected to the House of Representatives.[182] The constitutions of Westminster Model democracies adopted from the 1960s onwards reflected this convention and embodied it in their constitutional texts. The Constitution of Jamaica is typical, prescribing (Section 70) that the Prime Minister must be appointed from the House of Representatives, while other ministers shall be appointed 'from among the members of the two Houses'. It is notable that the Jamaican constitution was adopted in 1962, the year before Home became Prime Minister in the United Kingdom. This is a good example of the way in which New Commonwealth Westminster Model constitutions led, rather than followed, British practices.

While most such constitutions prescribe that ministers must be Members of Parliament, and that the Prime Minister must be a member of the lower or popularly elected House, there are usually exceptions allowing ministers who were Members of Parliament before a dissolution to continue in office for a limited period notwithstanding the dissolution (if this were not the case, all ministers would be ejected from office when Parliament is dissolved, which would clearly be unworkable). The Constitution of Trinidad & Tobago, for example, provides (Section 76) that:

> Where occasion arises for making an appointment to the office of Minister while Parliament is dissolved, a person who immediately before the dissolution, was a Senator or a member of the House of Representatives may be appointed Minister.

There may be a period of grace during which a minister may hold office pending election. The Constitution of Australia (Section 64), for example, provides that, no minister 'shall hold office for a longer period than three months unless he is or becomes a senator or a member of the House of Representatives'. That means any non-parliamentarian appointed to ministerial office has three months during which to try to obtain a seat in Parliament (usually in a by-election). Such provisions allow for some flexibility: to return to the example of John Gorton mentioned earlier, there was a period, between his resignation from the Senate on 1 February 1968 and his election to the House of Representatives on 24 February 1969, during which he took advantage of this rule.[183] Nevertheless, the general principle upheld by these constitutions is that ministerial office in a Westminster Model democracy comes from, and is additional to, parliamentary duties. There is an important idea at stake here: that ministerial office is essentially a political office, and that ministers are *politicians*. This is quite distinct from some continental European democracies, where ministers are not required to be MPs, and are frequently appointed from the civil service.

Another design consideration is a constitutional limit on the number of ministers. Those who hold ministerial office are bound, by the doctrine of collective ministerial responsibility, to vote in accordance with the government's 'whip' (party line). The principle is that ministers who are of Cabinet rank have a right to free discussion in Cabinet, but once a Cabinet decision is taken all ministers must assume collective responsibility for it; if they cannot reconcile the decision with their consciences (or the calculation of their political interests) then they must resign from office. This is probably a good system, in terms of being able to deliver coherent policies and providing responsible government. It does create problems in small Parliaments, as found in some South Pacific and Caribbean states, where recruiting enough ministers to fill the Cabinet can result in all, or very nearly all, of the government's MPs being given ministerial office. The 'friendly-but-critical' government backbenchers, who in Westminster Model Parliaments have such a vital if underappreciated role in ensuring accountability and improving the quality of legislation,[184] are squeezed out. In Tuvalu in 2018, for example, there were 15 Members of Parliament, of which eight held office, leaving only seven MPs to perform all scrutiny and oversight functions. Such numbers are, of course, extreme. Yet even in a relatively large Parliament there may be tendency to increase the number of ministers in order to swell the guaranteed bloc of government support.

The expansion of this so-called 'payroll vote' is open to abuse. Several Westminster Model constitutions have therefore introduced provisions to prevent it. In some constitutions, this limit is can be determined by law. In the Solomon Islands, for example, the constitution (Section 33) states that the number of ministers shall not exceed 'eleven or such greater number as Parliament may prescribe'. The Australian Constitution limits the number of ministers to just seven 'until Parliament otherwise prescribes'. Such flexible restrictions are likely to be ineffective in limiting the size of the payroll vote since the parliamentary majority can always evade or nullify the effect of these restrictions by statute. In Australia, the Ministers of State Act 1952, as currently amended and in force, sets the number of ministers at 30, plus 12 Parliamentary Secretaries.[185]

Other constitutions set more realistic – but less flexible – limits on the number of ministers. Under the Constitution of Belize (Section 40), the limit is 'not more than two-thirds of the elected Members of the party that obtains the majority seats in the House of Representatives following the holding of a general election' and 'not more than four Senators'. With the government having at the time of writing 19 seats in the 31 seat lower House, this means the number of ministers is limited to 12 – a little less than 40 per cent of the total membership of the House. The rule in Belize only applies, however, to members of the Cabinet, not to junior ministers. This, too, evades the intent of the rule. A better formulation is found in India, where the Constitution (article 75) limits the number of persons holding ministerial office (including Cabinet ministers and junior ministers outside the Cabinet) to 15 per cent of the total membership of the House of the People. The draft constitution for an independent Scotland drafted by the SNP in 2002 proposed limiting the number of ministers to 20 per cent of the Members of Parliament.[186] Whether the constitutionally prescribed maximum number of ministers should be 15 per cent, 20 per cent, or some other figure depends in part on the size of Parliament: in a small country, with a small Parliament, it might be necessary for a relatively higher percentage – perhaps up to one-third of the total – to hold ministerial office, simply so that the cabinet posts can be filled; in a relatively large country, for a Parliament measured in the hundreds and not in the dozens of members, limiting the number of ministers (including right down to Parliamentary Private Secretaries) to about 15–20 per cent of the total number of MPs is appropriate.

There are many other aspects of cabinet government to be regulated by the Constitution. Most Westminster Model constitutions are remarkably similar in these provisions. They provide for, example, for the allocation of functions to each minister. They formally establish the Cabinet as an executive committee of senior ministers having 'general direction and control of the Government', and state that the

Cabinet is collectively responsible to Parliament. Most provide for the performance of the duties of the Prime Minister in situations where the Prime Minister is absent or incapacitated, or if the office of Prime Minister suddenly becomes vacant by reason of the Prime Minister's death in office. The oath to be taken by ministers is prescribed. The relationship between ministers and Permanent Secretaries (the senior civil servants in each department) is also defined, as is the office of 'Cabinet Secretary' or 'Secretary to the Cabinet'. The following selected provisions, taken from the Constitution of Antigua & Barbuda (just because it is at the top of the alphabetical list), are typical of the standard formulae found, with minor variations, in almost all New Commonwealth Westminster Model constitutions:

> There shall be a Cabinet for Antigua and Barbuda which shall have the general direction and control of the Government and shall be collectively responsible therefor to Parliament. The Cabinet shall consist of the Prime Minister and such number of other Ministers (of whom one shall be the Attorney-General) … as the Prime Minister may consider appropriate. (Section 70)

> The Governor-General, acting in accordance with the advice of the Prime Minister, may, by directions in writing, assign to the Prime Minister or any other Minister responsibility for any business of the Government, including the administration of any department of government. (Section 71)

> Where the Prime Minister is absent from Antigua and Barbuda or is unable … to perform the functions conferred on him by this Constitution, the Governor-General may authorise some other member of the Cabinet to perform those functions. (Section 74)

> There shall be a Secretary to the Cabinet whose office shall be a public office. The Secretary to the Cabinet, who shall have charge of the Cabinet office, shall be responsible in accordance with such instructions as may be given him by the Prime Minister, for arranging the business for, and keeping the minutes of, the Cabinet and for conveying the decisions of the Cabinet to the appropriate person or

authority and shall have such other functions as the Prime Minister may direct. (Section 77)

Where any Minister has been assigned responsibility for any department of government, he shall exercise direction and control over that department; and, subject to such direction and control, the department shall be under the supervision of a Permanent Secretary whose office shall be a public office. (Section 78)

Here are some of the bare bones of a flat-pack, export-ready, Westminster Model system of cabinet government. In writing down the basic principles, conventions, practices and norms, in a way that made it possible to establish Westminster Model democracies all over the world, the constitution drafters of the decolonization era have paved the way to constitutional renewal in the United Kingdom. They have identified what is crucial and essential. These are the things that make the system of government understandable, both to the public and to those engaged in politics and public administration at the highest levels. In so doing, they have left a landmark to which, when distracted, divided, and demoralized, we can be recalled. It might seem like dreary stuff – and much of it is – but these are the rules, the practices, the institutions, that have sustained democracy and delivered acceptably good government in many parts of the world, wherever they have been faithfully adhered to. Departure from these fundamentals – as happened, for example, in those African countries where populist leaders were impatient with the old colonial ways – never resulted in a better democracy or a better administration. In part that is because the Westminster Model is not simply a parliamentary political system. It is also an administrative system and a judicial system. It works together as a package. Within its core principles, many variations can be made, but that core must be preserved – by writing it down, clearly and simply, in a constitution.

8

Parliament I: Functions, Powers and Composition

Roles and functions of Parliament

Westminster Model constitutions around the world have a lot to say about Parliament. Typically, the constitution will prescribe the composition of Parliament, the manner in which members are chosen, qualifications and disqualifications for being a member, their terms of office, the circumstances under which a member can be removed, the procedure for the resignation of members,[i] the election and removal of the Speaker, the privileges of Parliament and of its members, rules concerning adoption of standing orders, the quorum, remuneration of members, summoning and sessions of Parliament, rules for dissolution and the timing of elections, the procedure for the enactment of legislation, and much else. Where there are two Houses, some of this will be covered in duplicate, and the relationship between the Houses laid out.

Before proceeding to consider those specific design choices, it might be helpful to make some introductory remarks on the functions that a Parliament is expected to perform in a Westminster Model democracy. Synthesizing several classic authorities on this subject, including Walter Bagehot's *The English Constitution*, John Stuart Mill's *On Representative Government* and Sir Ivor Jennings' *Parliament*, seven main functions can be identified: (1) selecting, sustaining and removing governments; (2) legislation; (3) influencing and restraining governments in policy

---

[i] The farcical British practice of applying for the Stewardship of the Chiltern Hundreds as a way of leaving Parliament is, thankfully, not one that has been replicated by the Westminster Model constitutions.

making; (4) representing the people; (5) ensuring public accountability; (6) being a discursive forum for the formation and education of public opinion; and (7) enhancing the legitimacy of government.

Parliament in a Westminster Model democracy does not actively govern, but it does make and break governments. In so doing, Parliament determines what general direction of policy can be pursued. Policy making is directed by the Cabinet and takes place through individual ministries and Cabinet committees, but Parliament determines – through its votes of confidence and no confidence – who shall have the authority to make those decisions, and the conditions on which they shall do so. This, as Bagehot identified, is the first function of Parliament in a parliamentary democracy. Parliament (specifically the House of Commons) is like a permanent electoral college, which can not only 'choose' a Prime Minister, but also remove a Prime Minister from office – or at least force a general election and let the people decide.

The second function of Parliament is to legislate. The government will normally set the legislative agenda and propose most bills that have a chance of passing, but Parliament has the power to scrutinize legislation, to discuss its principles, to pick it over in detail, and to propose amendments. As bills go through their various legislative stages, Parliament may accept, amend, strengthen, improve and sometimes reject them. It is rare, of course, for Parliament to reject government bills outright. The principle of confidence means that the government will usually be backed by a loyal parliamentary majority and can usually count on parliamentary support for its proposed legislation. It is wrong, however, to conclude from this that Parliament is a mere 'talking shop' or 'rubber stamp'. Parliament has real and vital role in shaping legislation and policy; the Opposition, backbench members, committees, and cross-party groups, can all influence and constrain the government's action, particularly when they are able to engage with the media and to mobilize external pressure groups.[187]

The third function is to deliberate and debate public issues. Democratic government is government by discussion. Parliament acts a sounding board, not only for the people to speak to the government, but also for different parts, sections and classes of the people to speak to one another. These deliberations are not merely theatrical. They can raise issues, set the agenda, and influence and restrain government policy. The government must set out a policy, but it is up to Parliament to debate and scrutinize that policy, and to shape and develop it through such means as questions, debates, committee reports and lobbying both by individual members and by cross-party groups – at all stages of the policy-making process. For the policy intention of the government to be defeated outright on the floor of the House – as happened for example in 2013, when the House of Commons voted against the government's policy of bombardments in Syria – is rare enough to make headlines, but it is not unusual for a minister to review a policy decision after an unfavourable committee report, or to offer concessions on the implementation of policy in response to hostile questioning.

Fourth, Parliament is an instrument of accountability. It probes and peeks into the workings of the government, using ministerial statements, debates, committee investigations and reports, and oral and written questions, to hold the government to account. The government can govern, but it must be prepared to explain and justify its decisions in Parliament. This searchlight of accountability better enables the public, as citizens and voters, to judge the conduct and behaviour of the government at the next election. It also ensures that the decisions of public authorities are taken in the light of public reason: the very act of having to explain, justify and give account reduces the risk of arbitrary government and increases the likelihood that the government will use its great powers in responsible, publicly defensible, ways.

Fifth, aside from its tangible effects on policy and legislation, Parliament also has a representative role. It is the 'mirror of the people', reflecting their interests and opinions.[188] This mirroring should reflect not only differences of ideology, opinion or programme, but also the geographical, economic and demographic variety of society. In Bagehot's words, it 'ought to represent the various special interests, special opinions, special prejudices, to be found in that community'.[189] As a representative embodiment of the people, Parliament's existence is a persistent reminder that government work is public business. When standing at the despatch box to make a statement or answer a question, a Minister of the Crown is in the midst of 'the people' – who cannot be physically present to deliberate on public affairs, but are virtually, symbolically, one might almost say sacramentally, present by representation. This is why the current trend of ministers giving press conferences and the Prime Minister making policy statements from a podium in front of 10 Downing Street is so inconsistent with representative democracy; it symbolizes a power that has become detached from its parliamentary moorings.

The sixth role of Parliament is to be a practical school of civic education. Parliamentary proceedings are reported, televised, and available to livestream on the internet. Debates provide opportunities for issues to be explored from different angles. In the cut-and-thrust of debates, if Parliament is doing its job well, flawed arguments can be exposed, group-think bubbles punctured, and public opinion educated. It is not only the place where the people speak to the government and the government speaks to the people; it is also the place where the people speak to one another. The correct image here is that of the ancient Greek theatre: not just a place for staged comedy and tragedy, but the centre of public and civic life, where public debates are held and where public opinion is developed, educated and expressed.

Finally, Parliament is a legitimating body, conferring public legitimacy on the decisions that are taken. No organized political society could subsist if we had to give unanimous consent, or even majority consent, to each and every decision. The important thing is that the decision-making process as a whole must enjoy public legitimacy. Decisions must be seen: (a) to emerge from an inclusive representative institution that faithfully embodies a diverse people; and (b) to be reached through a deliberative process that enables these diverse viewpoints to be expressed, weighed and considered.

These functions are not always cleanly distinguishable – the boundaries between them are ragged and porous – but taken together they make Parliament an indispensable element of the polity. A strong, well-functioning, properly representative Parliament will promote the wellbeing of the polity as a whole; a weak, corrupt, poorly-functioning, unrepresentative Parliament will undermine the country. A new constitution must therefore seek to maximize the effectiveness of Parliament in each of its roles. The following sections of this chapter concentrate on how that might be achieved, in terms of the composition, powers and organization of Parliament. In each of these aspects, the experience of Westminster-derived Parliaments can be highly instructive.

Legislative powers of Parliament

Under a written constitution, Parliament's legislative power must be exercised only subject to, and in accordance with, the constitution. The constitution not only defines and limits the ordinary legislative power, but also creates and authorizes that power in the first place. This can be seen in plain terms in many Westminster-derived constitutions. The Constitution of Australia states (Section 51) that 'The Parliament shall, subject to this Constitution, have power to make laws for the peace, order, and good government of the Commonwealth with respect to [a list of federal legislative powers]'. The Canadian Constitution Act 1867 (Section 91) likewise declares that

> It shall be lawful for the Queen, by and with the Advice and Consent of the Senate and House of Commons, to make Laws for the Peace, Order, and good Government of Canada, in relation to all Matters not coming within the Classes of Subjects by this Act assigned exclusively to the Legislatures of the Provinces.

These are both federal examples, where the legislative power of Parliament is limited by the existence of other – state or provincial – legislatures. Similar terms can be found in the unitary Constitution of Jamaica (Section 48), which states that, 'Subject to the provisions of this Constitution, Parliament may make laws for the peace, order and good government of Jamaica.' (Constitution of Jamaica, Section 48). The Constitution of Malta (article 61), to cite just one more example, declares that, 'Subject to the provisions of this Constitution, Parliament may make laws for the peace, order and good government of Malta in conformity with full respect for human rights, generally accepted principles of international law and Malta's international and regional obligations …'

The recurring formulaic phrase 'peace, order and good government' is the term used to confer legislative power in many Westminster Model jurisdictions. Its origins can be traced to instructions to colonial governors issued at least as early as 1673, and was established as the standard formula for conferring legislative power by the end of the 19th century.[190] It implies a plenitude, or at least a very near-plenitude, of legislative power, subject only to the constitution. According to Mohammed Khan, it 'has been held that the words peace, order and good government connote, in British constitutional language, the widest law-making powers appropriate to a sovereign legislature'.[191]

The phrase 'peace, order and good government' was always related to a specifically named jurisdiction or political community, and there was historically some question as to whether it contained a restriction on the power of a legislature to pass extra-territorial legislation. In practical terms, any such restriction that might once have existed has been explicitly denied in relation to those Dominion Parliaments which have adopted the Statute of Westminster (Section 3, read together with Section 10). The Australia Act 1986 (Section 2) likewise lifted any restriction on the extra-territorial effect of legislation by Australian states. Some Westminster-derived constitutions confer the power to enact laws with extra-territorial effect in express terms, and it seems sensible, for the avoidance of doubt, to adopt this approach in a constitution for the United Kingdom. For example, the Constitution of Tuvalu (Section 86(a)) provides that, 'Subject to this Constitution, Parliament may make laws, not inconsistent with this Constitution, including laws having effect outside Tuvalu'.

There may be, embedded somewhere deep within this formulaic grant of a near-plenitude of legislative power, an implicit restriction against egregiously illegitimate, arbitrary and tyrannical abuse. By way of illustration, and not in an attempt to argue the matter conclusively, it is notable that in a case related to the expulsion of Chagos Islanders from their land, the High Court found that a grant of powers for peace, order and good government 'while broad, did not include a power to remove people from their homelands'.[192]

In some Westminster-derived Constitutions, the traditional 'peace, order and good government' formula has been abandoned in favour of a blank and bold statement conferring legislative power. The Constitution of Samoa, for example, provides (Art. 43) that 'Subject to the provisions of this Constitution, Parliament may make laws for the whole or any part of Samoa and laws having effect outside as well as within Samoa'. Even if the courts are reluctant to give any legal effect to the traditional formula in limiting gross abuses of legislative power, it seems wise to steer away from such a change. Constitutions are not only legal documents. They are also political covenants and sociological expressions of identity and hope. The term 'peace, order and good government' may help shape expectations and influence for the better the tone of public debate. It declares – in a vague, mostly dormant but nevertheless influential way – that public power is not supposed to be arbitrary, capricious or self-interested, but exists for the sake of the public good and should be used responsibly.

Much of the work of government takes place through secondary legislation: regulation, Orders-in-Council or statutory instruments adopted by ministers under a general framework established by Act of Parliament. Within their proper scope, and with proper procedural safeguards for scrutiny and approval are in place, secondary legislation is a necessary expedient that facilitates effective and efficient government.

However, there is a particularly dangerous type of delegated legislative power – the so-called 'Henry VIII powers', by which ministers are given the authority to make secondary legislation that amends or repeals Acts of Parliament. The ability to make law in this way has been expanded by the Legislative and Regulatory Reform Act 2006, which enables ministers to make 'regulatory reform orders' sweeping aside statutory provisions. According to Lord Judge, such Henry VIII powers are unnecessary, damaging to democracy, and should be 'confined to the dustbin of history'.[193] A written constitution could limit the use of secondary legislation, taking a firmer stand against 'Henry VIII powers'. At a minimum, the constitution should require secondary legislation amending or repealing Acts of Parliament to be passed only by the so-called 'affirmative procedure', which requires positive authorization by a vote of both Houses of Parliament, rather than the usually ineffective 'negative procedure' which merely enables Parliament to vote for the annulment of orders that have already been made.

The House of Commons

If the House of Commons[ii] is to perform its functions adequately, it must be properly representative of the people. Its legitimacy and its authority depend on its being a faithful reflection of the society it represents. The composition and mode of election of the House has, at various points in the past, been changed to improve its representative character. The 1832 and 1867 Reform Acts, by extending the suffrage and redistributing seats from rotten boroughs (those subject to blatant corruption) and pocket boroughs (those effectively in the 'pocket' of a rich patron) to the new towns, changed the composition of the House to bring it more into line with the people. Subsequent reforms, from the establishment of a Boundaries Commission to provide for the periodic review of constituency boundaries, to the extension of the right to vote to women on the same terms as men in 1928, have had the same end in view. While the House of Commons is indeed an ancient and venerable institution, it has not been a static one.

The current First Past the Post (or, as it is sometimes known to comparative scholars, 'Single Member Plurality') electoral system is a relatively recent innovation. It was only introduced for the election of 1885 (under the Representation of the People Act 1884). By this time, the system of parliamentary government was already well-established and had already begun to spread across the self-governing parts of the Empire. When Canada achieved responsible government

---

[ii] The name of the popularly elected House varies between Westminster Model constitutions. In the Bahamas, Barbados and Saint Lucia, it is known as the 'House of Assembly'. In Australia, Jamaica and Trinidad & Tobago, it is the 'House of Representatives'. India uses the name 'House of the People' (*Lok Sabha*). Canada follows the English custom and uses 'House of Commons'. If 'House of Commons' has any particular merit, besides the weight of tradition, it is that it contains, buried somewhere in its etymology, the idea that it represents the commonality (ordinary people) and the Commonweal (the common good, the public interest). It does no harm to be reminded of these things.

in 1867 under a parliamentary system 'similar in principle to that of the United Kingdom', First Past the Post was still nearly two decades into the future. There is nothing uniquely British about it, and nothing to say that the First Past the Post system is integral to the Westminster Model of parliamentary democracy. By the early 20th century, it was already being superseded in some parts of the Empire. Alternative Vote (also known as 'instant run-off', or 'preferential majority') system was adopted in Australia for the 1919 federal general election. Ireland has used the Single Transferable Vote system since 1922.

Today, Westminster Model constitutions using a wide variety of electoral systems can be found. Malta has used Single Transferable Vote since before it achieved independence in 1964. New Zealand switched to the Additional Member ('Multi-Member Plurality') system in 1996 – a system that, closer to home, is also used for the Scottish Parliament, the National Assembly for Wales, and the London Assembly. Alternative Vote has been used in Papua New Guinea and in Fiji, although the new (2013) constitution of Fiji provides for a simple party-list system of proportional representation. A change of the electoral system to better represent the people would not, therefore, be contrary to the Westminster tradition, but entirely in keeping with it. It is true that the majority of Westminster Model democracies use First Past the Post, but plenty of other tried and tested options are available.

The faults of First Past the Post are well known: it over-rewards the largest party, while under-rewarding third and minor parties. Likewise, the standard arguments for electoral reform on grounds are fairness have been rehearsed many times, and there is no need to repeat them here. It is necessary only to draw attention to some of the standard arguments against electoral reform that no longer stand up to scrutiny. For a long time, the orthodox opinion was that the faults of First Past the Post were more than compensated for by the virtues of the system. This view has recently been restated with some force by Frances Rosenbluth and Ian Shapiro.[194] However, these arguments are less credible now than they used to be. There are four particular weaknesses that have become increasingly apparent: (a) First Past the Post does not always deliver strong and stable governments; (b) First Past the Post does not ensure moderation, and can in fact increase polarization; (c) First Past the Post does not in practice provide effective local representation; and (d) First Past the Post no longer reliably produces a broadly supported government with sufficient democratic legitimacy.

Firstly, it might be argued that we should not focus too much on the character of Parliament as a representative body, but should instead be concerned with the stability and effectiveness of the government, and on the responsibility of the government to the people. First Past the Post has often been praised for delivering strong, stable government, with single party majority governments able to carry out their manifesto commitments. Proportional representation, in contrast, was traditionally thought to result in weak, divided, incoherent government, and blurred lines of accountability. However, this is not always the case. The examples of Ireland and New Zealand, in particular, show that a Westminster Model political system can operate successfully with a proportionally elected Parliament. The political realities of coalition government do curtail the freedom of action of Prime Ministers, who have to keep their coalition partners on-side, and whose ability to unilaterally dictate terms to Cabinet colleagues is thereby restrained. However, this does not prevent the Cabinet from exercising leadership, nor does it result in weak or unstable governments. In fact, across a range of government performance and outcome measures, countries with proportional electoral systems and coalition governments do better, not worse, than countries with majoritarian systems.[195] There is no trade-off, as once was thought to be the case, between representative democracy and responsible government.

Besides, the assumption that First Past the Post would deliver strong and stable government has not always held true. It only really describes the operation of the electoral system during the second half of the 20th century, when the two-party system was sustained by a broad social consensus on many issues, and when socio-economic class was the main determinant of voting behaviour.[196] That brief period of two-party dominance may have been the aberration, not the norm. From 1885 to 1945, there were several hung Parliaments and minority governments, as well as national coalition governments during times of crisis. In recent years, even on its own terms, by its own measure of success, First Past the Post seems to be failing – it failed in 2010 and 2017. That is not to say it will not deliver single party majority governments in the future (as it did in 2015 and 2019) but the rise of new forms of identity politics, the dealignment of class voting, and the emergence of new sociological and ideological cleavages, have made it less reliable. If hung Parliaments, minority governments and coalitions are the 'new normal', or at least a recurring possibility, we might as well sort out the arithmetic and have a House of Commons in which governments are formed on the basis of how people have actually voted.

A second traditionally cited advantage of First Past the Post is that it has a moderating effect, promoting alternation in power between two moderate, big-tent parties. This also seemed to hold in the decades following the Second World War: although orientating to the centre-right and centre-left, both major parties had to compete for centrist swing voters, whose effect was to prevent splintering to the extremes. However, when there are two big parties who alone have a realistic possibility of forming a government, and when these parties are pushed to the extremes, First Past the Post seems to reinforce, and not to moderate, polarization. In the aftermath of the Brexit referendum, this polarization has reached unprecedented levels. Thatcher and Foot in the 1980s had deeply polarized and antagonistic views on policy issues, but were both working in the context of a political system with fairly stable and well-established institutional foundations; by 2019, at the time of the prorogation crisis, Boris Johnson and Labour leader Jeremy Corbyn had no such institutional consensus to fall back on. In contrast, proportional electoral systems, although traditionally criticized for allowing small extremist parties to establish a toehold, may actually be more effective at limiting the influence of extremists, who can be isolated by the formation of centre-spanning grand coalitions.

Thirdly, the First Past the Post system is conventionally praised for the strength of its local representation through the constituency link between voters and Members of Parliament. In reality, the concerns of voters living outside highly targeted marginal constituencies are often ignored. The total number of votes received is less important that where those votes are cast. Election results can be quite arbitrary, since a small swing, if in the right places, can make all the difference. This causes the parties to concentrate on a small number of marginal constituencies, while ignoring others. A Conservative government has no incentive to try to minimize the damage it does in Scotland; a Labour government has no need to concern itself with rural voters in the South; in each case, large swathes of the country are written-off as politically and electorally irrelevant.

Finally, First Past the Post was viewed as being responsive – albeit in a very approximate, rough-and-ready way – to public opinion. A general election would, on the whole, reflect deep shifts in the public mood. The government could be held responsible because there was a clear choice: keep that government in office or kick it out and put in the other lot. The government, if not based on an absolute majority of the votes, would at least be based on a near-majority. During the period of two-party dominance, governing parties routinely won more than 45 per cent of the popular vote. Governments could legitimately and with some justification present themselves as the 'people's choice', even if only the choice between just two viable options. This is no longer the case. An increasingly complex and diverse society cannot be adequately represented by a two-party system. Attempting to squeeze it artificially into that mould through an electoral system that penalizes all but the biggest parties produces results that are not only unfair, in some abstract and theoretical sense, but also of dubious democratic legitimacy. A majority for one party might rest on a very thin section of the electorate – in 2005 Labour won a majority on 35 per cent of the vote, and in 2015 the Conservatives won a majority on 36 per cent of the vote. Governments no longer have to appeal to 'most of the people, most of the time'; they can win and hold office by appealing only to their specific voters in specific constituencies. This might – and does – win elections, but it weakens the moral authority of the political system as a whole. Governments based on such narrow electoral foundations cannot claim broad public legitimacy. They seem – and are – out of touch and unresponsive. They do not enjoy public trust. Everything is brittle, fragile, precarious. First Past the Post is government of a minority, by a minority, for a minority. The pressures and resentments that cannot be vented through such an exclusionary electoral system inevitably build up and fester until, at the first opportunity for release, they explode in a burst of vitriol – as, one could argue, happened in the 2016 referendum on leaving the European Union.

A key part of Rosenbluth and Shapiro's argument in favour of First Past the Post is that it supposedly forces parties to cater to the general public, and not to small, specific interests.[197] If this was once the case, in the era of mass two-party politics, it is not today. Elections under First Past the Post are no longer a competition between two large blocs, each of which hopes to speak convincingly in the name of a majority. Instead, they are contests between minority parties trying to build artificial parliamentary majorities by gaming the system through the strategic delivery of votes in marginal constituencies. Politics under First Past the Post revolves around the needs of 'Mondeo Man' and 'Worcester Woman'; general public demands, outside the needs of these key demographic target audiences, are easily ignored. 'Big data' and 'micro-targetting' techniques help those with the best financial resources and the best connections to the technology and surveillance industries to do this more effectively than their competitors. The result is no different, in effect, from the Parliament of the 18th century packed full of placemen from rotten and pocket boroughs; it has ceased to be a broadly acceptable, representative, responsible legislature that adequately reflects the public and has become a den of narrow particular interests. Now, as then, it is calling out for major reform.

Proportional representation is the only way to ensure that the House of Commons adequately represents the people. The exact form of proportional representation is a secondary issue. There is no perfect electoral system, and all have their advantages and disadvantages.[198] Three considerations, however, should be borne in mind – not as absolute criteria, but as desirable features of any electoral system that is likely to win widespread public approval in a country long used to First Past the Post. The first is that some constituency link should be maintained, even if this is in larger constituencies or in multi-member constituencies. The second is that the electoral system should avoid excessive splintering and fragmentation of the party system. Providing a broadly proportional outcome is good enough. There is no need to obsess about mathematical purity. Forms of proportional representation that *slightly* over-represent larger parties, or that exclude very tiny parties, would still be an advance on First Past the Post, without making coalition formation impossible. The third is that there should be some personal choice – the ability to vote for individuals at some level, and not merely to vote for impersonal party lists. At the same time, however, it should not encourage too much intra-party (as opposed to inter-party) competition: it should maintain the unity and cohesion of political parties.

There are basically two ways in which these three features can be realized: by the Single Transferable Vote system in moderately sized constituencies of, say, five or six members; or by means of the Additional Member System with about half the seats allocated in single member constituencies and about half the seats allocated on a 'top-up' basis from regional lists. Both have their shortcomings. Single Transferable Vote is complex and not always very transparent; manual counting can take days, and it is hard to trace how individual preferences are redistributed. It can also lead to intra-party competition, which in the Irish context has tended to result in clientelistic politics as candidates from the same party seek to distinguish themselves from their colleagues by the ability to win 'pork' for their constituencies. The Additional Member System (also known as the Mixed Member Proportional system) creates a distinction between two types of MPs, constituency members and 'top-up' list members, with the latter sometimes seen as 'second class'. On balance, the Additional Member System is probably preferable, if only because it promotes more coherent parties and is already familiar to voters in Scotland, Wales and London. Yet, the key principle is to end 'winner takes all' politics; either of these electoral systems would be a great improvement on First Past the Post.

Mention should also be made of the 'Alternative Vote Plus' system, recommended by the Jenkins Commission in 1998.[199] This system, which was never implemented, would have used the Alternative Vote (preferentially ranked ballot in single member constituencies) to elect constituency members, with a small top-up list portion (between 15 per cent and 20 per cent of the total membership of the House), chosen in grouped county-wide or city-wide constituencies, to lessen the degree of disproportionality. This proposal is not, however, fully proportional: the small number of top-up members, and the small areas in which they are chosen, together render the system semi-proportional at best. If adjusted so that the number of top-up members was around 40 per cent to 50 per cent of the total, and if these members were elected in larger constituencies (for example, those formerly used for the election of members of the European Parliament), it would be a promising combination of Alternative Vote and the Additional Member System.

The design of the electoral system is always a contentious issue in constitution-building. It directly influences who wins and who loses. With the stakes so high, decisions based on calculations of partisan advantage, rather than considerations of the public good, are perhaps unavoidable. In any future constitution-building process, the decision to adopt proportional representation is likely to be up there with federalism, or the decision to adopt a written constitution with a proper bill of rights in the first place, as one of the grand-strategic, state-redefining, power-recasting decisions that a Constituent Assembly would have to take as an essential pillar of the new constitutional bargain. It need hardly be mentioned that the rejection of Alternative Vote – which is not a proportional system – in the 2011 referendum should not be seen as an obstacle to that decision, nor as a mandate for First Past the Post.

In designing an electoral system to represent 'the people', it is important to remember that 'the people' are not one indistinguishable or homogeneous mass. The people are old and young, men and women, rich and poor, urban and rural, religious and secular, graduates and non-graduates, conservative and progressive, able-bodied and disabled, omnivores and vegetarians, water-skiers and bird watchers, motorists and cyclists. It is difficult for any institution to capture all these different aspects of representation. Decisions must be made about which of these beliefs, identities and roles are more important in designing a representative body. While many politically relevant interests and identities can be represented through a proportional electoral system, some Westminster Model Parliaments feature additional mechanisms designed to produce a House that not only thinks as the people think, but also looks – in all its diversity – as the people looks.

One such mechanism is a gender quota, or reserved seats for women. Gender quotas are rare in Westminster Model constitutions, being found only in Bangladesh and Samoa, although other British-influenced constitutions in sub-Saharan Africa do use them. Quotas can take various forms. In Bangladesh, a number of women members (50) are co-opted by the (300) directly elected members, thereby ensuring that women will have at least 14 per cent of the seats. The Constitution of Samoa (article 44), uses a 'best loser' system, in which women candidates who have not been directly elected, but have received the highest number of votes from among the runners-up, are awarded seats in Parliament, if necessary, to bring the total number of women in Parliament to 10 per cent of the total number of seats. Whether such arrangements are needed, or beneficial, in a British context is an open question. There are sound arguments – practical and theoretical – both for and against gender quotas, which it is not necessary to go into here. It is sufficient to note that such mechanisms do exist, and that if desired they can be ingrafted to a Westminster Model political system. In general, a proportional electoral system is thought to help ensure more gender-balanced representation anyway,[200] so changing to proportional representation may render superfluous additional measures intended specifically to address gender imbalance.

Another such mechanism is the ethnic quota, or reserved seats for certain ethnic groups. Three examples can be drawn upon: from New Zealand, India, and Mauritius. New Zealand's electoral system provides for a separate optional electoral role for the Maori, who thereby have an assured presence in the New Zealand Parliament. At present this is seven seats, out of a total of 120 seats, reflecting the number of voters who choose to register on the Maori electoral roll; Maori voters can also choose to register on the general roll and to vote in general constituencies. In India, the constitution provides for reserved seats for Scheduled Castes and Tribes in the House of the People (article 330) and in the Legislative Assemblies of the States (article 332). Initially this reservation was intended to be temporary, but it has subsequently been extended, several times, by constitutional amendments, and is still in effect today. In addition, there is scope for up to two nominated members to be appointed to the House of the People to represent the Anglo-Indian community (article 331). The Constitution of Mauritius (First Schedule) provides for 12 per cent of the seats in Parliament (8 out of a total of 70 seats) to be allocated so as to 'ensure a fair and adequate representation of each community' – the communities in question being the 'Hindu community', the 'Muslim community', the 'Sino-Mauritanian community', and the 'General Population'. If a requisite number of members have not been elected, in the directly elected constituency seats, from a community, the parliamentary candidates belonging to that community who were the 'best losers' become Members of Parliament. The Mauritanian arrangement has not been wholly satisfactory – at the time of writing, a constitutional amendment bill to abolish it was under consideration.[201] It may well be that in the United Kingdom, particularly with proportional representation, such measures would not be needed, and parties would have a sufficient electoral incentives to offer a diverse slate of candidates.

The one group that is often overlooked, when discussions on identity focus on gender and race, is the working class. It is a speculative point, and a somewhat provocative one, but the working class are now perhaps the most under-represented group in politics. What if the same sorts of measures that in Samoa are used to ensure the adequate representation of women, or in India are used to ensure the representation of Scheduled Castes and Tribes, were applied to the working class? Could a certain percentage of seats be reserved for those who do not have a university degree, do not own their own home, and who in the period of five years before entering Parliament earned less than median income? All sorts of difficulties arise – these are not, perhaps, practical suggestions. Yet it is important to recognize that Parliament cannot be a club for people – regardless of gender or ethnicity – with private incomes, or with lucrative careers in law or business; it also has to represent bricklayers, lorry drivers, waiters and cleaners. To achieve that by constitutional means might be an innovation that takes us somewhat beyond the tried and tested forms of the Westminster Model, but that would not prevent parties from seeking to broaden their appeal by recruiting more candidates from working class backgrounds.

The second chamber

Until 1911 the House of Lords had an unlimited and unconditional legislative veto. No bill could be passed by Parliament and become a law unless approved by both Houses. There was no mechanism – beyond political pressure and the ability of the government to nominate new peers – for resolving disputes or breaking deadlocks that might arise between the two Houses. As the Hanoverian constitutional settlement morphed gradually – through expansion of the suffrage, the rise of the party system, and the emergence of parliamentary conventions – into parliamentary democracy, it became increasingly evident that the will of the House of Commons should ultimately prevail. By the late 1860s, Walter Bagehot could describe the House of Lords as one of the 'dignified' rather than 'efficient' parts of the constitution – a decorous chamber, whose advice might be beneficial, but whose formal powers had to be exercised with restraint.[202] However, on certain issues, most notably Irish Home Rule, the Lords could and did use their formal powers to the full. This came to a head over the 'People's Budget', a radical budget to 'wage implacable warfare against poverty and squalidness',[203] proposed by the Liberal government in 1909 and vetoed by the House of Lords later in that year. The result was the Parliament Act 1911, which clipped the wings of the House of Lords: henceforth, it would be able to delay money bills only for one month, and other bills only for two years (later reduced to one year by the Parliament Act 1949).

The Parliament Act 1911 was intended as a temporary measure, to resolve the urgent crisis at hand. It was recognized by the early 20th century that a chamber consisting mostly of hereditary nobles, with a sprinkling of bishops ('Lords Spiritual') and judges ('Law Lords', or 'Lords of Appeal in Ordinary'), was difficult to defend on grounds of democratic principle, and would sooner or later have to be replaced by a chamber with a different composition. There has been no shortage of proposals to that effect ever since. In 1918 Viscount Bryce recommended a House in which three-quarters of the members would be indirectly elected by MPs grouped into regional electoral colleges; one-quarter of the members would be chosen by a Joint Standing Committee of both Houses. Members would serve for 12-year terms, with one-third of their number being elected every fourth year. The Law Lords would sit *ex-officio*. These proposals are worth detailing because they show the extent to which heredity was rejected as a valid principle of selection, even 100 years ago. Although the Bryce proposals were not fully accepted by the government, proposals for reform on similar lines were repeatedly included in the government's legislative agenda, albeit without any legislative result, from 1922 to 1927.[204]

The reforms that did take place – notably through the Life Peerages Act 1958 and then the House of Lords Act 1999 – were more limited in scope. Their effect was to transform the House of Lords from a chamber representing the hereditary aristocracy to one in which members of the 'great and good', politically nominated for life from among those with practical experience in high office, in the professions or in civil society, would predominate. This has strengthened the House of Lords, turning it into a body which, while lacking a democratic mandate, has partially overcome its early 20th century crisis of legitimacy. Within the limited bounds allowed by the 1911 and 1949 Parliament Acts, it has achieved substantial policy influence and has been able to inflict defeats that have caused governments to modify or withdraw their proposals.[205] It might even be argued that as a revising and scrutinizing body, which brings expertise and experience to bear in a relatively impartial way for the moderation and improvement of government policy, the House of Lords is today the least dysfunctional part of the whole constitutional system.

The global expansion of Westminster Model constitutionalism between the middle of the 19th and the middle of the 20th centuries reflects changing views over time on the role, status and desired composition of a second chamber. Five approaches can be identified: (i) a wholly appointed chamber in which the great and good, and people with expertise and experience from various walks of life, are represented; (ii) an indirectly elected chamber chosen by sub-national or provincial legislatures; (iii) a directly elected chamber chosen by the people; (iv) some hybrid concoction of two or more of these; or (v) to have no second chamber, and make do with one House.

Canada provides the textbook example of an appointed Senate in the Commonwealth. Although inspired by the House of Lords, the Canadian Senate differs from its British progenitor in four respects. First, it lacks a hereditary element and has no bench of bishops. It is a purely nominated body, Senators being appointed by the Governor-General on the advice of the Prime Minister. For most of Canadian history, the Prime Minister has used this power of appointment in an overtly partisan way; third parties and regional parties, which have played such an important role in Canadian politics and have always had a presence in the Canadian House of Commons, have hardly been represented in the Senate.

A second feature of the Canadian Senate is that these appointments are made – at least nominally – on a regional basis. Twenty-four Senators are appointed from each of four regions: (a) Ontario, (b) Quebec, (c) the Maritime Provinces (ten each from New Brunswick and Nova Scotia, and four from Prince Edward Island), and (d) the Western Provinces (six each from Manitoba, Saskatchewan, Alberta and British Columbia); a further six are appointed from Newfoundland, and one each from Yukon Territory, the Northwest Territories and Nunavut. Thus, the Canadian Senate does double duty, on the one hand as a scrutinizing and revising chamber very much like the House of Lords, and on the other as a federal chamber representing the provinces and territories of Canada. This aspect has generally been unsatisfactory. Although Senators must be chosen *from* the provinces they represent, they are not chosen *by* them; the Governor-General appoints Senators on the advice of the Prime Minister, not on the advice of provincial premiers.

Third, the number of Senators is limited. The normal size of the Senate is set at 105 members. New appointments can be made only when seats become available. This means that the government cannot just 'swamp' the Senate by the appointment of new members. As a primitive deadlock breaking mechanism, there is a rule that allows the government to appoint either four or eight new Senators in times of need, but the total must never exceed 113. Further appointments cannot then be made until the number of members has been reduced again (by death, retirement or disqualification) to less than 105.

Fourth, although Canadian Senators were originally appointed for life, since 1965 a mandatory retirement age of 75 has been in effect. A mandatory retirement age, provided that it is set high enough to dissuade any retiree from seeking subsequent office or employment, does not affect the general principle of appointments 'for life', nor does it undermine the independence of appointees. It simply ensures the benches are not cluttered up by those who are long past the peak of the intellectual faculties and no longer able to fully contribute the work of Parliament. The retirement age also helps to create a regular supply of vacancies and opportunities for new appointments.

Reform of the Senate has been an ongoing theme in Canadian constitutional politics. In 2015 Prime Minister Justin Trudeau established an Independent Advisory Board for Senate Appointments, on whose recommendation future appointments would be made. The Advisory Board consists of three permanent members, and two additional members for the province in respect of which an appointment is being made: for example, if a Senator is to be appointed for the province of British Colombia, two British Colombian members will be included on the appointments board for the purpose of making that appointment. Although this does not go as far as giving the provincial governments direct voice in the appointment of Senators, it is at least a partial recognition of the principle of provincial representation.

Perhaps the most beneficial aspect of Canada's new appointment mechanism is that the Advisory Board has formally set out the criteria that merit appointment. These include 'a high level of experience, developed over many years, in the legislative process and public service at the federal or provincial/territorial level', 'a lengthy and recognized record of service to one's community, which could include one's Indigenous, ethnic or linguistic community', or 'recognized leadership and an outstanding record of achievement in the individual's profession or chosen field of expertise'; candidates must also demonstrate 'solid knowledge of the legislative process and Canada's Constitution, including the role of the Senate as an independent and complementary body of sober second thought, regional representation and minority representation', as well as 'independence and non-partisanship'. It is further stated that 'Priority consideration will be given to applicants who represent indigenous peoples and linguistic, minority and ethnic communities, with a view to ensuring representation of those communities in the Senate', and that 'fluency in both official languages will be considered an asset'.[206] Such criteria, clearly stated, are important in an assembly whose legitimacy depends on the personal qualities of its members.

That said, Trudeau's scheme has its weaknesses. It is not written into Canada's Constitution, nor even established by statute. The Advisory Board is simply set up by the executive and can therefore easily be changed by any successor in the office of Prime Minister. The members of the Advisory Board are chosen by the Prime Minister – after consultation with the provincial authorities, in the case of provincial members, but ultimately at the Prime Minister's discretion. Also, the recommendations of the Advisory Board are not binding on the Prime Minister, who may simply ignore the board and make a personal recommendation to the Governor-General as of old. Arguably, the Prime Minister's control over appointments is not relinquished, but merely passed off to 'arm's length'.

Other classic examples of appointed Senates are found in the Commonwealth Caribbean. These also differ from the House of Lords, and from the Canadian model, in having short terms of office. Senators are appointed for the life of one Parliament and cease to hold office (although they may be re-appointed) whenever Parliament is dissolved. This completely changes the nature of senatorial office. Senators appointed for life or until a ripe age of retirement – as in Canada – might have an initial loyalty to those by whom they were appointed, but Prime Ministers come and go, while Senators continue practically forever, and over time those loyalties wane. Moreover, those appointed for life (or until retirement) have nothing much else to gain; sitting comfortably in a position of honour, privilege and influence, with parliamentary allowances that render paid employment unnecessary, they are, to a much greater degree than most, immune from both ambition and corruption.

Members appointed for short terms, dependent on the continued approval of those who select them, enjoy no such independence. This was very evident in New Zealand. Under the New Zealand Constitution Act 1852, the New Zealand Parliament included an upper House, known as the Legislative Council, whose members were appointed for life by the Crown on ministerial advice. The method of appointment was neither impartial nor democratic; every form of political patronage and partisan favouritism was employed. Nevertheless, their life tenure gave them some independence from political pressure once appointed. In 1891, however, the right to membership for life was removed from new appointees, and replaced with seven-year renewable terms.[207] The predictable effect of the abolition of lifetime tenure was to make the Legislative Council into a virtually useless body, wholly dependent on the government of the day. It was abolished without mourning in 1950.[208]

Caribbean constitutions also prescribe the number of government, Opposition, and 'crossbench' (independent) Senators. In almost all cases, the government has a slim built-in majority over both Opposition and crossbench members. In Barbados, for example, twelve Senators are appointed on the advice of the Prime Minister, two on the advice of the Leader of the Opposition, and nine at the Governor-General's discretion to 'represent religious, economic or social interests or such other interests as the Governor-General considers ought to be represented'. Thus, the government has an in-built working majority of two (assuming the President of the Senate, who does not normally vote, is chosen from the government side).[209] Senates so composed will be ineffective legislative bodies. While they might perform other useful functions (such as enabling the recruitment of expertise from among those who would not otherwise enter politics), their influence over ordinary legislation is 'negligible'.[210]

Westminster Model constitutions offer some examples of indirectly elected upper Houses. The Indian Raya Sabah, whose members are elected by state legislatures for six-year terms, with one-third of their number chosen every second year, is the main example today. Historically, the Senate of the Union of South Africa was also for the most part indirectly elected, with members chosen from each province by an electoral college consisting of the members of the provincial council and the MPs representing the province in the House of Assembly.

Indirect election by the state legislatures is also used to choose 26 (of a total of 70) members of the Malaysian Senate. India and Malaysia are federal systems – albeit relatively centralized federations – while the Union of South Africa had a form of provincial devolution and was in any case a composite country made up of formerly British colonies and formerly independent Boer republics. This may be a relatively effective way of representing regional diversity and of giving voice to regional elites in national legislation. It is frequently regarded as an important part of the principle of 'shared rule' inherent to federalism.

Australia specializes in directly elected second chambers, with both the Australian Senate and the Legislative Councils of several states being chosen by direct election. Directly elected second chambers do introduce a certain difficulty: that the mandate conferred by direct election may tempt a second chamber to go beyond its allotted role, and start to challenge the primacy of the lower house. At the federal level in Australia, the solution to the problem of what might happen when two directly elected Houses disagree has already been mentioned: double dissolution triggering new elections to both Houses. This has been resorted to several times since 1901. Invoking it is a risky strategy for the government since it may lose an election and fall from office. The effect, more often than not, is therefore to encourage the government to compromise with the Senate, rather than to push the confrontation to the point at which a double dissolution becomes necessary.

At the state level in Australia, other means of restraining the powers of directly elected second chambers have been adopted. The state constitution of Victoria declares (art. 16A) that the Legislative Council is a 'House of Review' and that it must 'exercise its powers in recognition of the right and obligation of the current government to implement' both 'the policies, promises and initiatives which were publicly released by or on behalf of the government during the last election campaign' and its 'general mandate to govern for and on behalf of the people of Victoria.' In other words, although both Houses in Victoria are directly elected by the people, it is made clear by the constitution that the Legislative Council, while an important check and balance, is not to usurp the primacy of the lower House, to which the government is responsible.

In New South Wales, a referendum is used to resolve disputes between the two directly elected Houses of the State Parliament. If the Legislative Council rejects a bill passed by the Legislative Assembly, and if after a joint sitting of the two Houses agreement cannot be reached, then the Legislative Assembly may trigger a referendum to resolve the matter. This does not really preserve the legislative supremacy of the lower House, but does nevertheless avoid the deadlock of competing mandates by allowing the people – who are the ultimate principals of both Houses – to decide.

An interesting feature of Australian bicameralism is that lower Houses are normally elected by a preferential majority electoral system (Alternative Vote), while upper houses are elected by proportional representation. This is a neat compromise: majoritarian politics dominated by two large parties alternating in office in the lower House to deliver strong government, balanced by multiparty politics in the upper House to ensure broad representation and inclusion of minority perspectives.

Malaysia is perhaps the best example of a second chamber with a mixed composition. In addition to the 26 indirectly elected members mentioned earlier, the other 44 members are appointed – four to represent the federal territories of Kuala Lumpur, Labuan, and Putrajaya, and 40 appointed by the Head of State.[211] The weakness of the Malaysian Senate lies, like that of Caribbean Senates, in the short duration of appointments: serving for terms of just three years, appointed members remain politically dependent have no opportunity to develop neutrality or objectivity.

An example of a mixed Senate in a unitary system is provided by Ireland. Eleven of the sixty members are nominated by the Taoiseach (Prime Minister); six are elected by graduates of the University of Dublin and the National University of Ireland – a legacy of the old university seats, which have since been abolished in the United Kingdom – and 43 are indirectly elected by an electoral college consisting of members of the Dáil and local councillors, nominally from candidates representing functional or vocational interests, such as language, culture and the arts, agriculture and fisheries, labour, industry and commerce, and public administration and the voluntary sector.[212]

Honourable mention could perhaps be made of the old Senate of Malta, under the Amery-Miller constitution of 1921. This consisted of seventeen members: seven elected by the people, and ten chosen by distinct functional or vocational electoral colleges – two each by the clergy, nobility, university graduates, the chamber of commerce, and the trade unions.[213]

The 1970 Constitution of Fiji divided Senate seats between nominees of the Prime Minister and the Leader of the Opposition in a way similar to the Caribbean constitutions already discussed, but probably counts as a mixed model because it reserved more than a third of the seats (8 out of 22) for the nominees of the Great Council of Chiefs; these held the balance of power between the Government and Opposition, and had an effective veto over constitutional amendments and also over legislation affecting indigenous rights.[214]

Some Westminster Model constitutions have dispensed with a second chamber. Historical examples include Sierra Leone (1961), the Gambia (1965) and Sri Lanka (1972). Currently unicameral Westminster Model constitutions are found in Samoa (1962), Malta (1964), Mauritius

(1968), Bangladesh (1972), Dominica (1978), Solomon Islands (1978), Tuvalu (1978) and Fiji (2013) – among others.

It is notable that some of these unicameral constitutions made provision for the inclusion of nominated members, alongside the elected members, in the one House. In Dominica, the single House consists of Representatives, elected by the people, and Senators who are appointed by the Prime Minister and the Leader of the Opposition – in effect, allowing for the 'co-option' of additional members. The Constitution of the Gambia (1965) made provision for both nominated members, chosen on the advice of the Prime Minister, and special members elected by the tribal chiefs. In this way, some of the features and characteristics of a bicameral system, such as having more than one means of representation, and allowing those who would not normally be elected to be present in Parliaments, are found in a unicameral context.

Having nominated members in a single chamber to which the executive is responsible is arguably less democratic than keeping them cordoned-off, as it were, in a Senate with limited powers. To avoid this, nominated members may (as in the Gambian constitution of 1965) have non-voting status – although then one might ask what the point of them is at all.

Finally, Botswana, the Cook Islands and Vanuatu have bodies of an advisory nature, which are not quite fully-fledged second chambers, but do perform some of the functions usually associated with them. These consist of traditional leaders (chiefs), with special responsibility for advising on traditions and customary law.

With that survey of options complete, we now turn to the composition of a reformed second chamber in the United Kingdom. That there should be further reform of the House of Lords has been a consistent demand since Charter 88 – and indeed, going back to before the Parliament Act 1911. That it remains stubbornly intact reflects not satisfaction with its existing composition, so much as an inability to settle on an alternative form. To solve the impasse, we must remember that form follows function: if we can reach a consensus of agreement about what the second chamber is *for*, we can then discern what its composition should be.

There are three options. The first is for the second chamber to be, as it currently is, a 'House of Review'. Such a chamber would perform scrutinizing functions, would improve the quality of legislation through technical amendments, and would bring different spheres of expertise and experience to bear on public affairs. From time to time it might require the government to pause, think again, and perhaps compromise on its proposals. It might, in the context of a written constitution, act as a constitutional safeguard, having a veto over constitutional amendments but not over ordinary laws.

If a simple House of Review is desired, then a wholly appointed Senate would be most appropriate. As in Canada, this would have a fixed maximum number of members, who would be appointed for life, subject to a constitutionally mandated retirement age. An independent commission would be established by the constitution to make nominations. It would even be possible to write into the constitution a requirement for the commission to recognize, in making recommendations, the need for political balance, gender equality, and professional, regional, religious and ethnic diversity.

The constitution could set out qualifying criteria, similar to those prescribed by the Independent Advisory Board in Canada. This would not be unprecedented. The Constitution of Malaysia specifies that the appointed Senators are to be selected from among those who 'have rendered distinguished public service or have achieved distinction in the professions, commerce, industry, agriculture, cultural activities or social service or are representative of racial minorities or are capable of representing the interests of aborigines'.[215] The 1925 Constitution of Iraq (admittedly, a 'British-influenced' constitution, perhaps, rather than clearly in the Westminster tradition) refers to Senators being appointed from 'among persons whose conduct has secured the confidence and esteem of the public and those who have served the State and nation with distinction in the past'.[216]

Such a Senate would merely take the longstanding trend of minor reforms to the House of Lords that have been incrementally adopted over the last century to their logical conclusion. It would create an independent chamber noted for its expertise and experience, consisting of appointees selected on merit from the various branches of the 'great and good', who – shorn of the hereditary element and reduced to a more manageable size – might continue to do what the House of Lords currently does well. It would not, however, complete the federal remake of the United Kingdom; it would be suitable, perhaps, for an independent England, but hardly adequate for a union comprising England, Scotland, Wales and Northern Ireland. In Canada, the deficiency of the Senate is chiefly attributed to its failure, despite the regional apportionment of appointments, to adequately represent provincial interests.

The second option, therefore, is for the Senate to act as a 'House of Federation'. This would be a necessary part of any genuinely federal reorganization of the Union. Assuming a federal union of four equal national states, as will be discussed in Chapter 10, the members of such a Senate could either be directly elected by the people from state-wide constituencies (as in Australia), or indirectly elected. If indirectly elected, they could be chosen either by state Parliaments (following the examples of India, Malaysia and Pakistan), or by state electoral colleges made up of the members of each state Parliament and the House of Commons representing each state. The latter approach has no extant examples, but was previously used in the Union of South Africa.

Indirect election is preferable. This is because direct election would prioritize party politics. Those elected to a directly elected Senate will be indistinguishable from those elected to the Commons. Indirect election by state Parliaments or state electoral colleges, although by no means free of partisanship, would better reflect the interests of the state Parliaments and would help to establish closer ties between state legislators and the Union Parliament. It would enable the election of those whose disposition does not incline them to stand for popular election, but who would nevertheless by well placed to contribute, by virtue of their experience, to the improvement of legislation and policy. Those who have served in the Parliaments of England, Scotland, Wales and Northern Ireland, or perhaps as mayors of major cities or as leaders of English regional authorities with devolved powers, would be natural candidates for election to such a Senate, as would persons of note in culture, the arts, academia, the law, industry, or similar walks of life, in each state. Such people would be equipped both to defend state interests and to contribute constructively to Union-level legislation. The elections should be conducted in each state electoral college by proportional representation, such that those of the minority, as well as the majority party, can be elected.

The Wakeham Commission (2000) recommended a 15-year term for the elected members of a second chamber, with one-third of their number being elected at each general election.[217] This proposal was also adopted by the House of Commons Political and Constitutional Reform Committee's draft constitution published in 2015.[218] While it is by no means unusual for members of a second chamber to serve for longer terms than those of the primary chamber (in India, for example, members of the Lok Sabha serve for five years, but members of the Raya Sabha for six), a fifteen-year term is too long, and would weaken any representative connection between the Senate and the national and regional legislatures. A term therefore of eight years, with half the elected Senators being chosen every fourth year, would be a sensible solution, especially if the state Parliaments of England, Scotland, Wales and Northern Ireland are to be elected – as they probably should be – on a four-year cycle. Any longer, and the representative mandate would be so diluted as time as to be untenable; much shorter, and the cool, calm, reflective, senatorial aspect of the chamber might be lost.

One of the most sensitive aspects of the design of a Senate representing the constituent parts of a federal union is the number of members to be elected from each unit. The two principles in play are proportionality (each state, region or province should return a number of members in proportion to its population) and equality (each state, region or province, in recognition of its equal status in the Union, should return an equal number of members). The old South African Senate operated on the principle of equality-of-provinces, each electing eight Senators. The Senate of Pakistan has 23 members from each province. The Australian Senate – although directly elected – is also based on the principle of equality, with each state electing 12 Senators. The Indian Rajya Sabha, in contrast, is composed partly on the basis of population, with larger states electing more members than small states – although the formula is not strictly proportional, and *per capita* the small states are somewhat over-represented. In a United Kingdom context, the most important balance may be that of England – taken as a whole – against the other three parts of the Union. One might imagine, for example, an arrangement whereby, of say 200 elected Senators, 100 are elected from England, 40 from Scotland, and 30 each from Wales and Northern Ireland. This would give the English members half the elected seats, over-representing the other three parts, but not to the point of parity. The crucial point, assuming a two-thirds majority rule for constitutional amendments, is to give non-English Senators a veto over constitutional change.

The third option, and the best, is to combine these two approaches: a reformed second chamber should be both a 'House of Review' and a 'House of Federation'. In this case, the Senate might consist of two classes of members: (a) 'elected Senators', indirectly elected by members of the state Parliaments as discussed; and (b) 'nominated Senators', appointed for life (or until reaching the prescribed retirement age) on merit by Her Majesty acting on the advice of a non-partisan commission established by the constitution for that purpose.

The crucial design choice in that case would be to determine the members in each category. The Malaysian Senate (in its current form) tilts this balance decisively in favour of the appointed members, who have around two-thirds of the seats, while members chosen by the state legislatures have only around one-third of the seats. The Wakeham Commission recommended that nominated members should be in the majority.[219] However, if the 'House of Federation' function of a second chamber is to be taken seriously, the balance should be tilted the other way, to give the elected members a clear majority. A workable Senate in a four-nation United Kingdom might therefore consist of 300 members, with 200 being indirectly elected and 100 appointed. This is put forward as a suggestion, not as a final prescription, but it shows the general lines on which to proceed.

This assumes, of course, that the House of Commons under the new constitution is elected by proportional representation. If it is not politically feasible to achieve that, another option arises: not a 'House of Review', or a 'House of Federation', but 'House of Democracy'. In this case, the purpose of the Senate would be to mitigate the unrepresentative character of the Commons, providing a toehold for third and minority parties and broadening representation beyond a two-party duopoly. Any reticence about direct election, and all arguments made in favour of a more expert, experienced and independent second chamber, would have to yield to the over-riding need to ensure that at least one House reflects how people actually vote.

Having settled its function and composition, the powers of a second chamber must now be considered. In the old dominions, there is considerable variation in the formal powers of the second chamber. This is because their constitutions were adopted at time when the relationship in Britain between the House of Lords and House of Commons was still evolving. The Canadian Senate had (and has) on paper near identical powers to the Canadian House of Commons – just as, in 1867, the House of Lords had in relation to the British Commons. In practice, of course, and by convention, the Canadian Senate uses this power sparingly.[220] By the time the Australian Constitution was adopted in 1901, a complex 'double dissolution' mechanism had been developed, allowing deadlocks between the two Houses to be resolved – in a dramatic but democratic way – by means of a general election to both Houses.[221] The South African constitution of 1909 allowed for the resolution of disputes between the Senate and the House of Assembly by means of a joint sitting.[222] A similar approach was taken by the Indian Constitution of 1950.[223]

Later Westminster Model constitutions were adopted after the powers of the House of Lords had been clipped, leaving it with merely the ability to delay, but not ultimately deny, the passage of legislation. The Constitution of Trinidad & Tobago is quite typical. A bill (other than a money bill) that has been passed by the House of Representatives and rejected by the Senate may be presented to the Head of State for assent, notwithstanding the fact that the Senate has not consented to the bill, if it is passed again by the House of Representatives, in the following session of Parliament, after an interval of not less than six months.[224] Similar rules are found throughout the Commonwealth Caribbean, such as in Belize[225] and Grenada.[226] Occasionally there are slight variations in the permissible length of the Senate's delay: in Barbados, for example, it is seven months rather than six.[227] Money bills usually have even tighter restrictions. Money bills may only be introduced in the lower House. The period of permissible delay that the Senate might inflict on a money bill, in all the countries listed in this paragraph and many others besides, is but one month. In many cases, however, the Commonwealth Caribbean Senates have an absolute (not merely suspensive) veto power over constitutional amendments. These three different levels of legislative authority – almost no power over money bills, a suspensive veto over ordinary legislation, and an absolute veto over constitutional amendments – reflect the different roles of the Senate: not to restrict the ability of the government to govern by 'withholding supply' (that is, refusing to pass the budget), but to provide a means by which the government can be caused to pause, to think again, and perhaps to accept amendments to ordinary legislation, while acting as a constitutional safeguard.

These formal powers must be understood in their political context. A House with little democratic legitimacy is likely to be circumspect in the use of its powers, even if on paper these are extensive. Paradoxically, a House with limited powers (like the House of Lords) may be persuaded to use them, secure in the knowledge that confrontation will ultimately be decided in favour of the lower House, while a House with broader powers of paper (like the Canadian Senate) might not dare push its luck.

In effect, this is an argument for limiting the powers of a second chamber, to the point at which, being non-threatening, and unable to cause fatal disruption, they might safely be used as milder check and balance. The House of Lords, since the Parliament Act 1949, seems to have got this about right: defeat in the Lords is enough to inhibit the government, to bring a matter into the public eye, to give time for the public and civil society to make their views heard, and to enable the government – without loss of face – to accept amendments to a bill; but it is never so drastic as to thwart the legislative intent of a government with a clear majority in the Commons. The power to scrutinize, to delay, and to propose but not to insist on amendments, enables the House of Lords to contribute to democratic deliberation without hindering democratic responsibility.

In terms of general legislative powers, including powers over approval of secondary legislation, the best course of action would therefore be for the new second chamber to have the same powers as the current House of Lords. In one respect, however, its powers should be strengthened: it should have an absolute veto over constitutional amendments. This is discussed further in the final section of this chapter, but the principle is that as a House of Review it should provide a stable safeguard against hasty or destructive change, and that as a House of Federation it should ensure any constitutional changes enjoy support not only across party lines, but also across the geographical diversity of the United Kingdom.

Royal assent and consent

The power of the Crown to refuse assent to legislation has long been a paradoxical feature of the unwritten constitution. On the one hand, we are assured that this power is purely nominal, that the royal assent is a formality, never to be denied. On the other hand, royal assent is presented as the last bastion against tyranny – a sort of substitute for a written constitution and supreme court, which in the final analysis would allow the Queen to step in to protect our freedom. Clearly, it cannot be both. A power that is so harmless that it can never obstruct the parliamentary majority is also so useless that it can never defend the public from the abuse of power by that majority. The crucial distinction between interference with policy choices and defending the constitutional order, which it is possible to make with a written constitution, is imperceptible in an unwritten system. It would be impossible for the Queen to exercise the power of refusing assent, even in defence of liberty against tyranny, without violating the conventional foundations of democracy.

Yet, for practical purposes, it was enough to say that the royal assent would never in the normal course of things be withheld. The power to refuse assent to legislation was last exercised in 1706 and was widely believed to have fallen into disuse. Recent debates around the enactment of the 'Cooper Act' (European Union (Withdrawal) Act 2019) and the 'Benn Act' (European Union (Withdrawal) (No.2) Act) – legislation seeking to constrain the power of the Prime Minister in relation to Brexit-related processes and so prevent a 'No Deal' Brexit – have challenged that assumption. These two pieces of legislation were passed by the House of Commons against the wishes of the government, which had lost its working majority but not been defeated in a formal vote of no confidence under the terms of the Fixed Term Parliaments Act. When the bills for these Acts were going through Parliament, some members on the government side suggested that the Cabinet might forestall their enactment by the exceptional ploy of advising the Queen to withhold assent.

This sparked a lively debate among constitutional experts. Some – such as Robert Craig – argued that the convention that the Queen acts on ministerial advice should prevail, and that assent to legislation might be withheld on the advice of the government. The fact that refusal of assent is so rare is a reflection of the fact that the government normally commands the confidence of a parliamentary majority, and that is truly exceptional for a government to be faced with legislation passed by the House against its will. Others – such as Philippe Lagassé – argued that the Queen acts on ministerial advice in relation to her executive powers, but on the advice of Parliament in relation to legislative powers. The Queen-in-Parliament is the legislature, and the Queen is bound, in the granting of assent, to defer to Parliament's wishes. According to this view, the convention is that the Queen can never refuse royal assent to legislation passed by Parliament.

This difference of opinion, as to the proper interpretation of unwritten and unenforceable rules, merely highlights the inherent problem of an unwritten constitution based on conventions. A credible and principled argument can be made in favour of both positions. What matters most is that there is a clear, known, accepted rule. Without it, uncertainty is generated. In the end, the government decided not to test the point. Perhaps we could argue that its power in this regard has now, by evolving convention, been curtailed. But we do not know how a future government might act in a similar situation, or what the Queen, faced with advice to from Parliament to enact a law and with advice from her responsible ministers to refrain from enacting it, might decide to do. In any event, the lack of constitutional clarity and certainty would only make matters worse.

Westminster Model constitutions around the world show this lack of certainty to be quite unnecessary. It is perfectly easy to cut through the mess by stating the constitutional rules in clear, authoritative, unequivocal terms. The Constitution of Saint Lucia states (Section 47) that 'When a bill is submitted to the Governor-General for assent in accordance with the provisions of this Constitution he shall signify that he assents.' The Constitution of Malta (article 72) provides that 'When a bill is presented to the President for assent, he shall without delay signify that he assents.' These provisions remove the power to refuse assent to legislation. The role of the head of state or Governor-General is simply to acknowledge and give formal assent to what Parliament passes.

The Constitution of Fiji (article 48) goes a step further. It provides that if the Head of State fails to assent to a bill within seven days, it comes into effect anyway:

> When a Bill has been passed by Parliament, the Speaker must present it to the President for assent. Within seven days after receipt of a Bill, the President must provide his or her assent. If the President does not assent to a Bill within the period set out in subsection (2), the Bill will be taken to have been assented to on the expiry of that period.

The Constitution of Malaysia contains a rule (article 66) with a similar effect, although the time allotted for the granting of assent is 30 days, not seven; if after that time the Head of State has not granted assent, the bill nevertheless comes into effect as if assent had been granted.

There are other possibilities, allowing a more extensive and more autonomous role for the Head of State. The President of Ireland (article 26) can, after consulting with the Council of State (an advisory body analogous to the Privy Council), refer a bill to the Supreme Court for review of its constitutionality. If the Supreme Court rules that the bill is repugnant to the constitution the President must withhold assent. This power is not a dead letter. It has been used several times.[228] In Mauritius, the President is permitted by Section 46 of the Constitution to return a bill, other than a money bill or a constitutional amendment bill, to Parliament for reconsideration. If after reconsideration Parliament passes the bill again, with or without amendment, the President must assent. This is a very weak, easily overridden, and mostly symbolic form of presidential veto. It gives the President the power to signal concern and cause Parliament to debate the matter again, but it does not allow the President to stand in the way of a majority that has made its mind up.

Arrangements like those in Ireland or Mauritius may be beneficial in a republic, where an elected Head of State is entrusted with their exercise. They would be too controversial, however, in a constitutional monarchy. Even though in both cases the Head of State is not a decision maker or a policy maker (all they can do is refer a bill either to the Supreme Court, in the Irish example, or back to Parliament, in Mauritius), such intimate involvement in the legislative process would be democratically unacceptable. Other checks and balances – the written constitution being the most important, followed by the proportional electoral system and the reformed second chamber – would be better placed, in a United Kingdom context, to prevent the enactment of bad laws. If the monarchy is to be retained, the role of royal assent should be reduced in explicit constitutional terms to that which it has long been in implicit understanding: a ceremonial, formal marker of the completion of the legislative process, by which a parliamentary bill is enacted as law, without any scope for the personal discretion, either of the monarch or the ministers, getting in the way.

Finally, a word must be said about royal consent. Royal assent and consent are often confused, but they are distinct in three respects. Firstly, royal assent must be granted to all bills before they can become laws, whereas consent applies only to bills that concern Crown prerogatives, the Crown Estate, or the personal rights or interests of the Queen or the Prince of Wales (including those belonging to the Duchy of Cornwall or Duchy of Lancaster). Secondly, while royal assent takes effect at the end of the legislative process, after a bill has been passed by Parliament, the consent of the Queen (or Prince of Wales in some cases) is required in the middle of the legislative process, usually before the third reading debate.[229] Thirdly, refusal of royal assent, as already noted, has not occurred for more than three centuries, but consent is occasionally refused on ministerial advice. A report by *The Guardian* in 2013 showed the power to refuse consent had been used to block the Military Actions Against Iraq Bill 1999 – a private members' bill seeking to limit the prerogative of waging war by requiring parliamentary approval for any military strikes against Iraq.[230]

Consent is a democratically highly dubious process. It personally involves the Queen, and in some cases the Prince of Wales, in giving approval, before Parliament has been able to have a final say, on the minutiae of legislation across a vast range of topics. We do not know what sort of discussions take place in those meetings between ministers and royals. Even if there is nothing untoward, the process contradicts principles of openness and accountability. If consent is denied on ministerial advice, its effect is to increase the power of the government by enabling it to keep bills that would diminish its powers, by constraining the prerogative, from being enacted. That is a sort of 'pocket veto', less visible than refusal of royal assent, but potentially just as damaging.

There are two arguments advanced in favour of maintaining a requirement for consent. The first is that consent on matters concerning the prerogatives of the Crown are necessary 'to protect key executive authorities and the constitutional powers of the sovereign from ill-advised statutory infringements and alterations'.[231] This argument is irrelevant, however, once we have a written constitution. Under a written constitution, the test of constitutionality and the procedural hurdles required to amend the constitution would be a sufficient guarantee against legislation that would affect the fundamentals in this way. Philippe Lagassé gives as an example that 'a bill that attempted to terminate the Sovereign's power to dismiss a prime minister might not be given the Crown's consent unless it included alternative means of removing a head of government under certain situations'.[232] Such a bill, under a typical New Commonwealth Westminster Model constitution, would either be flatly unconstitutional, or else a constitutional amendment bill that would have to be passed in accordance with a rigorous super-majoritarian procedure.

The second argument is that consent in relation to the Crown Estate or the personal rights and income of the monarch and the heir to the throne is necessary to preserve the independence of the Head of State.[233] This hardly seems credible. Perhaps in the 18th century, under the old Hanoverian settlement in its original form, it made sense to preserve a source of revenue for the Crown that Parliament could not touch without consent. In a parliamentary democracy, where the Head of State performs a primarily ceremonial and symbolic function, and where the reserve powers of the Head of State are narrowly defined and tightly restricted, such protection for a private stream of revenue is superfluous. In any case, the effectiveness of the requirement for consent, as a means of protecting the independent of the monarch, depends on its being exercised by the Queen at her own discretion – which would be undemocratic to an intolerable degree. Alternatively, if as suggested consent is granted or withheld only on ministerial advice, it is hard to see how this could protect the independence of the monarchy from the government.

The solution is simply to abolish the requirement for consent. It adds nothing but mires the monarchy in potential political controversy. Since the requirement for consent is only a matter of parliamentary procedure, which is established by no statute, it could be abolished very easily by amending parliamentary standing orders. However, for greater reassurance and avoidance of doubt, it would be better for the constitution to explicitly abolish the requirement for consent.

War-making and treaty-making powers

In most Westminster Model constitutions control over the deployment of the armed forces, declarations of war and peace, and the ratification of treaties, are still largely treated as prerogative powers of the Crown (or President, in republics) that can be exercised on ministerial advice and do not require further constitutional specification. Many of the New Commonwealth Westminster Model constitutions do specifically address the appointment of ambassadors and High Commissioners, but only in the context of allowing the Prime Minister to have some additional say in their appointment, in contrast to the majority of appointments that are handled by a Public Service Commission. Parliamentary control over these powers is exercised indirectly – ultimately through votes of no confidence, but more often through the usual parliamentary mechanisms such as debates, questions, select committee reports, and the budget process.

In the United Kingdom, two relatively recent developments have given Parliament a greater degree of control over such powers. Firstly, although the government has resisted any attempts to increase Parliament's statutory control over war powers, it has been a practice to hold authorizing votes in the House of Commons before initiating major military action.[234] On a point of principle, it seems right that such important decisions as committing people to armed conflict should be made, in a democracy, by means of a formal parliamentary debate and vote before the action is taken, and not afterwards; that the permission, and not merely approval, of Parliament should be sought. There are of course practical difficulties – arising in part from the definitional problem of establishing what, exactly, constitutes military deployment. Does it apply only to the decision to put 'boots on the ground', or also to airstrikes, or the deployment of a warship near a hostile coast but in international waters? There is a danger that urgent action might be delayed not only for Parliament to vote on the matter, but also for the courts to decide whether a vote is, in any particular circumstance, constitutionally necessary. One compromise might be to require prior approval as the norm, but to allow the government to take urgent action without prior approval if they deem it necessary, subject to a substantive debate as soon as may be practicable.

Secondly, the Constitutional Reform and Governance Act 2010 incorporated the so-called 'Ponsonby rule', which had conventionally required treaties to be laid before both Houses for 21 days. Under the Act, a treaty (with certain exceptions) cannot be ratified unless it has been laid before Parliament for a 21-day period, during which time either House may by resolution veto ratification of the treaty. Incorporation of that statutory rule into a written constitution would be one way forward. Apart from the length of time allowed, the rules under the Constitutional Reform and Governance Act 2010 are similar in principle to those found in the Constitution of Papua New Guinea (Section 117(3)). However, the current system allows treaty ratification by default – unless Parliament moves to block it during the allotted time, ratification can go ahead. Some Westminster Model constitutions demand a more active endorsement of treaties. In Ireland (article 29) the Constitution requires every international agreement to be laid before Dáil Éireann, while those 'involving a charge upon public funds' (other than 'agreements or conventions of a technical and administrative character') must be approved by Dáil Éireann. It also clarifies that 'No international agreement shall be part of the domestic law of the state save as may be determined by the Oireachtas [Parliament].' Belize (Section 61A) for example requires the Senate to actively approve the ratification of any treaty. Likewise, the Constitution of Fiji (Section 51) provides that, 'An international treaty or convention binds the state only after it has been approved by Parliament'. Whether such changes would be a major improvement on the current statutory scheme is secondary to the principle that the rules, one way or the other, should be clearly laid down in the constitution, in a way that the government of the day cannot evade.

Constitutional amendment rules

Having a written (supreme and fundamental law) constitution necessarily implies a distinction between the ordinary law-making power of Parliament and the process for constitutional amendments. Although this principle is quite universal, there is considerable variation, among Westminster Model constitutions, in how it is applied in terms of the extra steps or precautions required in the amendment of constitutions. In general terms, these amendment rules can be divided into three main types: (a) super-majoritarian rules, requiring approval of a constitutional amendment by a larger than 50%+1 majority in the national Parliament; (b) referendum rules, requiring a direct vote by the people; (c) sub-national approval rules, requiring approval by state or provincial legislatures. Some Westminster Model constitutions use one of these rules; many combine two or even three.

The principle of a super-majoritarian rule is that a government with an ordinary working majority in Parliament should not be able to impose unilateral constitutional changes. This principle goes to the very core of the constitution's function and identity as a set of ground-rules that underpin the political system and are binding on the government. To amend constitutional provisions protected by a super-majoritarian rule, one of two conditions must be met: either the government must have won a landslide majority, enabling it to claim an extraordinary mandate for constitutional change; or the government must agree with the Opposition (and perhaps other third or minor parties), thereby demonstrating a broad political consensus in favour of change.

The usual super-majority rule, in many Westminster Model constitutions, is a two-thirds majority vote. For example, the Constitution of Bangladesh (article 142) states that 'no such Bill [to amend the constitution] shall be presented to the President for assent unless it is passed by the votes of not less than two thirds of the total number of members of Parliament'. The Constitution of Tuvalu (Section 7) similarly provides that 'a Bill for an Act to alter this Constitution is not passed by Parliament unless it is supported at its final reading in Parliament by the votes of two-thirds of the total membership of Parliament'. Elsewhere, a three-fourths majority vote may be required. In Fiji, for example, a constitutional amendment is not deemed to have been passed by Parliament unless, 'at the second and third readings, it is supported by the votes of at least three-quarters of the members of Parliament' (Constitution of Fiji, article 160). In countries with bicameral Parliaments, a two-thirds majority in both Houses may be required. The Constitution of Malaysia (article 159), for instance, provides that 'A Bill for making any amendment to the Constitution … shall not be passed in either House of Parliament unless it has been supported on Second and Third Readings by the votes of not less than two-thirds of the total number of members of that House.' In India, most of the constitution can be amended (article 368) by 'a majority of not less than two-thirds of the members of [each] House present and voting'. It is important to note here the distinction between a two-thirds majority of the total membership of the House (as in Malaysia) and a two-thirds majority of those present and voting (as in India). This latter is potentially a weaker protection. A minority in India must vote actively against a constitutional amendment if they seek to prevent it, whereas in Malaysia abstention is sufficient.

The degree of constitutional rigidity or flexibility obviously depends on the size of the super-majority required. A lower threshold makes for a more flexible constitution, which is more open to beneficial change and updating, but also more vulnerable to destructive changes. Higher thresholds makes for a more rigid constitution, which is harder to improve but also more resilient against attempts to undermine it. Much also depends on the electoral system and party system. A two-thirds majority may be relatively easy to achieve in a small Parliament elected by First Past the Post. In 2018, in Antigua and Barbuda, Barbados and Grenada, single party governments won 'clean sweep' elections, taking all or very nearly all the seats in the lower House.[235] In a more diverse Parliament, building a two-thirds majority will almost certainly involve reaching agreements across the aisle. In a Parliament elected by proportional representation it is possible that even a combination of the government and official Opposition may not be enough to reach higher (such as a three-fourths majority) thresholds without the agreement of third or minor parties.

Many Westminster Model constitutions combine two different super-majority rules, which are applied to different parts of the constitution. The fundamentals of the constitution may typically be amendable by a three-fourths majority, while other parts of the constitution – which are still important, but perhaps a little less crucial – are amendable by a two-thirds majority. In Belize, for example, the Constitution (Section 69) provides that a three-fourths majority vote in both Houses of Parliament is required to amend those parts of the constitution concerning fundamental rights, the composition and election of Parliament, the dissolution of Parliament, the Electoral and Boundaries Commission, constituency boundaries, electoral rules and the conduct of voting, the judiciary (including judicial appointments and tenure), the prerogative of mercy, the independence of the Director of Public Prosecutions and the Auditor-General, the Public Service Commission and the rules for the appointment of public officers, and of course the rules on constitutional amendment themselves. The other provisions of the constitution can be amended by a two-thirds majority. Similarly, the Constitution of the Solomon Islands (Section 61) requires a three-fourths majority in Parliament to amend provisions relating to fundamental rights, the election and composition of Parliament, the Constituency Boundaries Commission, the right to vote and the conduct of elections, the judiciary and the Ombudsman, the Auditor-General, and the rules on constitutional amendment. The details vary, but the general principles are common: that those parts of the constitution protecting basic human rights, judicial independence, the composition of Parliament, the Electoral Commission, and the integrity and impartiality of the electoral system must receive the greatest protection. This two-track approach enables a nuanced balance to be struck between rigidity and flexibility, protecting the core of the constitution without making the constitution as a whole unwieldy.

The super-majority rule uses the Opposition as the veto point to protect the constitution against unilateral changes imposed by the government or any slim parliamentary majority. The referendum rule, in contrast, uses the people as a veto point to protect the constitution from being changed by elected representatives – even by overwhelming majorities of elected representatives, against the will of the people. Some constitutions require the consent of the people for all constitutional amendments no matter how insignificant. Within the Westminster tradition the constitutions of Ireland, Australia and Fiji are of this type.

In the Irish example, the constitutional amendment rule has no super-majority requirement at all. The constitutional amendment process requires only a simple majority in Parliament followed by majority approval in a referendum. Such arrangements may be acceptable in a relatively homogenous society where the constitution serves more as an instrument of delegation from the people to the institutions of state than as a pact or bargain between different communities. In Australia, in contrast, the referendum is used as part of a constitutional amendment process which recognizes the composite nature of Australia as a federation of states. Constitutional amendments must be first be passed by an absolute majority in the Federal Parliament, and then approved by a double majority in a referendum: firstly by a majority of the voters across Australia as a whole, and secondly by a majority of the voters in at least four of the six states. The result is to make the constitution rather more rigid that it should be.

Fiji is an interesting case. A constitutional amendment in Fiji requires a three-fourths majority vote in Parliament, followed by a three-fourths majority – not just of the votes cast, but of the total registered electorate – in a referendum. That is very high threshold for amendment, and there is a danger that such excessive rigidity may result in a brittle constitution which, because it cannot bend, is likely to break. However, in its context, these high barriers to amendment make sense. Fiji has struggled to achieve constitutional solidity after two decades plagued by military coups. The root of this instability lies in the contest for power between the two major communities in Fiji – the indigenous Fijians, or iTaukei, and the Indo-Fijians. By raising such high barriers to amendment, the present Fijian constitution ensures that each of these two communities has a veto over any proposed change to a carefully balanced constitutional bargain.

Other Westminster Model constitutions use the referendum only for certain amendments, concerning those parts of the constitution deemed to be of greatest importance, while relying on super-majority rules in Parliament for other parts of the constitution. The Constitution of Antigua & Barbuda, for example, can be amended by a two-thirds majority vote in Parliament, but certain provisions concerning fundamental rights, the basic structures of Parliament and the electoral system and the independence of the judiciary cannot be amended except if the amendment bill, after having been passed by Parliament, is approved by the people in a referendum (Section 47). A similar arrangement was found, for example, in the 1965 Constitution of the Gambia (Section 48). Such reliance on a combination of super-majoritarian rules at the parliamentary level for some amendments and insistence on a referendum for other amendments is another attempt, like that discussed earlier, to achieve a fine balance between the flexibility that enables a constitution to adapt and the rigidity that protects it from majoritarian manipulation or passing whimsy.

The third form of amendment rule found in Westminster Model constitutions requires approval by sub-national legislatures. The best examples of this arrangement are Canada and India. In Canada, the general formula for amendment is the so-called 7–50 rule; having been passed by Parliament in the usual manner a bill to amend the constitution must be submitted to the provincial legislatures and approved by those of not less than seven of the ten provinces, with those approving the amendment having, in total, at least 50 per cent of Canada's population. Again, there are multiple layers of entrenchment with some fundamental provisions being amendable only with the unanimous consent of all provincial legislatures. In India, the consent of the state legislatures is required for amendments principally concerning the powers of the states and the federal distribution of competences. These require, in addition to approval by a super-majority vote in Parliament, the approval of a majority of the state legislatures.

In addition to these three main forms of constitutional entrenchment, most Westminster Model constitutions also include other procedural rules to protect the integrity of the constitution. Constitutional amendment bills must be specifically intended for that purpose and must be designated as such in their title. This ensures that a parliament cannot amend a constitution, as it were, by accident without recognizing that the bill is one of constitutional significance. There may be requirements for a constitutional amendment bill to be published a certain number of days in advance of its discussion in Parliament to enable time for civil society and the general public to comment on the bill. Often a bill, before receiving assent, must be accompanied by a certificate signed by the Speaker, certifying that the provisions of the constitution have been complied with.

From this bewildering array of options, rules and processes, three general themes stand out. Firstly, there must be a balance between rigidity and flexibility, making the constitution difficult to change, but not impossible. The amendment rules must be onerous enough to protect the constitution from hasty, one-sided or destructive change, and must ensure that any change really does enjoy broad cross-party support. At the same time, even the best constitution, using a tried and tested model, may need some amendment to improve its operation in the light of experience, respond to newly emerging needs and challenges, or to correct such abuses as inevitably arise. Perhaps the door to change should for good reason be a narrow one, but it should never be barred.

Secondly, that to achieve this balance, many Westminster Model constitutions have more than one amendment rule. This allows rigidity where necessary and some flexibility where possible. A distinction can therefore be made between the provisions amendable by a two-thirds majority and 'entrenched' provisions which are amendable only by a three-fourths majority. The 'entrenched' provisions might include those on, say, the principle of universal suffrage, the maximum term of a Parliament, fundamental human rights and the principles of judicial independence.

Thirdly, that the amendment rule reflects something of the nature of the original bargain by which the constitution is established: when the constitution is a pact between states or provinces, whose autonomy must be preserved within a federal scheme, it is right that the states or provinces should have a voice in constitutional amendments. In a federal United Kingdom, there should be a class of 'specially entrenched' provisions which require approval by the national and regional legislatures. This would apply to any amendment concerning the composition of those legislatures, the scope for their powers, or their relationship with the Union.

When a constitution emanates from a highly developed sense of popular sovereignty, it is right that the people, through a referendum, should have a direct voice in amendments. Referendums have been used in recent decades for major institutional change in the United Kingdom. According to a House of Lords report, the use of referendums has become part of the conventional constitutional order, and there are at least six issues on which a referendum would be deemed appropriate: to abolish the monarchy, to leave the European Union, for any country to secede from the Union, to abolish either House of Parliament, to change the electoral system for the House of Commons, to adopt a written constitution, and to change the UK's system of currency.[236]

The record of such referendums in the United Kingdom is, however, mixed at best. They have been divisive and subject to unscrupulous manipulation. While not precluding the use of the referendum as a means of consulting the people on certain types of policy decision (see Chapter 11), they are unsuitable for constitutional changes a situation like that of the United Kingdom, where the constitution would not express a single, unitary 'national will', but an agreed compact across the parts of the Union; to require approval by referendum in all four, or three of the four, nations might be to make the constitution too rigid (like Australia); to allow it to be amended by a simple Union-wide majority would undermine federalism.

Two exceptions to this general scepticism of constitutional referendums apply. The first is in the case of alteration of state boundaries – for example, if Berwick-on-Tweed wished to join Scotland – where the people of the area concerned should be consulted by referendum. The second is in the case of secession. Northern Ireland has an existing, recognized right under the Good Friday agreement to leave the United Kingdom and to reunite with Ireland. Scotland's national sovereignty under the Claim of Right demands that there should always be provision, for as long as Scotland is part of the Union, for a referendum of this type. It is unclear whether Wales, as its condition for participation in such a Union, would demand the same guarantees. In any case, the principle of self-determination should apply equally to all.

Specific provisions for referendums on secession should be made accordingly, as in the Constitution of St Kitts and Nevis (Section 113) and the 1947 Constitution of Burma (sections 201 to 206). It should be made clear that the secession of one state will be supported by the goodwill of the remainder of the union, and that suitable arrangements for negotiating the division of assets and debts, dual citizenship, free movement and rights of residence, free trade, military cooperation, and so forth, would be agreed to give effect to any independence referendum. Also, it should be provided that the constitution would continue in effect, in so far as it affects the remaining parts of the United Kingdom, with only such consequential changes as may be required by the secession of one of its states. These changes might be made by Order-in-Council, without having to follow the normal constitutional amendment rules; thus, if for example Scotland were to be independent, parts of the Constitution could amended by Order-in-Council to the extent necessary to remove references to Scotland, and no further.

9

Parliament II: Privileges, Organization and Procedures

Parliamentary privileges

The privileges of Parliament – freedom of speech, the immunity of its members from legal liability for statements made in the House, and the freedom of each House to order its own affairs without interference by the Crown – are an integral part of the Westminster System, going back to Article 9 of the Bill of Rights 1689. The immunity of members has occasionally been used to good effect by 'whistleblowers' seeking to expose wrongdoers whose actions might otherwise be difficult to express under English libel and slander laws. Such freedom of speech, however, is but 'one facet of the broader principle that what happens within Parliament is a matter for control by Parliament alone'.[237] Parliament regulates its own proceedings. Each House adopts its own standing orders and enforces its own rules.

Most Westminster Model constitutions replicate these privileges, either by directly specifying and enumerating them in the constitution, or by conferring on Parliament the power to determine its own privileges – usually with the proviso that, until it does so, the privileges of the House of Commons shall apply. The Constitution of Trinidad & Tobago is a typical example. This states that 'subject to the provisions of this Constitution, each House may regulate its own procedure' (Section 56) and that 'there shall be freedom of speech' in both Houses 'subject to the provisions of this Constitution and to the rules and standing orders' of each House (Section 55). It further provides (Section 55(2)) that 'No civil or criminal proceedings may be instituted against any member of either House for words spoken before, or written in a report to, the House of which he is a member' or 'for the publication by or under the authority of either House of any report, paper, votes or proceedings'.

Beyond this, the Constitution gives Parliament the power to prescribe 'the powers, privileges and immunities of each House and of the members and the committees of each House' – but until Parliament defines them, those of the United Kingdom House of Commons apply. Similar references to the House of Commons are found in the Constitutions of Nauru (Section 90), and formerly in India (Section 105). Other Westminster Model constitutions frequently include similar wording with respect to freedom of speech in Parliament, the immunity of members, the right of each House to determine its rules of procedure or standing orders, and the right of Parliament to determine – subject to those constitutional requirements – its own powers, privileges and immunities.

The power of each House to determine its own standing orders often means in practice that the government, having the support of a disciplined majority, controls the parliamentary 'order paper' – the ordering and agenda of business – on most sitting days. The UK House of Commons, under Standing Order 14, follows this rule as the default. It allows a certain number of days in each session to be reserved for the Opposition ('Opposition days'). At present, there are 20 Opposition Days in each session: 17 are allocated to the official Opposition and 3 to the other opposition parties. On all other days, the government controls the agenda of the House – although, in practice, it usually does so in consultation with the Opposition.[238] Since 2010, certain days have also been allocated to backbench business, as determined by a cross-party Backbench Business Committee. This innovation was introduced on the proposal of the 'Wright Committee' (the Select Committee on Reform of the House of Commons, under the chairmanship of Dr Tony Wright MP).[239]

The allocation of parliamentary time is not normally specified in Westminster Model constitutions. Perhaps because the allocation of parliamentary time is a *practice* (in the sense defined by Phillipe Lagassé)[240] and not a *convention*, it escaped codification. However, there is a strong case for codifying at least the general principles. Opposition and Backbench Business Days provide crucial opportunities for the House to debate issues of public concern that the government might otherwise prefer not to find the time for. Much in a Westminster Model constitution depends on this back-and-forth between the government and Opposition (including, within the Opposition, any third and minor parties). The government must have *primacy*, but not *supremacy*. The government is principally responsible for leading Parliament and setting the policy-making and legislative agenda, but opposition parties and backbenchers must also have the right to criticize, oppose, suggest, and present alternatives. One draft constitution to have considered this issue was that prepared by the Scottish Provisional Constituent Assembly, an offshoot of the early Scottish independence movement, in the 1960s: this proposed that government business should 'take precedence', but that at least 'a quarter of the time in each session' must be reserved for non-government business (it did not distinguish between Opposition business and backbench business).[241] In the context of a UK constitution, the best course of action would simply be to constitutionally enshrine the current practice by which a certain minimum number of days are allocated to the Opposition parties and backbenchers, and so protect this practice against attempts by any future government to undermine it.

Westminster Model constitutions deal with other elements of parliamentary organization. Most provide for the appointment of the Clerks and other staff of Parliament. They also regulate the resignation of members (which is theoretically impossible in the United Kingdom and has to be bizarrely circumvented by applying for a sinecure under the Crown). Constitutions likewise set out rules for the disqualification of members. All these provisions are quite standard across Westminster Model constitutions. The details vary (Does a twelve-month prison sentence cause a member to lose his or her seat, or a six-month sentence?) but the principles are generic, universal, and tried and tested.

Some constitutions expressly enable Parliament to make provision by law for the payment of Members of Parliament (Constitution of Pakistan, Section 250; Constitution of Malaysia, Section 64). Others (Constitution of Papua New Guinea, Section 261A; Constitution of the Solomon Islands, Section 69A) establish independent commissions to determine the salaries and allowances of parliamentarians.

Committees

The committee system is another aspect of parliamentary practice which contributes to maintaining a healthy degree of parliamentary scrutiny and oversight, both of legislation and administration. Many Westminster Model constitutions refer, at least in passing, to the power of Parliament, or each House, to establish committees and define their functions. Some go further, setting out some of the purposes of the committee system in the text of the constitution. The Constitution of Bangladesh (article 76), for example, mandates the appointment of a Public Accounts Committee and a Privileges Committee. It also specifies the powers of committees, which may include the ability to: 'examine draft Bills and other legislative proposals', 'review the enforcement of laws and propose measures for such enforcement', 'investigate or inquire into the activities or administration of a Ministry' and 'perform any other function assigned ... by Parliament'. The Constitution of Fiji (article 70), in terms that are suitably broad and open, states that 'Parliament must, under its rules and orders, establish committees with the functions of scrutinizing government administration and examining Bills and subordinate legislation and such other functions as are specified from time to time in the rules and orders of Parliament.'

The value of putting the powers or functions of parliamentary committees into the text of the constitution is twofold. Firstly, it prevents the courts taking a too-narrow view of the role and investigatory powers of committees. This has been a problem in Ireland, where the Irish Supreme Court ruled in 2002 that it was unconstitutional for a parliamentary committee to make a finding of fact that could damage the reputation of any person who is not a member of the Parliament.[242] This limits the ability of committees to conduct investigations into serious policy failures. An attempt was made to amend the constitution in 2011 to expand the investigatory powers of committees, but this was rejected. Putting the powers of committees in the constitution should prevent that. The second reason to state, in broad and general terms, the powers of committees in the constitution is that creates norms and expectations. It shows everyone, from the general public to Members of Parliament themselves, what committees can do and should do. It makes it clear that the scrutiny and investigatory functions of committees are valid, necessary parts of the constitutional order.

Some other basic principles of committee organization ought to be written into the constitution. For example, the Constitution of Papua New Guinea (Section 118) constitutionalizes the principle that ministers cannot be members of parliamentary committees. This is a sound rule, recognized in many Westminster Model jurisdictions, that avoids the absurd charade of ministers sitting on committees scrutinizing their own bills or investigating their own conduct. An exception is usually made for committees that deal with the internal workings of the House, such as a Privileges Committee or Ethics Committee, since these do not deal with policy matters but with the administration and self-government of Parliament, of which ministers are members.

Papua New Guinea's Constitution, in the same section, also requires membership of committees to 'be spread as widely as practicable among the back benchers'. The Constitution of Malta (article 65) similarly expressly requires that 'Committees of the House to enquire into matters of general public importance shall be designed to secure that, so far as it appears practicable to the House, any such Committee is so composed as fairly to represent the House'. The intent of these provisions is to ensure that the Opposition parties are adequately represented on committees. It might be worth further specifying that committees should, in so far as it is practicable to do so, reflect the gender balance and regional balance of the House.

Under a reform introduced on the proposal of the Wright Committee, select committee Chairs in the United Kingdom House of Commons are elected by the whole House, albeit in a way that respects the partisan balance, allocating a certain number of Chairs to each party. This reform has done much to strengthen the House of a whole. In the spirit of preserving what we have lest we lose it, it might also be wise to explicitly include this rule in the new constitution.

The Speaker

The Speaker plays a vital role in ensuring the proper functioning of Parliament's legislative, deliberative and scrutinizing functions, as well as in the organization, administration and operation of Parliament as an institution. Speaker John Bercow was elected by the House of Commons in 2009, in the aftermath of the expenses scandal and amidst a general sense of public distain for Parliament, on a reforming agenda. Standing up for Parliament as a whole, and for the rights of backbenchers in particular, so that the House can effectively debate issues and express its will on them, was a consistent characteristic of his tenure. Replying to a Point of Order in the House in January 2019, he explained, 'As far as I am concerned, I am a member of the legislature. My job is not to be a cheerleader of the executive branch. My job is to stand up for the rights of the House of Commons. And the Speaker will assuredly do so.'[243]

In the United Kingdom the office of Speaker of the House of Commons has no statutory foundation. The election of the Speaker – subject to the nominal formality of approval by the Crown – is recognized as one of the privileges of the House, but it is regulated only by standing orders and not by statute. In most other Westminster Model constitutions, in contrast, the office of Speaker does not depend on the custom of Parliament but is explicitly established in the text of the constitution. The written constitution also regulates the election of the Speaker. The usual practice is to require the election of a Speaker as the first item of business of a new Parliament at its first sitting after a general election. If the office of Speaker becomes vacant between general elections, a new Speaker must be elected as soon as practicable. The wording of such provisions is remarkably consistent, at least among the set of New Commonwealth documents. The Constitution of Malta (art. 60(1)) provides a typical example:

> When the House of Representatives first meets after any general election and before it proceeds to the despatch of any other business it shall elect a person to be Speaker of the House; and, if the office of Speaker falls vacant at any time before the next dissolution of Parliament, the House shall, as soon as practicable, elect another person to that office.

These provisions are reproduced, almost *verbatim*, in the constitutions of Dominica (sect. 36), Belize (sect. 60(1)), and many other countries. Occasionally, subtle variations appear. For example, the Bangladesh (art. 74) does not prescribe the election of new Speaker 'as soon as practicable' after a vacancy arises, but more specifically 'within seven days or, if Parliament is not then sitting, at its first meeting thereafter'. However, despite such variations in wording, the gist and intent of such provisions is consistent. The House is in some sense incomplete, and unable to proceed to substantive business, until the Speaker is elected.

Most Westminster Model constitutional also establish the office of Deputy Speaker, in recognition that the job of Speaker is an onerous one with a wide range of duties, and that is usually necessary for the House to elect at least one Deputy Speaker to whom some of these duties can be delegated. In almost all countries where there are two Houses, the presiding officer of the upper house is likewise elected by its members, although in Canada the Speaker of the Senate is appointed by the Governor-General (Constitution Act (Canada) 1982, sect. 34).

The usual practice in countries with relatively large Parliaments is for the Speaker to be, first and foremost, a member of the House. The House is presided over by one of its own. This is the rule, for example, in Australia, Bangladesh, Canada, Ireland and India. Some countries, however, allow the Speaker to be chosen from outside the House – as in Antigua & Barbuda, Bahamas, Fiji, and the Solomon Islands. In a system based on single member constituencies, there may be some advantages to the external recruitment of the Speaker: voters in the constituency of the Speaker are effectively unrepresented (since the Speaker does not vote, except to exercise a casting vote) and disenfranchised (because of the convention that the Speaker is returned unopposed, and that the major parties do not put up a candidate in the Speaker's seat). The force of these arguments is very much diminished, however, in a system based on proportional representation, using multi-member constituencies.

A written constitution must also provide rules for the removal of the Speaker. In countries where the Speaker must be a member of the House, ceasing to be a member of the House, other than by reason of the dissolution of Parliament, automatically disqualifies a person from the office of Speaker. It must also be possible – but not easy – to remove a Speaker on grounds such as incapacity, gross misconduct, or neglect of duty. A super-majority requirement helps to ensure that the Speaker is not dependent on the government, and that removal can take place only with broad cross-party support. For example, the 1970 Constitution of Fiji (Section 36(1)) required a two-thirds majority to remove a Speaker, as does the Constitution of the Solomon Islands (Section 64). The 1963 Constitution of Kenya (Section 45(4)) required a three-quarters majority.

The functions and duties of the Speaker are recognizably similar across the family of Westminster Model Parliaments and it is still possible – despite many national variations – to speak of a shared set of parliamentary norms, conventions and practices, which includes a set of rules and formal and informal expectations around the role, functions and conduct of the Speaker.[i] The Speaker is expected to perform their duties, while in the chair, in an impartial manner; they are required to treat members equally regardless of their party, and to uphold the privileges and procedures of the House as a whole. In most cases, this requirement to act in a politically neutral manner is not expressly stated in the constitution but depends, as in the UK, on convention, practice, and parliamentary tradition, aided in places by sub-constitutional rules such as parliamentary standing orders.

The degree to which Speakers are expected to be non-partisan when *not* in the chair varies between jurisdictions. The strong conventions of impartiality that have emerged in Britain since the speakership of Arthur Onslow in 1728 – which today require Speakers to cut all ties to their former party and renounce forever any ambitions for ministerial office – are not always replicated; neither is the practice by which the office of Speaker informally alternates between the two main parties honoured. In many cases, the government seeks to propose its own candidate as Speaker, and the voting takes place as a straight partisan

---

[i] This was memorably demonstrated at a meeting with the Speaker of the Parliament of Tuvalu in September 2017. On being asked how he dealt with situations for which Standing Orders made no clear provision, the Speaker replied 'By consulting Erskine May, of course!'

vote. Despite conventions of impartiality in the chair, this alliance with, and dependence on, the government must colour the Speaker's judgement from time to time.

One way to guard against such influence is to provide for the election of the Speaker by secret ballot. This is currently the case in the United Kingdom under Standing Order 1B. This rule is of inestimable benefit, helping to keep the Speaker at arm's length both from the ministers and the party whips. Although most Westminster Model constitutions do not do this, it seems sensible to preserve and enshrine this rule in the text of the constitution; otherwise it would be too easy for the government to use its majority to amend standing orders, remove the shield of the secret ballot, and impose its own candidate for Speaker.

Aside from clearly establishing the office of the Speaker, providing for the election of the Speaker by secret ballot, and requiring a super-majority vote to remove the Speaker, it might be wise, for the avoidance of doubt, and to better secure the impartiality and independence of the Speaker, to explicitly declare these principles in the Constitution. The Constitution of Tuvalu provides an example, stating (Section 106(7)) that 'The Speaker shall perform his functions impartially, and has a duty to ensure that in the conduct of the business of Parliament there is a reasonable opportunity for all members present to be fairly heard.' Including such provisions in the Constitution shapes expectations and helps to reinforce and protect good conventional practices.

Leader of the Opposition

The office of Leader of the Opposition is an established part of the Westminster Model. Older Westminster Model constitutions do not expressly provide for the office in the constitutional text – it exists as a matter of parliamentary practice, which is often reflected in parliamentary standing orders, and perhaps in ordinary legislation (for example, in a statute making provision for the salary of the Leader of the Opposition). Newer Westminster Model constitutions, as a rule, do explicitly provide for the office.

The Constitution of Fiji (article 78) provides that the Leader of the Opposition shall be formally elected by all Members of Parliament who do not belong to the Prime Minister's party or otherwise support the government. This is an unusual formulation, because it means that the leader of the largest opposition party does not automatically become Leader of the Opposition; in a multiparty Parliament, it is at least theoretically possible that some other person, who is able to win the votes of third or minor parties, might be elected. More typically, the Governor-General or Head of State appoints the Leader of the Opposition, being constitutionally bound to appoint the leader of the largest opposition party. The Constitution of Saint Lucia (Section 67) contains the standard wording, generally representative of that found in the majority of such constitutions:

> ... the Governor-General shall appoint the member of the House who appears to him most likely to command the support of a majority of the members of the House who do not support the Government; or, if no member of the House appears to him to command such support, the member of the House who appears to him to command the support of the largest single group of members of the House who do not support the Government.

As well as the traditional roles and privileges accorded to the Leader of the Opposition in Parliament (such as opening proceedings at Prime Minister's Question Time), many Westminster Model constitutions confer on the Leader of the Opposition a right to be consulted in the making of certain appointments to independent, non-partisan offices. The Prime Minister of Jamaica, for example, must consult with the Leader of the Opposition before nominating a candidate for appointment as Chief Justice or President of the Court of Appeal. Likewise, the Leader of the Opposition in Jamaica must be consulted before appointing certain members of the Judicial Service Commission and the Public Service Commission. Some such appointments might even be made on the advice, or with the concurrence, of the Leader of the Opposition. Under the Constitution of Belize (Section 88), two members of the Elections and Boundaries Commission are 'appointed by the Governor-General acting in accordance with the advice of the Prime Minister given with the concurrence of the Leader of the Opposition'. The difference in this case is that the Leader of the Opposition not only has the right to be consulted, but to veto appointments. The Constitution of Dominica (Section 56) allows the Leader of the Opposition to nominate two members of the Constituency Boundaries Commission, balancing the two other members of that Commission nominated by the Prime Minister.

In drafting a written constitution for the United Kingdom, it would be advisable to establish the office of Leader of the Opposition in this way, and to confer certain powers and privileges, in relation to bi-partisan or non-partisan appointments, on the office. Beyond this, the Leader of the Opposition in the United Kingdom is sworn in as a Privy

Councillor, and as such is able to receive briefings from the Prime Minister on 'Privy Council terms' – that is, discretely and in absolute confidence. The advantage of this is that it enables the Prime Minister and the Leader of the Opposition to have frank behind the scenes discussions on sensitive matters of high national policy, particularly in relation to military or diplomatic matters. This too should be written into the Constitution, as the Leader of the Opposition's membership of the Privy Council should be a right of office, and not something that depends on the Prime Minister respecting conventions.

As with the other constitutional prescriptions previously discussed in this chapter, including these rules and principles in the written constitution is primarily intended to protect them against the roll-back that a future government, impatient of parliamentary scrutiny, might otherwise impose. Secondarily, it is intended to send a clear signal that Parliament is not a winner-takes-all arena in which the government dominates, but a place of deliberation, debate and scrutiny where the Opposition – including third and minor parties – have a chance to participate and contribute.

Dissolution

Dissolution is the process that ends the life of the current Parliament and makes way for a general election. In Westminster Model constitutions, Parliaments are generally dissolved in one of two ways. The first is by the passage of time. Parliament continues for a certain time and is then dissolved. A standard formulation is that 'Parliament, unless sooner dissolved, shall continue for five years from the date of the first sitting of Parliament after any dissolution and shall then stand dissolved'. Those words – or very similar ones – are found in the Constitutions of Antigua & Barbuda (sect. 60), the Bahamans (sect. 66), Bangladesh (art. 72), Belize (sect. 84), Grenada (sect. 52) and Jamaica (sect. 64), among many others. The older Westminster Model constitutions used a slightly different formula, but with a similar effect.

On the ordinary duration of Parliaments, the range of variation in Westminster Model constitutions is from three to five years, with five years being most common. A balance here has to be found between two valid principles – the principle that there should be regular and not infrequent accountability to the people, and the principle that a government should have long enough in office to fulfil most of its major manifesto commitments. If this second principle is ignored, the result would be not more democracy, but less; for democracy to be effective, there has to be time for a government to formulate and implement policy in response to public demands, and time for the effects of policy decisions to become evident. Three-year terms in Australia and New Zealand are probably more of a burden and an inconvenience than a democratic strength. If shorter terms and more frequent elections are desired, a four-year term seems best; otherwise, a five-year term is acceptable, but no longer.

The usual rule in Westminster Model constitutions is to allow Parliament to extend its own life in times of war, but only in specified increments, and for a maximum allowable time. The rationale is twofold. Firstly, that during a major war there has to be a united front against the enemy, and the often-divisive nature of party politics might appear to weaken and distract the country at a crucial time. Secondly, that during a major war there are too many logistical and administrative obstacles to the holding of a general election. The Constitution of the Bahamas (Section 66) is a typical example, stating that, 'At any time when The Bahamas is at war, Parliament may extend [the five-year life of a Parliament] for not more than twelve months at a time: Provided that the life of Parliament shall not be extended under this paragraph for more than two years.' The Constitutions of Barbados (Section 61) and Jamaica (Section 64) are almost identical. In these examples, the total maximum period of delay must not exceed to years. That seems a sensible rule. Malta (article 76) allows extension for up to five years in total, which is too long. A two-year delay allows sufficient time to deal with even a severe crisis. With sufficient notice, which a two-year delay would allow, it should possible to hold a general election even in the midst of a major war – as New Zealand did in 1943.

Adapting such provisions to the United Kingdom, two modifications should be made. Firstly, as demonstrated by the 2020 coronavirus pandemic, there are situations other than war in which it may be necessary, in a democracy, to delay elections. A broader formulation, as in India, Bangladesh and Papua New Guinea, allowing elections to be postponed when a state of emergency is in effect, would be preferable. Secondly, there should be some counter-majoritarian safeguard; delaying elections is not a decision to be taken by the ruling majority alone, without the concurrence of, say, the Leader of the Opposition or a two-thirds majority vote in both Houses.

Parliament might also be dissolved before the end of its prescribed maximum term. In older Westminster Model constitutions, premature dissolution was a Crown power governed by convention. The monarch dissolved Parliament on the advice initially of the Cabinet, although by the early 20th century the power to advise dissolution had shifted decisively to the Prime Minister.[244] Major constitutional works of that period – including Bagehot's *English Constitution* and J.S. Mill's *Considerations on Representative Government* – were unanimous in their view that the Prime Minister's power of dissolution was essential to the stability and effectiveness of the British system of government. It meant that no Prime Minister could be removed from office by a vote of no confidence without first having an opportunity to appeal directly to the people in a general election. That made the Prime Minister far more *primus* than *inter pares* and contributed to the emergence of a 'prime ministerial' democracy. Agnes Headlam-Morley, in her 1928 account parliamentary democracy in continental Europe, laid much of the blame for the weakness and chronic instability of parliamentary institutions on the lack of a dissolution power in the hands of the Prime Minister.[245] Conversely, those who criticize the Westminster Model for concentrating too much power in the hands of the Prime Minister, have often sought to limit the power of dissolution. The Fixed Term Parliaments Act is often seen merely as a quick-and-dirty fix to shore-up the coalition between the Conservatives and the Liberal Democrats after the 2010 general election – and to some extent it was – but the desire for fixed terms also had more principled purpose: to empower Parliament as a whole, and weaken the grip of the Prime Minister.

Yet while the right of the Prime Minister to request a dissolution – and normally to receive one – was recognized, it was also recognized that under prevailing constitutional conventions the monarch might, in certain circumstances, refuse such a request. In particular, the monarch might refuse a dissolution requested by a Prime Minister who does not enjoy the confidence of Parliament, allowing an alternative Prime Minister (most naturally the Leader of the Opposition) an opportunity to try to form a working majority government. This power to refuse dissolution was exercised in Canada in 1926.[246] The Canadian Prime Minister, Mackenzie King, led a precarious minority Liberal government, which was dependent on the fickle support of the Progressive Party. When defeated in the House, King requested a dissolution of Parliament. The Governor-General, Viscount Byng, refused the request, and instead appointed the erstwhile Leader of the Opposition, the Conservative leader Arthur Meighen, as Prime Minister. Meighen was also unable to form a stable majority government, and in turn asked for a dissolution, which was granted. The Liberals won the ensuing general election, and King was returned to office as Prime Minister. Perhaps the episode could have been avoided, had Byng seen that the chances of Meighen forming a majority government were slim, and granted King a dissolution when requested. To that extent, perhaps Byng misjudged the political situation. He did not, however, misjudge the extent or the proper use of his reserved power under prevailing conventional understandings. He was quite within his constitutional rights to refuse dissolution to a Prime Minister who did not command the confidence of the majority of the House. The loss of confidence, under conventional rules, forces the Prime Minister to resign unless a dissolution is both requested and granted. If dissolution is not requested, or not granted at the discretion of the Queen or Governor-General, then the Prime Minister must resign, or else be dismissed.

A similar understanding of conventional constitutional principles was applied in South Africa – then a dominion – in 1939. On the outbreak of the Second World War, the Prime Minister, General Hertzog, wanted South Africa to remain neutral, and supported resolution of neutrality in the House. His Minister of Justice, Jan Smuts, moved an amendment, turning the resolution into a declaration of war. This amendment succeeded by 80 votes to 67 – a clear statement that the House had no confidence in the Prime Minister's policy. Hertzog advised the Governor-General, Sir Patrick Duncan, to dissolve Parliament. The Governor-General refused. Hertzog duly tendered his resignation, which Duncan accepted only once it was clear that Jan Smuts, succeeding Herzog as leader of the United Party, could indeed form a viable government.[247]

Perhaps the most authoritative statement of the conventional rule was that articulated, in a letter to *The Times* from Sir Alan Lascelles, the King's Private Secretary, in 1950. This stated that the monarch might refuse a dissolution of Parliament if three conditions were met, namely, that the existing Parliament was still 'vital, viable, and capable of doing its job'; that a general election would be 'detrimental to the national economy'; and that another Prime Minister could be found who could govern 'for a reasonable period, with a working majority in the House of Commons'.[248] The first and third prongs of this test elide: a Parliament that is 'vital, viable and capable of doing its job' is, in practice, one that can support a government, 'for a reasonable period, with a working majority in the House of Commons'. Under the old conventional rules, a Prime Minister who lost the confidence of the House had the right to request a dissolution. The Queen had the right to grant or refuse a dissolution. In the calculation of whether to refuse, the most important criterion was whether another Prime Minister could be appointed, and a government formed that would be able to command the confidence of the House. The second test, that of detriment to the national economy, would be only a subordinate consideration in such circumstances, although it might be a more pressing consideration if a Prime Minister who had not lost the confidence of the House wanted to call an election at time of national crisis or emergency. In any case, the right to a dissolution was not an automatic one, and the Queen's power to refuse dissolution very real.

The authors of later Westminster Model constitutions took different approaches to the conversion of these conventions into explicit constitutional rules. In Barbados and Jamaica, any uncertainty over the extent of discretionary power to refuse dissolution was removed by explicitly requiring the Governor-General to dissolve Parliament at any time when so advised by the Prime Minister. There are no exceptional circumstances when the Governor-General might refuse a dissolution. These two constitutions also provide that a vote of no confidence in the government leads automatically to a dissolution of Parliament. A slightly different rule applies in the case of a 'vote to revoke the appointment of the Prime Minister'; in such cases, the Prime Minister has a choice between resignation and dissolution, and if a dissolution is requested it cannot be refused. This approach – which tilts power towards the Prime Minister to an extent far beyond what old conventional rules allowed – puts the Prime Minister in an overbearing position, and Parliament in a correspondingly weak one. It is almost impossible to remove a Prime Minister from office under such rules without risking a dissolution.

A second approach is to let Parliament vote on its own dissolution. The Constitution of the Solomon Islands, for example, (Section 73) states that 'If at any time Parliament decides by resolution supported by the votes of an absolute majority of the members of Parliament that Parliament should be ... dissolved, the Governor-General shall forthwith ... dissolve Parliament'. The Constitution of Tuvalu (Section 118) similarly provides that 'The Head of State, acting in accordance with a resolution of Parliament may at any time dissolve Parliament.' The effect of such a rule is the opposite of that seen in Barbados and Jamaica: it strengthens Parliament, since Parliament cannot be dissolved without its own consent, and it makes the position of the Prime Minister that little bit more precarious. This formulation makes for easy changes of government, as factions realign in Parliament, without any risk of dissolution to discipline members. Instability is exacerbated, in these South Pacific countries, by weak or non-existent parties, but the same risk might appear in the United Kingdom with a proportionally elected Parliament. There is also the chance that this rule could lead to a stymied, paralyzed relationship between the government and the parliamentary majority, of the sort that we saw in the United Kingdom during the Parliament elected in 2017.

A third approach is exemplified by the Constitution of Ireland (article 13). This states that 'The President may in his absolute discretion refuse to dissolve Dáil Éireann (Lower House) on the advice of a Taoiseach (Prime Minister) who has ceased to retain the support of a majority in Dáil Éireann.' A very similar, perhaps even neater, solution appeared in the Burmese constitution of 1947, which stated that

> The Chamber of Deputies shall be ... dissolved by the President on the advice of the Prime Minister: provided that, when the Prime Minister has ceased to retain the support of a majority in the Chamber, the President may refuse to prorogue or dissolve the Chamber on his advice and shall in that event forthwith call on the Chamber to nominate a new Prime Minister; provided further that, if the Chamber fails to nominate a new Prime Minister within fifteen days, it shall be dissolved.

The Irish and (former) Burmese rules do not prevent a government with a working majority from calling a snap election. As long as the Prime Minister commands the confidence of the House, the Head of State has no discretion, and must grant a dissolution if requested. Only if the Prime Minister has lost the confidence of the House may the President refuse a dissolution, potentially enabling a change of government during the lifetime of a Parliament.

The fourth approach – and the most common one – is for the constitution to attempt to transcribe the Lascelles principles into constitutional writing. The Constitution of Saint Lucia (Section 55), provides a typical example:

> In the exercise of this powers to dissolve Parliament, the Governor-General shall act in accordance with the advice of the Prime Minister: Provided that ... if the Prime Minister advises a dissolution and the Governor-General, acting in his own deliberate judgment, considers that the government of Saint Lucia can be carried on without a dissolution and that a dissolution would not be in the interests of Saint Lucia, he may, acting in his own deliberate judgment, refuse to dissolve Parliament.

Near identical wording is found in the Constitutions of Belize (Section 85), Malta (article 76) and Saint Vincent and the Grenadines (Section 48). Such provisions are a balanced, reasonably comprehensive, flexible, yet robust, way of incorporating traditional conventional rules into a written constitution. However, unlike the Irish and Burmese provisions, this rule does not explicitly anticipate the refusal of dissolution on the grounds that the Prime Minister has ceased to command the confidence of a majority in the House. On the other hand, again in contrast to the Irish and Burmese provisions, these rules allow the Head of State to prevent a snap election being called in circumstances that would not be 'in the public interest'. This is a somewhat broader exception than the 'economic detriment' test in the Lascelles letter, but it has a similar intent. A wise Head of State would be circumspect in refusing a dissolution on those grounds, but the risk of refusal might at least cause a Prime Minister to think twice.

New Commonwealth Constitutions also typically delineate two other 'reserve powers' in relation to dissolution. The first is the power to dissolve Parliament without a request from the Prime Minister if the Prime Minister attempts to 'squat' in office following a loss of confidence – that is, refusing to resign or to request a dissolution. If that situation were to arise, the initiative would pass to the head of state or Governor-General, who would have the reserve power, clearly articulated in the Constitution, either to dismiss the Prime Minister (and appoint another Prime Minister who does enjoy the confidence of the House), or else to dissolve Parliament and let the people decide. The second additional reserve power is the discretionary right to dissolve Parliament if the office of Prime Minister is vacant and there appears to be no prospect, within a reasonable time, of being able to appoint a Prime Minister who is able to command the confidence of the House.

In a constitution for the United Kingdom, there is much to commend a mixture of the Irish-Burmese rules with the Lascelles principles: make it explicit in the constitution that the Queen may dissolve Parliament at any time on the advice of the Prime Minister, but also make it clear that the Queen may refuse a dissolution if requested by a Prime Minister who does not command the confidence of Parliament, or if 'the Government can be carried on without a dissolution and a dissolution would not be in the public interest'. If the House of Commons passes a vote of no confidence in the government, and a dissolution is either not sought or sought but refused then the government would have to resign (or be dismissed) and a new Prime Minister appointed in the usual way; if that appointment cannot be made after a certain constitutionally prescribed interval, then the Queen would be permitted by the constitution to dissolve Parliament in her own deliberate judgement in order to break the deadlock.

Such discretion, both to refuse a dissolution when asked and to force a dissolution when not asked, is admittedly an awesome power to entrust to a hereditary monarch. The situations in which that power might be used, however, would be narrowly defined by the constitution. The role of the Queen, when called on to exercise such power, is not to impose her own will, but merely to apply the rules of parliamentary democracy as a neutral umpire.

If it is nevertheless felt that such discretion cannot with safety or democratic propriety be entrusted to a hereditary monarch, then the approach taken by the Solomon Islands would be the appropriate one: to let the House of Commons decide on the dissolution of Parliament by means of a resolution. This would be the essence of rule established by the Fixed Term Parliaments Act 2011, without the two-thirds majority requirement that gives the opposition a veto.

In either case, these formulations would normally enable a Prime Minister, with a solid majority in the House of Commons to seek and to obtain a dissolution. Dissolution would be denied only if the Prime Minister does not have such a majority or is acting in a reckless and inappropriate way. Thus, a powerful tool would be returned to the Prime Minister's hands. In the context of a constitutional design that otherwise shares power – through proportional representation, federalism, a reformed second chamber, and a stronger judiciary – this would be an important counterbalance, enabling a Prime Minister to 'appeal to the country'.

Prorogation

The Fixed Term Parliaments Act 2011 did not change the rules on prorogation.[249] It remains a matter of royal prerogative, which by convention has since the development of parliamentary democracy been exercised on the advice of the Prime Minister. Prorogation is an interruption of Parliament's session. Normally, it is a routine and uncontroversial procedural device used to formally end one session of Parliament so that a new session can be held; a new session means a new Queen's Speech and therefore an opportunity for the government both to set out its policy agenda and to prove that it enjoys the confidence of the House of Commons. Since the Parliament Act 1949 requires a bill rejected by the House of Lords to be passed again in another session of Parliament, prorogation has been used on occasion to fast-track legislation through Parliament. Prorogation also causes any bill currently going through Parliament to lapse, but since in normal circumstance the government has overall control of Parliament's legislative timetable, this has not generally given rise to any problems. When prorogation occurs in a planned way, by a government enjoying the confidence of a majority in the House of Commons, it is usual for any uncontroversial legislation to be wrapped up, and to receive royal assent, before prorogation takes place.

On 28 August 2019, the Queen made the necessary Order-in-Council to authorize the prorogation of Parliament. The newly appointed Prime Minister, Boris Johnson, having only faced Parliament for one sitting day since taking office, and with a shaky and unproven parliamentary majority, was keen to minimize the number of sitting days during which opposition to a No Deal Brexit could effectively express itself, whether in the form of a vote of no confidence or an opposition-sponsored bill requiring the Prime Minister to seek another extension to the Brexit deadline. For the Queen to refuse prorogation in such circumstances would have been a bold move because the conventional rules on this point are far from clear. Seen from the perspective of the overriding principle of parliamentary democracy, to refuse prorogation might nevertheless have been the proper course of action. My intent here is not to criticize the Queen's actions, so much as to show the inadequacy of conventional rules that make the exercise of a reserve power, even in democratically appropriate circumstances, very difficult. The Queen and the country would have greatly benefited from clearer, more explicit, constitutional rules.

In particular, there is a strong case to be made for a rule that would explicitly deny the right to prorogue Parliament to a Prime Minister who does not command the confidence of a majority of the members of the House of Commons. The Prime Minister only attains the moral right to advise the Queen by virtue of the fact that he or she enjoys the confidence of a majority in the House of Commons. If the Prime Minister does not enjoy the confidence of the House of Commons, then that authority is weakened. Likewise, if a Prime Minister were to request a prorogation of Parliament in order to avoid holding, and potentially losing, a vote of no confidence it could be argued that the Queen has a conventional duty to refuse prorogation.[250]

In Canada, where constitutional conventions remain uncodified, the issue of prorogation arose in 2008. The Conservative Government of Stephen Harper seemed poised to lose its majority to a loose coalition of Liberal, New Democratic Party, and Bloc Quebecois MPs. Harper advised the Governor-General to prorogue Parliament, buying the Prime Minister some time to shore up his majority. The Governor-General, Michaëlle Jean, acted in accordance with this advice. However, she made it clear that acting on such advice was no mere formality.

She considered that advice might legitimately be refused, and she understood that the decision rested with her alone. In an interview with *The Canadian Press* in 2010 she explained, 'I had the duty to make a decision. It couldn't be dealt with in just a few minutes. So I had to analyze, I had to anticipate what my decision would imply — whatever it was.'[251] This was a correct reading of the situation – not necessarily that she was correct to agree to prorogation, but that she was correct to recognize that in such cases, where the Prime Minister's legitimacy as the one who enjoys the confidence of the House of Commons is in doubt, a reserve power to refuse prorogation exists. A survey of 25 constitutional scholars conducted by Johannes Wheeldon concluded that a majority of those surveyed argue that the Governor-General does have a limited discretion to refuse the advice of the Prime Minister, even if this is limited to 'ensuring any such advice is given by a prime minster whose government holds (and is seen to hold) the confidence of the House'.[252] This is in accordance with the principle of responsible government, which requires that the House should not be frustrated by the Crown in its attempt to test, and perhaps withdraw, confidence.

However, when we examine those post-WW2 constitutions in which the conventions of parliamentary democracy are constitutionalized, we see that such a reserve power to refuse prorogation is not usually recognized. Prorogation is near-universally vested in the Head of State (or Governor-General) acting on the advice of the Prime Minister, without any explicit authority to refuse. The Constitution of Barbados (sect. 61) states that 'The Governor-General, acting in accordance with the advice of the Prime Minister, may at any time by proclamation prorogue Parliament.' The same words occur (sect. 66) in the Constitution of the Bahamas. Another common formula (Constitution of St Christopher and Nevis, sect. 47; Constitution of Saint Lucia, sect. 55) is to treat both prorogation and dissolution together, as powers that must normally be exercised on the advice of the Prime Minister, and then to make specific exceptions for the reserve powers of the head of state or Governor-General's with respect to dissolution, but not to prorogation.

In other words, in terms of prorogation most Westminster Model constitutions have until now erred on the side of Prime Ministerial power. Such formulations are unsurprising. Given the generally restrained, uncontroversial and predictable use of prorogation during the British constitution's majoritarian heyday, it was not felt necessary to introduce specific limitations. As we have seen by the September 2019 prorogation, such trust has been abused and the Supreme Court has had to step in. This could have been avoided, had the rules been clearer – a good example of how written constitutions can reduce reliance on the judiciary.

A future written constitution for the United Kingdom could solve this problem in one of two ways. The first would be to adopt the rule contained in the former (1947) Constitution of Burma, which allowed the Head of State to refuse to prorogue (as well as dissolve) Parliament on the advice of a Prime Minister who had lost the confidence of the House. This rule would prevent a Prime Minister who has lost control of the House of Commons from proroguing Parliament in order to avoid a vote of no confidence – although its use depends on the discretion, and perhaps courage, of the Head of State. The second would be to adopt the rule of the Solomon Islands, where responsibility for prorogations is completely taken out of the hands of the Prime Minister and the Governor-General, and no prorogation is possible without explicit parliamentary approval (sect. 73). On balance, perhaps the Solomon Islands' rule is better, simply because the Head of State should have no more discretionary powers than are necessary. As discussed in the previous section, such discretion may be necessary in so far as it relates to dissolution, because other alternatives are too rigid, either giving the Prime Minister too much power or too little, but in relation to prorogation such considerations do not apply. Nothing goes wrong, and the system is not stymied, if prorogation is denied.

In addition, there should be a rule enabling Parliament to be recalled into session, at any time when it is adjourned or prorogued, by an authority other than the government. The former Speaker John Bercow has proposed a mechanism for recalling Parliament, according to which the Speaker would be able to recall Parliament directly on the request of one-quarter of the MPs.[253] The 1970 Constitution of Fiji allowed the Governor-General at his discretion to recall Parliament at the request of one-quarter of the members of the House of Representatives on the grounds that 'the Government no longer commands the confidence of a majority of the members of that House' or that 'it is necessary for the two Houses of Parliament to consider without delay a matter of public importance'. This is an admirable rule, with the exception that once again unnecessary dependence on the Head of State's personal discretion may be excised. In the United Kingdom, a better formulation would be to require – not merely permit – the Queen to recall Parliament when the Speaker, on the basis of a petition signed by one-quarter of the members of the House of Commons, so advises.

10

Nations, Regions and Local Democracy

The Union and the 'English question'

Sir Ivor Jennings, writing in the context of decolonization in the 1950s, observed that, 'before you can decide how the people are to govern themselves, you must first decide who are the people'.[254] The primordial question that any new British constitutional settlement must answer, therefore, is whether the Union is to continue, and if so which nations are to be included in it.

We should not prejudge this question. There is no reason to assume that the United Kingdom will, can or should continue in its current shape. The route to constitutional refoundation might well pass through the reunification of Ireland and Scottish independence. The Union was built by and for the Empire, and it is difficult to say, in a post-imperial age, what the United Kingdom is *for* anymore. It would not be unreasonable for the Scots and Northern Irish, and perhaps even the Welsh, to conclude (each in their own ways and for their own good reasons) that the constitutional future they desire no longer involves a union with England. That need not be seen as a disaster. It may be a natural next step. If so, the priority is to ensure that independence is achieved in a peaceful, orderly and democratic way, and that friendly post-independence relations are maintained. After all, there is nothing quite so in keeping with the best British constitutional traditions as a managed path to independence.

In any case, any constitutional renewal project must recognize that the United Kingdom is neither a homogenous 'nation state' nor an undifferentiated 'unitary state', but a complex 'Union state' made up of distinct nations.[255] It is a messy amalgam of two kingdoms, a principality and a dismembered province, forged together by civil wars, bribery and dynastic wrangling. It contains two established churches, three legal systems, four legislatures, and several national cultures and identities. Our official lives are bound up in this British 'Union state', into which our several proximate but distinct nations are absorbed. Thus we have a United Kingdom anthem, but only English, Scottish, Irish and Welsh folk songs. We have United Kingdom passports, but only English, Scottish, Irish and Welsh literature. There are also divergent political dynamics in the different countries of the Union: recent general elections have been won by the Conservatives in England, the SNP in Scotland, the Labour Party in Wales, and the Democratic Unionist Party in Northern Ireland.

This plurinational complexity has far-reaching consequences for constitution-building. Even when fairly standard off-the-shelf forms of Westminster Model constitutionalism are applied, the geographical, cultural, historical and demographic complexity of the polity being constituted will determine much of its constitutional architecture. This is illustrated by India and Bangladesh, two countries whose constitutions are thoroughly Westminster influenced and show many obvious similarities of form, but are so different in their design because of the demands of context: India being federal, multilingual and secular, while Bangladesh – except for limited autonomy extended to the Chittagong Hill Tracts – is unitary and monocultural.

The more complex a polity is, the harder it is to reach a constitutional settlement: more interests have to be reconciled, more interlocking compromises struck, and in consequence a wider array of provisions, embodying those compromises in enforceable constitutional terms, must be included. This applies not only to arrangements for territorial government (such as federalism or devolution), but also to other matters of constitutional design. For example, as discussed in Chapter 8, a suitable structure of the upper house intended to act as a House of Review in a unitary nation state might be quite different from that required for a chamber that is intended to represent constituent units of a federal union. Similarly, the constitutional amendment mechanism of a unitary state might enable the people to decide on constitutional amendments by referendum as the national constituent power (as in Ireland), whereas in a federal union the constitutional amendment rule might have to take into consideration the views of the different parts of the federation (as in Canada). It is also necessary to consider such things as judicial appointments and the structure of the judiciary (reflecting the needs and traditions of different jurisdictions), language rights (recognition of national and minority languages), and 'fourth branch' scrutiny and oversight institutions (for example, establishing distinct Ombudsman and Auditor-General institutions in each part of the Union).

All told, the range of viable and acceptable constitutional design choices available to a 'United Kingdom of Great Britain and Northern Ireland' will be quite different from those open to a 'United Kingdom of England and Wales', or even an independent England or an independent Scotland or Wales.[i] This foundational decision of who is 'in' and who is 'out' also affects the design of the constitution-building process itself; the Constitution of a United Kingdom of Great Britain and Northern Ireland would have to be negotiated and agreed not only between parties in London, but across the different parts of the Union. As will be discussed in the final chapter, this would tilt the design of the constitution-making body away from a centrally nominated commission and towards a Constituent Assembly elected from the four nations.

Another complication is that different parts of the United Kingdom are at different stages of their cultural and political journey towards a new constitutional settlement. Scotland has already begun to reconstitute itself in post-Unionist terms. Although at the time of writing there is only a slim majority support for Scottish independence, there has been a subtle but palpable shift in the conversation, to the point at which independence increasingly seems not just possible but inevitable.[ii] Northern Ireland is divided on the Union as on all other issues of political identity, but it is safe to say that a large minority in that province define themselves in opposition to the British state, and that with Brexit the idea of a united Ireland may one day reach a tipping point. Wales, too, has maintained and reasserted a sense of

---

[i] My views on the constitution of an independent Scotland have been set out in several of my earlier works, including *A Model Constitution for Scotland: Making Democracy Work in an Independent State* (Edinburgh: Luath Press, 2011); *A Constitution for the Common Good: Strengthening Scottish Democracy after the Independence Referendum* (2nd edition) (Edinburgh: Luath Press, 2015); *Constituting Scotland: The Scottish National Movement and the Westminster Model* (Edinburgh University Press, 2016).

[ii] My preference for Scottish independence is a matter of public record. However, it might be that a second independence referendum is not forthcoming, or that if it is, it might yield a result similar to that of the second Quebec referendum (where independence was defeated on a knife-edge – but nevertheless politically decisive – vote). In that case, it would be necessary to find a new form of Union that can work better for Scotland, and for all parts of the United Kingdom, than the current arrangement – a federal Union that would protect national autonomy and national identity to the fullest extent possible, while still maintaining common institutions and policies where necessary.

national identity that can disentangle itself from the Union, with growing support if not for independence then for significantly enhanced autonomy. Only in England is there no active, effective, mainstream political movement to loosen the country from the grip of 'British rule'.

There is a Campaign for an English Parliament, which recognizes that devolution has short-changed England, but it has not yet had much effect on the constitutional conversation, either at the policy level or in public consciousness. Instead, the procedural expedient of English Votes for English Laws ('EVEL') has been adopted. This procedure, which allows only Members of Parliament representing English constituencies to vote at certain decisive stages of England-only legislation, is a very poor substitute for an English Parliament. It merely adds to the anomalies, inconsistencies and complexities of a system that has lost all coherence. The Westminster Model of parliamentary democracy is based on a government that is responsible to Parliament, holding office because it enjoys the confidence of the parliamentary majority. It is not clear what happens in situations – not entirely hypothetical ones – in which a party has a majority in the Union Parliament but does not have a majority among English MPs.

As the largest country of the Union, and the one whose culture and interests dominate the rest, the very idea of English autonomy seems absurd to some. Yet England – as a nation, and not simply as the vast majority of the British electorate – is ignored. There is no English Parliament or English government, nor really any English national politics as distinct from the politics of the United Kingdom. With or without EVEL, the United Kingdom Parliament and government continue to do double duty as the only Parliament and government for England. It is easy to see why, psychologically, this arrangement encourages the perception that the United Kingdom is little more than 'Greater England'. There is no one to speak for England. It is hardly surprising, therefore, that so many of the English people clamour, in the words of the infamous Brexit slogan, to 'Take back control' – even if their ire is misdirected.

In Scotland, most folk are quite conscious of the difference between Scottish and British identities, even when these align. A Scottish Unionist, for example, might identify as 'Scottish and British', or even as 'British and Scottish', without ever losing sight of the differences – and tensions – been these identities. They might support the Union, but only because they see it as being in Scotland's national interest. In England, however, this internal personal tension between English and British identities has, at least until recently, been largely absent. English and British identities did not layer on top of one another, but blurred together as one, so that an English person can talk about England while meaning the United Kingdom, and talk about the United Kingdom while meaning England, without even being conscious of their error until corrected by someone from another part of the United Kingdom in whose ears it jars.

In consequence, there is very little English nationalism of the civic-democratic, liberal or progressive kind, comparable with the Scottish nationalism of the SNP or the Welsh nationalism of Plaid Cymru. The English left has tended to deny its Englishness and to cling to a post-1945 vision of what might be termed 'National Coal Board Britain'.[256] As the former Labour MP John Denham put it in a speech to the Young Fabians in 2019, if English identity is mentioned at all by the British left, 'it is to be disparaged and abused'.[257]

English nationalism certainly exists, but has generally expressed itself through a British identity that is, if not actually reactionary, at least nostalgic. There is some irony, although no surprise, in the fact that those who feel most strongly English have been most inclined to vote for parties, like the United Kingdom Independence Party and the short-lived Brexit Party, that promote a right-wing, Eurosceptic, 'Spitfires-over-the-Channel' form of British nationalism.[258] As Adam Ramsay, editor of Open Democracy, put it, 'England, specifically, desperately needs to find a way to escape the prison of imperial longing, and emerge as a modern democracy'.[259]

With those caveats in place, let us now consider three options for reconstituting the United Kingdom as a federal Union, assuming that its current boundaries, encompassing England, Scotland, Wales and Northern Ireland, are for the time being to be maintained.

The principle of federalism, as the basis for the re-constitution of the Union, is a necessary starting point. Federalism differs in kind, not merely degree, from devolution. Devolution works by delegation. Its operating principle is the unilateral, conditional, revocable delegation of power from a superior authority to subordinate authorities. The devolved authorities have only such powers as the United Kingdom Parliament chooses to grant them and can hold and exercise such powers only for so long, and in such manner, as that Parliament may prescribe. Any authority that is given to devolved legislatures can easily be taken away, and Parliament can – Sewel convention not withstanding – interfere unilaterally in devolved matters.

In a federal system, in contrast, both levels of government (the federal or Union level and the state, provincial or regional level) have constitutionally guaranteed and protected powers. Each has a degree of genuine autonomy within its allotted sphere. Powers allocated to each level are prescribed in a written constitution, the fundamentals of which cannot be unilaterally changed by either level. This division of powers between different levels of government has to be policed by an independent judiciary, with authority to ensure that neither level of government can encroach upon the other's sphere.[260] In this way, federalism offers secure autonomy-as-right; devolution offers only conditional autonomy-by-permission.

S.A. de Smith, surveying the wide variety of federations within the Commonwealth, noted that there might seem to be 'a characteristic British bias in favour of federalism – a bias which, however, corrects itself north of the channel'.[261] This predilection for federalism, he argued, was not the result of any dogmatic scheme, but a pragmatic and sometimes reluctant response to the political demands and governance needs of diverse societies. Federalism is beneficial in situations where different territorial entities cannot live apart, because they have too many economic, security, and other interests in common, but cannot live together under a unitary government because they have too many differences in interest, identity, culture or policy preference. In such situations, federalism can be a strategic compromise that reconciles 'shared rule' with 'self-rule', allowing a measure of guaranteed autonomy for each territorial unit in its own affairs, while also establishing inclusive and legitimate mechanisms of 'shared rule' over common affairs.[262]

However, for all the talk about federalism in principle, relatively little detailed work has yet been done on filling out the picture with a comprehensive federal plan that can serve at least as a basis for negotiations. The Labour Party, in particular, has tended to use the word 'federalism' without defining in any concrete and practical way what it would look like. This section seeks to remedy that by setting out three federal models, which may be labelled as 'Special Autonomy', 'Nations and Regions', and 'Union of Four Equals', for consideration.

The 'Special Autonomy' model would constitutionally recognize and entrench special autonomy for Scotland, Wales and Northern Ireland, without extending similar autonomy either to England as a whole or to English regions. Commonwealth examples of this model can be found in Antigua & Barbuda, St Christopher & Nevis, and Trinidad & Tobago. In each case, the smaller entity (Barbuda, Nevis, Tobago) has its own legislature or governing council with a some degree of constitutionally protected autonomy, but – crucially – there is no legislature exclusively for the larger entity; instead, the Parliament of the Union acts as the legislature both for the whole and for the major part.

The degree of autonomy and the precise mechanism of constitutional protection vary. The Constitution of Antigua and Barbuda (Section 123) offers only minimal protection. It recognizes that, 'There shall be a Council for Barbuda which shall be the principal organ of local government in that island', and provides that a bill to alter any of the provisions of the Barbuda Local Government Act 1976 shall not be enacted except with the consent of that Council. This gives the Barbuda Council some degree of autonomy, in that laws affecting its powers cannot be passed without the consent of its own members. The constitution of St Christopher & Nevis goes much further. Firstly, it contains a list of 23 'specified matters' over which the Nevis Island Legislature has exclusive legislative authority. Except in a state of emergency, the Parliament of St Christopher & Nevis cannot legislate on these specified matters without the consent of the Nevis Island Legislature.[iii] Secondly, it provides a mechanism by which Nevis can, if it so chooses, transition democratically to independence.

The constitutional arrangements like those of St Christopher & Nevis, if applied to the United Kingdom, would transform the Union into a sort of lopsided federation. The 'Sewel' convention, which restrains the Westminster Parliament from legislating on devolved matters in 'normal' circumstances without the consent of the devolved legislatures, would be raised to the status of a firm and judicially enforceable constitutional rule. That would rectify one of the main weaknesses of devolution, ending the dependence of the devolved legislatures on the self-restraint, goodwill and political calculations of the United Kingdom Parliament.

Such arrangements would not, however, solve the problem of asymmetry. The special autonomy of Scotland, Wales and Northern Ireland would be assured, but only as particular exceptions in an otherwise centralized polity; England, and therefore the vast majority of the population of the United Kingdom, would still be governed directly by the United Kingdom Parliament and government. This would leave England, as at present, without a voice of its own. There would still need to be an EVEL procedure to deal with England-only legislation, with all that means for the disruption of normal patterns of responsible party government. Most of all, it would perpetuate the perception of the United Kingdom as 'England plus the Celtic

[iii] Trinidad & Tobago, at the time of writing, is in the midst of a constitutional reform process which might see it switch from a system rather like that of Antigua and Barbuda to one more like that of St Christopher and Nevis.

Fringe', which causes such misunderstanding in England and such offence outwith it.

It is notable that the examples of special autonomy arrangements are all two-part unions, where the entity having autonomy is but one small part of the whole. It might work, perhaps, in a United Kingdom of England and Wales, but it is difficult to see how this arrangement would be suitable or sustainable in a United Kingdom of Great Britain and Northern Ireland.

The second potential approach is to blend constitutional autonomy for Scotland, Wales and Northern Ireland with English regionalism, creating a complex federal scheme based on 'Nations and Regions'. Assuming the restoration of previous regional boundaries (those of former European Parliament constituencies and NUTS1 statistical regions), this would result in a federation of 12 parts: Scotland, Wales, Northern Ireland, and nine English regions.

The 'Nations and Regions' model depends on the viability of regionalism in England. There is much to be said for regional devolution. Regional authorities are essential to the task of rebalancing wealth, resources and power away from London; no new civic life and new economic hope will be possible for provincial England's 'left-behind' communities unless they have democratic institutions of their own, with policy and financial levers in their hands. The creation of regional authorities would open up the civic space to new political leaders and civil society actors, create new policy networks, and shift large numbers of graduate-level jobs out of London to the regional capitals, sustaining a more balanced geographical distribution of economic opportunity.[iv]

The rejection of a pilot scheme for regional devolution in the North East of England, in a referendum held in 2004 was interpreted by the government of Tony Blair as a sign that there was no demand for English regional authorities, and the idea was quietly dropped. Yet no such conclusion should be drawn from such a failed experiment. The scheme put forward was almost designed to fail. It amounted not to a transformative decentralization of power from the centre to a new regional authority, but an upwards concentration of power from local councils to the regional level. More recently, the generally

---

[iv] My conversion to English regionalism came in December 2018, during an advent tour of English cathedral cities. Even the picture-postcard places with the medieval cathedrals looked poor, tired, run-down and forgotten. Only a massive geographical shift of resources – and democratic power over those resources – can reinject life into the once proud cities and towns of provincial England.

warm response to the city-region 'devolution deals' under the Cities and Local Government Devolution Act 2016 – which enable some aspects of transport policy, regional, planning, education and skills, and regional economic development to be devolved to 'Combined Authorities' headed by elected mayors – shows that there is a public demand for greater autonomy at the city-region level.

One advantage of the 'devolution deal' arrangement, over previously envisaged forms of regionalism, is that its boundaries are organic, being negotiated and agreed from the bottom up. One of the main objections to regional authorities, as formerly conceived, stemmed from romantic notions about the ancient identity of English counties; to shoehorn them into new-fangled artificial regions, for the sake of mere administrative convenience, seemed horribly Napoleonic. This is not a concern to be brushed aside. Sentiments matter: the best institutional design will fail if it disregards the feelings and attachments of the people. If the intention is to create powerful English regional authorities, care should be taken to root them in some sense of existing historical identity. It is hard, in a country where the historicity of place is so highly valued, to love an administrative abstraction like 'The South West' or 'The North East'. At least counties have cricket teams and cities have football teams. Regions – at least as they are considered in the popular imagination – have nothing but statistical planning departments.

We must be clear, however, about the question we are answering and the problem we are solving. Devolution deals, patchwork and thin though they might be, do at least indicate a possible path to curing the chronic, debilitating, life-draining over-centralization in England; they are a response to an English domestic need for the re-ordering of governance in England. They are not, however, a solution to the imbalance of the Union. It is impossible to speak of Scotland and Sheffield in the same breath and to imagine that they are in any way equivalent.

Here we reach a conundrum. A variant of regional devolution that would be popular and workable in England does not translate into the kind of federalism that would solve the problems of the Union as a whole. Although less so than the 'Special Autonomy' model, a federation of 'Nations and Regions' would still be asymmetrical; elements of English domestic policy could be transferred to regional authorities, but much asymmetry between the 'nations' on the one hand and the 'regions' on the other would necessarily remain. As matter of pride and principle, a historic nation like Scotland or Wales, with its own culture and identity, should not be placed on the same level as a mere region of England. As a matter of practicality and politics, any set of powers minimally acceptable to Scotland, Wales or Northern Ireland might be unnecessary, unwanted or unworkable in English regions. For example, we would not expect English regional authorities to legislate separately across the broad scope of civil and criminal matters that are within the legislative competence of the Scottish Parliament. There would still be a considerable range of England-only legislation that would go through the Union Parliament, with all that means for the retention of the unwieldy EVEL procedure.

The third option, then, is to re-cast the United Kingdom as a federal 'Union of Four Equals'. Under this scheme, which would be similar to the major Commonwealth federations, the United Kingdom would consist of just four national states – England, Scotland, Wales and Northern Ireland – each having the same rights, powers and status. There would be a Union government, headed by the Prime Minister of the United Kingdom, responsible to the House of Commons as the lower House of the Union Parliament, with authority over defence, foreign affairs, and other aspects of Union-level policy. Alongside this there would be four state governments, each headed by a First Minister, responsible to a unicameral state Parliament, with responsibility for most matters of internal and domestic policy in each state.

A Union of four equals would still enable the establishment of regional authorities in England. Indeed, the creation of regions and the devolution of substantial powers to them could and should be an integral part of the scheme. All the arguments in favour of English regional devolution still stand. Regional authorities would help distribute power, resources and responsibility for public affairs more widely within England and create a thicker democratic tapestry that enables policy innovation and initiative, as well as reconnecting politics with people and place. The point is simply that in a Union of four equals these English regional authorities would be *devolved* rather than *federated*. Their powers, boundaries and sources of revenue would be prescribed by the English Parliament – whether by building on the existing scheme of 'devolution deals' and 'combined authorities' or otherwise. The regions would be integrated into the governance system of England, but would not be constituent units of the Union in their own right. Constitutionally speaking, therefore the English regions would – like the existing Greater London Authority – be conceived as a top-tier of local authority within England.

The main objection to this scheme is the vast inequality of size: England has around 85 per cent of the population of the United Kingdom. The classic 19th century texts on federalism all warn against such inequalities of size, but four-part unions between entities of unequal size are not totally unprecedented. Canada, when first confederated in 1867, comprised two big provinces (Ontario and Quebec) and two smaller ones (Nova Scotia and New Brunswick). The Union of South Africa, as constituted under the 1909 Act, also had four provinces – of which one, Cape Province, was considerably larger than the others. Besides, size discrepancy is not an insurmountable obstacle to a working federation. The English, having an overwhelming majority of votes, would of course dominate United Kingdom-wide matters – there is no way around that – but the English government would not. In terms of autonomy over its own affairs, touching most of the areas of domestic policy that affects people's daily lives, England would simply be one part of the Union, on equal terms with the other three. In the same way, the representatives of England would fill more than 80 per cent of the seats in the House of Commons, and the largest bloc of seats in the second chamber too, but when it comes to inter-governmental relations, the First Minister of England would just be one of four equals.

To reiterate what has been said in previous chapters, the design of the second chamber and the constitutional amendment rules would be crucial. These have to be arranged in such a way as to enable majoritarian decision making over normal legislation, while preventing an English-only majority from being able to change the constitution without broader consent.

Under such conditions, the size and power of England, rather than being a liability, could in fact help ensure a more balanced Union. In a federation of four equal parts, a Prime Minister of the United Kingdom would serve alongside a First Minister of England; they might belong to different parties, and be elected at different times, but would have a broadly similar electoral legitimacy. A First Minister of England will not be an inferior or a subordinate to a Prime Minister of the United Kingdom, but something very close to an equal. The English Parliament and English government would be protective of their constitutionally enshrined autonomy, and therefore have a strong stake in the maintenance of the constitution, protecting it from overreach by Union-level institutions. By this means, England would protect the autonomy of Scotland, Wales and Northern Ireland as well. The strength of England would add to the strength of all states, in a way that mere regional authorities, having fewer powers and being more financially dependent on the Union-level government, cannot do.

If the Union is to be maintained, this Union of four equals solution is not only the best one, but the only one with any realistic chance of long-term viability. It is the only approach that recognizes that England, too, is a nation. It enables England to have a healthy and responsible national political life, to develop a civic-democratic patriotism free from ethno-nationalist bitterness, and to achieve a national self-confidence that no longer hides its nationhood under the cloak of Britishness. England, in such a union, would be the equal of Scotland, Wales and Northern Ireland, in a federal constitutional order that is balanced, equitable and relatively simple. This would not preclude, of course, independence from the Union in the future, if the people of a state so desire – no democratic federation can be held together against the will of its members – but it might at least provide a framework for a stronger union based on equality and respect.

Flexible federalism

This section examines how a federal 'Union of Four Equals', as outlined earlier, might be framed in constitutional terms. There are many Westminster Model examples of federalism to guide us. Australia, Canada and India provide interesting contrasts. The Australian Constitution has but one list of federal matters (Section 51), on which the federal Parliament can legislate. Residual power over anything not on that list lies in principle with the states. In practice, Australia has become more centralized over time, with the federal government using fiscal transfers to influence state governments.[263] Canada has two lists: a list of federal powers (Section 91) and a list of provincial powers (Section 92). Canada's Parliament can legislate on any matter not expressly reserved to the provinces; the list of exclusive federal powers is included only 'for greater certainty' and 'not so as to restrict the generality' of the powers conferred upon the federal Parliament. Despite residual power belonging to the federal level, Canada's provinces have extended control over their own resources and have increased in power over time.[264]

When India became independent, its constitution makers had a dilemma. They were aware that they needed a federal system to accommodate the size and territorial diversity of their society. However, they were also acquainted with the disadvantages of federalism: it can be a slow, rigid, inefficient and expensive form of government. They recognized the need for a more efficient and adaptable federalism that would enable the central government to drive forward public works, major infrastructure projects, and the economic policies needed to re-industrialize India and bring it out of poverty.[265] The result was a

New Commonwealth form of federalism, more flexible and nuanced than that which had developed in the old dominions.

The Indian model of federalism specifies three lists of powers: a union or federal List, a State List, and a Concurrent List. Matters on the Union List are the exclusive preserve of the Union Parliament. Those on the State List are the exclusive preserve of the State legislatures. Matters on the Concurrent List can be legislated on by both the Union and the states, although in case of incompatibility, Union legislation prevails. The explicit identification of concurrent powers introduces an element of dynamic flexibility. The Union can extend its scope into concurrent matters when necessary, but can also leave space, if desired or demanded, for the states to act on their own initiative, provided that they do not conflict with Union law.

The Indian constitution also allows for the transfer of powers between different levels of government. Under article 249, the Union Parliament can legislate on state matters in the national interest if a resolution authorizing such legislation is passed a two-thirds majority of the upper house; such a resolution is in effect for up to one year, but may be renewed. Article 252 permits two or more states, by resolution passed by their legislatures, to transfer legislative authority over state matters designated in that resolution to the Union Parliament; it also allows another state to 'opt in' to that legislation. Under article 250, the Union Parliament can legislate on any state matter when a Proclamation of Emergency is in effect – enabling the temporary transformation of a federal state into a unitary one if required.

A workable solution for the United Kingdom might therefore be as follows. There would be three lists of legislative competencies: a Union List, a Concurrent List and a State List. The Union Parliament would have exclusive authority to legislate for the whole or any part of the United Kingdom in respect of the matters on the Union List. The legislatures of the four national states would have exclusive authority to legislate on matters enumerated on the State List. Both the Union and State legislatures would have authority to legislate on matters on the Concurrent List, but in case of an incompatibility between an Act of the Union Parliament and an Act of a State Parliament, the Act of the Union Parliament would prevail.

The powers allocated exclusively to the Union level would be those essential to the maintenance of the Union as a political entity in its internal and external aspects: defence and the armed forces, foreign relations, diplomatic and consular representation, succession to the Crown, the civil service, the United Kingdom Supreme Court and the Judicial Committee of the Privy Council, the Security Service and Secret Intelligence Service, citizenship and naturalization, immigration, asylum, passports, policing of borders, extradition, Overseas Territories and relations with Crown Dependencies, currency and coinage, weights and measures, shipping and navigation, and so forth. The powers allocated concurrently would be those related to the economy, including commercial law, employment law, social security and welfare benefits, elements of transport and infrastructure affecting more than one state, and environmental protection. All else – including culture and heritage, education, health, housing, policing, social services, transport within the state, public utilities and infrastructure, and local government – as well as the bulk of civil and criminal law – would be at state level. Certain taxes – income taxes, corporation taxes, and so forth – would be levied by the Union, while other taxes would be levied by the states. In contrast to India, any residual subject not enumerated on any of the lists would be a state matter. These lists are not exhaustive, and would of course have to be negotiated during the constitution-building process, but are indicative of the general approach to be followed.

In addition, the federal scheme should be subject to exceptions similar in principle to those of articles 249, 250 and 252 of the Indian constitution. There should be provision for the Union-level Parliament, in exceptional circumstances, and with explicit authorization by both Houses of Parliament (with a veto power for the Senate as a 'House of Federation'), to legislate on matters that would normally be state competencies. It would also be beneficial to allow two or more states to 'delegate upwards' on a matter of mutual concern (for example, one could imagine England and Wales delegating to the Union Parliament authority over certain matters, otherwise handled at a state level, in relation to the control of the Severn estuary). There should also be provision for a state to give authorization by resolution for an Act of the Union Parliament, which would otherwise relate to a state matter and therefore be beyond the legislative competence of the Union Parliament, to apply in that state; this would be a constitutionalization of the existing legislative consent motion procedure. Finally, in a public emergency, duly authorized by Parliament, the Union Parliament should have plenary power to enact necessary legislation even over what would normally be state matters. These rules would overcome most objections to the inherent inflexibility of federalism, without allowing the Union authority to overstep its bounds, except with consent or in cases of real necessity.

The constitution would have to establish the state Parliaments in England, Scotland, Wales and Northern Ireland. They should be elected by proportional representation, for four- or five-year terms, and should enjoy all the immunities and privileges properly belonging to a Parliament in a Westminster Model constitution. Provisions relating to the election of the Presiding Officer, the appointment and removal of the First Minister, votes of no confidence, dissolution, the rights of the Opposition, the qualification and of members, the declaration of interests, and so forth, would be similar to those applied to the Union Parliament.

Presumably, the state Parliaments of Scotland, Wales and Northern Ireland, being the successors to the existing devolved legislatures, would continue to meet in Holyrood, Cardiff Bay and Stormont. The location of the state Parliament of England is less obvious. There is a strong argument to be made for differentiating the seat of the Union Parliament from that of England, in order to visually symbolize their distinct functions, but also to spread access to power and wealth more evenly around the country. Perhaps it would be best for the Union Parliament to continue to sit at Westminster, while a new English Parliament building is located further north: Birmingham, Liverpool, Manchester and Leeds would be obvious contenders.

A modern federalism system requires not only mechanisms for the division of power between levels of government, but also mechanisms for coordination and consultation. In older federations, these mechanisms of cooperation and consultation exist informally, as a matter of para-constitutional practice, and are not recognized in the constitutional text. Some newer Westminster Model federal Constitutions do, however, establish such institutions. The Constitution of Pakistan establishes a Council of Common Interests (art. 153) and a National Economic Council (art. 156), creating a formal framework in which the Chief Ministers of States negotiate and cooperate, both among themselves and with the federal-level leadership. It also establishes a National Finance Commission (art. 160), bringing together the finance ministers of the states and the federal finance minister, to agree on the distribution of tax revenues between them. Such mechanisms of inter-ministerial cooperation are vital to the promotion of good governance and resource sharing in a federal United Kingdom and should be included in the Constitution. In outline, there would be two such cooperative bodies, one bringing together the Prime Minister and the First Ministers to deal with matters of general policy, and one bringing together state and Union finance ministers to agree the distribution of tax revenues.

Finally, constitutional provision should be made to ensure the equality of Welsh with English in Wales, and the recognition of Gaelic and Scots in Scotland and Irish and Ulster Scots in Northern Ireland.

Westminster Model constitutions abound in such linguistic provisions. Canada's Constitution Act 1982 provides (Section 16) that 'English and French are the official languages of Canada and have equality of status and equal rights and privileges as to their use in all institutions of the Parliament and Government of Canada'. This equality of status applies to proceedings in Parliament (Section 17), parliamentary statutes and records (Section 18), and the courts established by Parliament (Section 19). The former constitution of the Union of South Africa (1909–63) provided (Section 137) that 'Both the English and Dutch languages shall be official languages of the Union, and shall be treated on a footing of equality, and possess and enjoy equal freedom, rights, and privileges.' There is no reason why, as a symbolic gesture to the spirit of an equal Union, the United Kingdom could not do likewise. In the same way, the right of each state to have its own national flag and anthems should be recognized. Federalism is not simply a matter of constitutionally protected self-government; it also demands a level of mutual recognition and respect – a willingness to accept the other as an equal partner.

This is a detailed description of a complex federal model. It is proposed as a solution to the needs of the United Kingdom, giving maximum autonomy to England, Scotland, Wales and Northern Ireland consistent with the maintenance of an effective economic, diplomatic and military Union. No doubt various objections may be found against it. It would be improper, however, to be more than tentatively prescriptive. It will be the responsibility of a future constitution-making body to consider various proposals and to reach an acceptable constitutional settlement. Much will depend on the prevailing politics, in particular on whether – and on what terms – Scotland, Wales and Northern Ireland wish to remain in the Union. In an independent England, or in a rump two-part United Kingdom of England and Wales, much of this complex constitutional engineering could be simplified. For present purposes, it serves to demonstrate that a federal Westminster Model constitution is, on a legal and technical level, at least possible. Whether we get one or not will depend on the politicians.

Local democracy

Local government in the United Kingdom once enjoyed substantial autonomy. It gave rise to a lively sense of civic identity and local pride, as well as to innovative local policies, such as the 'municipal socialism' pioneered by Joseph Chamberlain, Mayor of Birmingham.[266] From its late Victorian apogee, this local autonomy has steadily atrophied. It has been hit by a triple blow, firstly from the centralizing tendencies of the two world wars, then by post-war social democracy – which in Britain was delivered and controlled from the centre – and finally by the disintegrating imposition of neoliberal capitalism since 1979. The powers once exercised, functions performed, and services provided by democratically elected local authorities were lost either to Whitehall or the market.[267] The effects are easily seen: 'left-behind' towns with town halls stripped of funds; bleak districts denuded of local leadership, public services, and civic life; and whole parts of the country suffering from decades of under-investment, both public and private. The geographical disparities of socio-economic opportunity exacerbate the widening cleavage between metropolitan 'anywheres' and provincial 'somewheres'.[268]

In recent decades, local authorities have been seen as instruments of local *administration*, whose purpose is to ensure service delivery, and to which standardized measures of outcomes and cost-efficiency can be applied. The deeper civic purposes of local *democracy*, including its role as what John Stuart Mill called a 'school of political capacity and general intelligence',[269] have been lost. Centralization not only undermines policy initiative and responsiveness to local needs, but also corrodes civic sentiment and democratic vigour. Some communities – like Frome in Somerset – have been able to use limited local powers to assert themselves and to revitalize civic life, but these are the exceptions.[270]

A federal Union with constitutionally enshrined state legislatures does not diminish the need for local democracy. As discussed in the previous sections of this chapter, a 'Union of Four Equals' would still have to make provision for devolution within England. The question, therefore, is how to incorporate devolution of power below the state level within the federal structure in a way that empowers the states to address their own local governance needs.

In some Westminster Model federations, the constitution says little or nothing about local government, because it is a function of the state or provincial authorities. Section 92 of the Constitution of Canada, for example, simply confers the power to make laws in relation to municipal institutions upon the provincial legislatures. Australia's federal constitution says nothing about local government – although some of the constitutions of the individual Australian states do. Leaving local government dependent on parliamentary majorities, even state-level parliamentary majorities in a federal system, offers no security or guarantee for their powers, funding or even existence. In Malaysia, for example, it has led to local elections being indefinitely suspended and the replacement of local councils by nominated bodies appointed by state authorities.[271] That sort of thing should not be constitutionally permissible.

Some unitary Westminster Model constitutions do make explicit provision for elected local authorities. The Irish constitution (article 28A) declares that 'The State recognizes the role of local government in providing a forum for the democratic representation of local communities, in exercising and performing at local level powers and functions conferred by law and in promoting by its initiatives the interests of such communities.' It provides that, 'There shall be such directly elected local authorities as may be determined by law' and that 'their powers and functions shall, subject to the provisions of this Constitution, be so determined and shall be exercised and performed in accordance with law'. It also regulates local elections, making provision for the franchise, five-year terms and the filling of vacancies.

The Constitution of Jamaica is another typical example. It states (Section 66) that 'There shall continue to be a democratic system of local government for Jamaica', the purposes of which are to, 'encourage and assist the effective participation of local communities in the affairs of local government', 'provide local public services and facilities and to carry out other related activities for the benefit of local communities and the wider public', 'perform such regulatory functions as may be conferred upon local authorities by law', and 'facilitate the management, improvement and development of the resources of local communities'. The Jamaican Parliament is constitutionally empowered to make provision, 'for local authorities to generate and spend their own revenue', 'for assigning functions between the various tiers of government', 'for the holding of local government elections'; and 'prescribing any other matter relating to the governance of local authorities'.

Although the Constitution of India includes a Directive Principle (article 40) calling for the establishment of village councils or *panchayats*, the organization of local government was originally left – as in Australia and Canada – to be decided by the states. This produced patchy results, with some states doing rather better than others in devolving power to elected local institutions. This led to the passage of the 73rd and 74th Amendments in 1992, which inserted provisions on the organization of *panchayats* and municipalities into the constitution.[272]

Constitutional provisions are not a shortcut to effective decentralization. Ireland and Jamaica remain highly centralized, with local government having only a subordinate role. The quality and effectiveness of Indian local government is still variable. Nevertheless, these three examples illustrate how Westminster Model constitutions can make a general commitment to the principle of local democracy and can establish at least the bare bones of an institutional structure for local authorities. Even if much of the detail is, perhaps rightly and necessarily, left to ordinary legislation, the constitutional recognition of local democracy performs three functions. Firstly, it establishes a baseline of protection for local government. It can ensure that local government exists and that local elections can take place. In countries without such protection, such as Saint Lucia[273] and Malaysia,[274] local democracy has simply been abolished. Secondly, it has a symbolic and proclamatory function. It signals that local democracy is integral to the constitutional order. It stands witness to the fact that citizens are not just part of an undifferentiated mass, to be administered by distant authorities; they live and work in towns, cities and villages, which have their own identities, their own local public interests, their own democratic and civic lives, which the constitution nurtures and promotes. Thirdly, it can establish a framework within which the decentralization of power is enabled, expected and encouraged to take place. In an English context, the powers and boundaries of regional level authorities might, for example, be left up to the English Parliament to decide, but the Constitution might provide a framework with which such legislation would have to comply.

11

Judiciary, Administration, Elections and Miscellaneous Provisions

The judiciary

The argument that written constitutions dangerously over-empower judiciaries has already been dismissed in the fourth chapter. Nevertheless, if the judiciary is to perform its functions properly, particular care must be taken to ensure that the mechanisms for the appointment of judges, the rules protecting their neutrality and independence, and the procedures for their removal from office are sufficiently robust. The apex judges in particular (those forming the Supreme Court, or in some jurisdictions a separate Constitutional Court) must be chosen in a way that ensures their professional legal competence, political neutrality and personal integrity. Just as the legitimacy and authority of a cricket umpire do not derive from popularity with the players, but from the umpire's knowledge of the Laws of Cricket, trained eye, and reputation for neutrality and independence, so likewise judges derive their legitimacy from these characteristics. An assessment of 'community standards' or what is 'reasonably justifiable in a democratic society' may come into their deliberations – and some will be more conservative, others more progressive – but ultimately they must have the professional integrity to adhere to the norms of legal reasoning, which are subject to peer review by the legal community, in applying democratically endorsed constitutional rules to particular cases.

On the other hand, if every international cricket umpire were from Pakistan, Indians might feel that they are unjustly discriminated against. Even if those Pakistani umpires are people of the utmost integrity and impartiality, the optics are wrong: justice must not only be done but be seen to be done. The legitimacy and authority of the judicial bench may therefore also depend on diversity in judicial appointments – gender balance, racial inclusion, and openness to suitably qualified and experienced candidates from working class and lower middle class backgrounds.

The practice in early Westminster Model constitutions was for judicial appointments to be made by the Crown, acting on the advice of the Prime Minister. It was usually the standard practice of the Prime Minister to consult with senior judges and with the Attorney-General before making such appointments, but there was no direct legal obligation to do so. The appointment process was closed, opaque, and not always above partisan patronage. In many places where such executive-centred appointment mechanisms are still constitutionally prescribed, they have been modified by the establishment, on a statutory basis, of appointments boards to recommend candidates. Notable examples of such bodies include the Ontario Judicial Appointments Board and the Judicial Appointments Advisory Board in Ireland. However, because these bodies are not constitutionally entrenched, their recommendations are usually non-binding, and their status and independence ultimately depend solely on the self-restraint of the parliamentary majority.[275]

India is a curious example. The Indian constitution sought to regularize the practice of informal consultations and to put it upon a constitutional footing. Thus Article 124 of the Indian constitution, as originally enacted, stated that judges of the Supreme Court are appointed by the President 'after consultation with such of the judges of the Supreme Court an of the High Courts of the states as the President may deem necessary for the purpose', provided that, 'in the case of a judge other than the Chief Justice, the Chief Justice of India shall always be consulted'. This has hardened over time, partly by practice and partly by judicial interpretation, into a 'collegium' system, whereby judicial appointments are made on the advice of a committee of senior judges.[i]

Elsewhere, in most New Commonwealth constitutions, special commissions were established with responsibility for judicial appointments, generally known as Judicial Service Commissions or Judicial and Legal Service Commissions. The size and membership of

---

[i] A recent amendment to the procedure for judicial appointments in India has been passed but found unconstitutional.

such bodies varies, but in general they have a mixed membership of senior judges and sometimes law officers sitting *ex-officio*, representatives of the legal professions, and lay members who are supposed to represent the general or public interest. The Constitution of Samoa (article 72) establishes a miniature Judicial Service Commission of just three members: the Chief Justice, the Attorney-General, and a person nominated by the Minister of Justice. That established by the Constitution of Jamaica (Section 111) is more typical, consisting of six members: the Chief Justice (as Chair), the President of the Court of Appeal, the Chair of the Public Service Commission, one former judge appointed by the Governor-General on the advice of the Prime Minister after consulting the Leader of the Opposition, and two members likewise appointed by the Governor-General from 'a list of six persons, none of whom is an attorney-at-law in active practice, submitted by the General Legal Council'.

Such bodies are intended to perform a triple function. First, they keep the appointment of judges at arm's length from the executive, reducing the scope for blatant partisan patronage. Second, they provide a forum in which those best placed to assess the quality of judges can do so – a relatively small, relatively intimate, and suitably experienced committee. Third, they should keep the judiciary from becoming too insular or self-referential: there should be some external influence that, in a filtered an indirect way, reflects the general public interest. The success of such institutions in performing these functions will depend in large measure upon their composition: very small commissions, or those dominated by executive appointees, as in Samoa, are likely to be less effective than larger commissions whose members have greater independence from the executive. The consultation of the Leader of the Opposition in making bi-partisan appointments may be a particularly beneficial mechanism if such consultation is real and not merely formulaic.

The Judicial Appointments Commission, established by the Constitutional Reform Act 2005, currently advises on judicial appointments in England and Wales. In a United Kingdom of England and Wales, it would be just as well to place this institution on a constitutional footing, and thereby to secure it against future attempts to abolish or undermine it. If Scotland and/or Northern Ireland were to remain in the United Kingdom, similar constitutional provision would have to be made for their own judicial appointments commissions, or equivalent – again drawing on existing statutory arrangements, but placing these above the reach of governing majorities. In a 'Union of Four Equals', Wales would also need its own jurisdiction, and perhaps therefore its own national judicial appointments commission.[ii]

The rules on judicial tenure are perhaps even more important. The protection of judges from removal at the pleasure of the Crown, finally secured in England by the Act of Settlement, is really the beginning of the institutional recognition of judicial independence. Under the Act of Settlement, which was influential throughout the family of Westminster Model constitutions, judges serve *quamdiu se bene gesserint* (during good behaviour). That means they must be immune from arbitrary dismissal. They do not depend for their continuance in office upon the goodwill of the government, nor change with the coming ins and going outs of Prime Ministers. At the same time, however, there must be some way to remove judges when there is compelling reason to do so, such as gross misconduct, neglect of duty or incapacity.

Among Westminster Model constitutions two main approaches to the removal of judges are found. In some, judges are removable, on such stated grounds, by a resolution of Parliament. The independence Constitution of Ceylon (Section 52) bearing the pen-marks of Sir Ivor Jennings, faithfully replicated the provisions of the Act of Settlement:

> Every Judge of the Supreme Court shall hold office during good behaviour and shall not be removable except by the Governor-General on an address of the Senate and the House of Representatives.

Normally a two-thirds majority vote is required to remove a judge, so that the decision is not that of the government alone but requires at least agreement between the Government and Opposition. The Constitution of Malta (article 97) is a typical example of this approach:

> A judge of the Superior Courts shall not be removed from his office except by the President upon an address by the House of Representatives supported by the votes of not less than two-thirds of all the members thereof and praying for

---

ii   The 2019 Report of the Commission on Justice in Wales (*Justice in Wales for the People of Wales*) recommended the devolution of lawmaking power on justice matters to Wales and a recognition that the Law of Wales is distinct from the 'Law of England and Wales' in certain respects; to enable Wales to establish – within broad constitutional limits – its own legal and judicial system in a 'Union of Four Equals' would not be a radical innovation, but a natural step along the existing direction of travel.

such removal on the ground of proved inability to perform the functions of his office (whether arising from infirmity of body or mind or any other cause) or proved misbehaviour.

The Constitution of India (article 124) establishes similar rules, but in a bicameral context. Obviously, since an address for the removal of a judge must be passed in two different Houses, this provides an additional check against arbitrary dismissal.

> A Judge of the Supreme Court shall not be removed from his office except by an order of the President passed after an address by each House of Parliament supported by a majority of the total membership of that House and by a majority of not less than two thirds of the members of that House present and voting has been presented to the President in the same session for such removal on the ground of proved misbehaviour or incapacity.

The second approach is to establish an independent tribunal to investigate any suspected incapacity or misbehaviour. The tribunal might be appointed by the head of state or Governor-General on the advice of the Prime Minister (as in Jamaica and Trinidad & Tobago) or at the Governor-General's own discretion (as in the Solomon Islands) – but must normally consist of other serving or retired senior judges. In Jamaica and Trinidad & Tobago, the independent tribunal recommends that the question of removal be referred to the Judicial Committee of the Privy Council, which then makes the final decision.

These two approaches may be usefully combined. Under the Constitution of Tuvalu (Section 127), the Governor-General appoints a tribunal if 'the Cabinet decides, or Parliament resolves, that the question of removing a Judge from office should be investigated'. The tribunal consists of 'a chairman and at least one other member, each of whom is qualified for appointment as a Judge of the High Court', who are appointed after consulting the Prime Minister and the Chief Justice. The tribunal reports to Parliament with a recommendation as to whether the judge should be removed. The decision to remove the judge is then made by a resolution of Parliament. A very similar procedure is used in Scotland, under Section 95 of the Scotland Act 1998.

A suitable process in the United Kingdom might be for judges to be removed by a two-thirds majority vote of both Houses of Parliament, in the case of the members of the United Kingdom Supreme Court, or in the case of the superior judges at state level by a two-thirds majority vote of the State Parliament concerned (assuming a 'Union of Four Equals' model). Such a vote would be permitted to take place, however, only on the recommendation of the appropriate Judicial Appointments Commission, which would first appoint a tribunal to investigate the matter.

Judicial independence and neutrality are also supported by constitutional rules on such matters as the salaries of judges and restrictions on their private interests and political activities. In most modern Westminster Model constitutions judicial salaries are a direct charge upon the Consolidated Fund (and therefore not subject to the political uncertainties of annual budgets) and cannot be reduced while they are in office. Likewise, judges are usually explicitly disqualified from serving as Members of Parliament. The retirement age for judges should also be specified in the constitution. Otherwise, unscrupulous governments might try to dismiss judges prematurely by forcing them into early retirement; this trick was attempted by the Government of Poland, but found unlawful by the European Court of Justice.[276] Declaratory phrases requiring judges to be independent in the exercise of their judicial functions, as found in Section 3 of the Constitutional Reform Act 2005 are, by themselves, insufficient. With all these things, constitutional rules alone, although important, can only go so far. A culture and ethos of constitutionalism, the rule of law, and judicial independence and integrity, must continue to be inculcated. Nevertheless, we can no longer rely on the unspoken sense of obligation or propriety that once, perhaps, was enough. There is much to be said for stating these principles clearly and explicitly, to give them solidity and public recognition, so that the norms of judicial conduct can be re-affirmed and reinforced.

'Neutral guardians' and institutional integrity

Westminster Model constitutions establish a set of independent institutions, sometimes referred to as 'fourth branch' institutions. These perform regulatory, oversight, administrative, appointive or advisory functions, and operate at arm's length from the Government and Parliament. S.A. de Smith recognized the emergence of these 'neutral guardians' as a distinctive feature of New Commonwealth constitutionalism.[277] These institutions are not policy-making bodies. They do not govern. Instead, they are intended to provide 'ongoing safeguards to restrain a [...] government once it wins office',[278] to prevent governments and Parliaments from making certain sensitive decisions according to their own 'self-seeking interests, inimical to the public interest',[279] and to 'deal more effectively with individual grievances, investigate claims of maladministration, enhance transparency, combat corruption, protect electoral democracy and regulate key services in the public interest'.[280]

The Westminster Model's 'efficient secret', the reciprocal relationship of mutual confidence between the government and Parliament under the leadership of the Prime Minister,[281] demands such institutions in order to provide an external check upon the majority – a new form of 'separation of the powers'.[282] In general terms, these institutions contribute to democracy, constitutionalism and good governance in one of three ways. Firstly, they promote the integrity, impartiality and professionalism of the permanent institutions of the state: 'The intention, it may be assumed, is to protect these offices from too overt political interference, and perhaps to foster some measure of impartiality in the operation, for example, of the Public Service.'[283] Secondly, they protect the fairness of the electoral processes on which democracy depends – whether as an Electoral Commission supervising the conduct of the election, or a Boundaries Commission to prevent gerrymandering. Thirdly, these institutions may bring attention to issues that might otherwise be overlooked – as in the case of Human Rights Commissions, whose role is not to adjudicate rights, but to monitor and oversee their realization.

The list of such institutions is quite long. In addition to the Judicial Service Commission discussed in the previous section, a Westminster Model constitution will typically include an Electoral Commission, Constituency Boundary Commission, Public Service Commission, Auditor-General and Ombudsman. Other institutions of this type found in Westminster Model constitutions include Fiji's Human Rights and Anti-Discrimination Commission (Constitution of Fiji, Section 45), the Police Service Commissions of Saint Vincent and the Grenadines (Section 84) or Trinidad & Tobago (Section 122), and Special Officer for Linguistic Minorities in India (article 350B).

Over successive waves of constitution-building, the tendency has been to place greater reliance on such institutions. Within sensible limits, this is commended by the Commonwealth Secretariat:

> The establishment of scrutiny bodies and mechanisms to oversee Government enhances public confidence in the integrity and acceptability of government's activities. Independent bodies such as Public Accounts Committees, Ombudsmen, Human Rights Commissions, Auditors-General, Anti-corruption commissions, Information Commissioners and similar oversight institutions can play a

key role in enhancing public awareness of good governance and rule of law issues. Governments are encouraged to establish or enhance appropriate oversight bodies in accordance with national circumstances.[284]

The demand for such institutions depends on the context. Very small countries, with small populations and a limited revenue base, might have to combine the functions of two institutions into one body (for example, combining the roles of Electoral Commission and Boundary Commission). In federal countries, parallel institutions may need to be set up at different levels of government: India, for example, has an Election Commission at the Union level and state Election Commissions. Countries with a single national police force might need a Police Service Commission to ensure that institution is kept tolerably free of political patronage, but this would not be appropriate in countries where the police is responsibility of sub-national governments.

Although these institutions are diverse and perform a wide range of functions, they have certain characteristics in common. In many ways, these are similar to those which apply to judges. The officers and commissioners performing these functions must be independent, non-partisan, professionally competent, and at the same time must enjoy broad public trust. Mechanisms of appointment and tenure similar to those used for judges are therefore often appropriate. In many Westminster Model constitutions, this includes bi-partisan appointment mechanisms. This may take the form of an appointment made by the head of state or Governor-General acting on the advice of the Prime Minister after consulting with (or even with the concurrence of) the Leader of the Opposition (as is the case, for example, of the Election and Boundaries Commission of Belize). Alternatively, some commissioners will be appointed on the advice of the Prime Minister and others on the advice of the Leader of the Opposition, as with the Electoral Commission of Dominica. There might also be scope for neutral, ex-officio members, or for members appointed by other independent commissions. The Ombudsman of the Solomon Islands, for example, is chosen by a committee consisting of the Speaker, the Chairman of the Public Service Commission and the Chairman of the Judicial and Legal Service Commission.

Members of these institutions typically serve for fixed terms and can only be removed from office by similar mechanisms. The Auditor-General of Jamaica, for example, can be removed after investigation and on the recommendation of an independent tribunal (Section

121), while a member of the Election Commission in India cannot be removed except 'on grounds of proved misconduct or incapacity' on an address from both Houses of Parliament passed by a two-thirds majority in each House (article 324, read in conjunction with article 124). Restrictions may be placed on their political activities; for example, any person who has been a candidate for election to Parliament may be disqualified for appointment. In many cases the salaries of the members of these institutions are made a standing charge on the Consolidated Fund, so as to protect them from the political pressures of an annual budget cycle.

A constitution for the United Kingdom should, as a minimum, provide for Judicial Service Commissions for each state or jurisdiction, an Electoral Commission, a Boundaries Commission, a Human Rights Commission, a Civil Service Commission, a Commissioner for Public Appointments, an Ombudsman (Parliamentary Commissioner for Administration), and an Auditor-General. The task is made easier because these institutions already exist under statute; the written constitution would not therefore have to create them, only to place them on a constitutional rather than statutory basis. This constitution should give them the clearly mandated powers, constitutional recognition, security of tenure and independence of operation that their functions demand. The constitution would also give us an opportunity to strengthen the neutrality and inclusivity of these bodies – and so to increase their legitimacy and effectiveness – by reforming the rules of appointment to give the Leader of the Opposition (and perhaps leaders of other parties) at least a consultative role in, and perhaps a veto power over, nominations.

It is particularly important to strengthen the Civil Service Commission and the Commissioner for Public Appointments. A democracy without an effective, efficient, well-led and well-trained civil service is all talk and no action. The 2020 coronavirus crisis reminded us of the need to increase what international development experts call 'governance capacity' – the ability of the state to act, and to act promptly, decisively, competently and fairly. Four decades of neoliberal 'New Public Management', with its emphasis on privatization, contracting-out services, and market-orientated structures, together with a tendency to recruit senior staff directly from business, management consultancy or public relations, have undone much of the work of the Victorian era state builders. As well as facilitating political patronage, creating potential conflicts of interest, and eroding the public service ethos of the civil service, these changes have seriously degraded the ability of the civil service to plan for, and respond to, crises and to ensure that ministers are well-briefed. A revitalization of our democracy also requires a renewal of the civil service on Northcote-Trevelyan[iii] principles: meritocracy, permanence, professionalism, political impartiality. Such a civil service is an integral feature of the Westminster Model and essential to its success.

Public ethics

Some Westminster Model constitutions contain provisions promoting ethical standards in public life. The Constitutions of Papua New Guinea (sections 26 to 31) and the Solomon Islands (sections 93 to 95), for example, include 'Leadership Codes' in which the ethical duties of those in office (such as acting with integrity and avoiding conflicts of interest) are laid own.

In the United Kingdom, the so-called 'Nolan principles' provide a softly-codified set of norms and expectations for how those in public office are supposed to perform their duties, covering the themes of selflessness, integrity, objectivity, accountability, openness, honesty and leadership.[285] Similarly, the requirement that Members of Parliament declare private interests are currently contained in a Code of Conduct enforced by the rules of the House of Commons. Such sub-constitutional regulation has two problems. Firstly, these codes can be swept away or manipulated at the convenience of the government. Secondly, because the rules and principles are hidden away in sub-constitutional documents they have not seeped into the public mind. Putting ethical rules and principles in the constitution would give them greater resilience and visibility, making them more effective and easier to enforce. This would reiterate an important point of democratic morality: that the state is a public entity, established for the public good, in which public officers exercise a position of trust on behalf of the public.

Public service broadcasting

Another public institution in need of constitutional recognition and protection is the BBC. There is an obvious need in a democracy for reliable non-partisan sources of information on news, politics and

---

[iii] The Northcote-Trevelyan Report (1854) laid the foundations for the home civil service from the late Victorian era until the 1980s – spanning the majoritarian heyday of British democracy.

current affairs. This must be in the hands of a trusted and competent public service broadcaster, free from both political control and the 'dumbing down' pressures of the market.

For a long time, the BBC was well-respected in this role, but like all British institutions its neutrality and independence always depended more upon self-restraint and tacit understandings than on firm constitutional rules. In recent years, these arrangements have become increasingly inadequate. The former Board of Governors was abolished in 2007 and replaced by the BBC Trust, which was in turn abolished and replaced by the BBC Board in 2017, but despite changes of nomenclature a lingering suspicion of partisanship has remained. Without criticizing any individual, genuinely constitutional questions are raised as to whether the process of appointments – which allows broad discretion to ministers – is able to deliver a politically impartial and independent BBC.[286]

A new constitution could provide an opportunity to ensure that the BBC has a clear constitutional mandate and a corresponding constitutional duty to act truthfully, impartially and with integrity. It could also reform its governance arrangements to bring the BBC out of the sway or influence of ministers. Such provisions are, admittedly, rare in other Westminster Model constitutions, but they are not without precedent; the Constitution of Malta (articles 118–119), for example, creates a Broadcasting Authority to ensure that public broadcasting is balanced.

Mechanisms widely used in Westminster Model for the appointment of members of other highly sensitive non-partisan institutions, like Electoral Commissions, could be applied to the BBC. The appointment of the Chair of the Board might have to be made by the Prime Minister with the concurrence of the Leader of the Opposition; a certain number of members of the Board might be appointed by the government, others by the Leader of the Opposition and the leaders of other parties, such that divergent views and interests are represented.

In a federal union, the presence of representatives from Scotland, Wales, Northern Ireland, and English regions could be strengthened. The reformed BBC must appreciate that it serves not one unitary nation state, but a union of nations, each with its own political situation as well as its own cultural needs. This can only come from a governance structure that gives proper weight – not token representation as at present – to each part of the Union. It might even be thought necessary to transform the BBC into a federal structure, with separate boards for the four nations. Furthermore, the BBC's funding could be made constitutionally secure by making it a standing charge on the

Consolidated Fund; that would free it from dependence on the license fee or annual appropriations and also protect it from privatization.

Elections, referendums and campaign finance

Free and fair elections are integral to representative democracy as we know it. While scope does exist for other forms of representation and participation, elections are the primary means, in a Westminster Model democracy, by which the people express their views and announce their judgement on both the 'people and policies' of the government. To rig elections is to deny democracy; to manipulate elections is to distort it. The Electoral Commission and Boundaries Commission, with their independent constitutional status and quasi-judicial autonomy, have already been introduced in the previous section. However, setting up the institutions and mechanisms, while important, is not the only way in which the constitution can protect the integrity of electoral processes. It is also important to constitutionally protect the right to vote; the question of who can vote is too important to be left to be settled by ordinary majorities, who might seek to selectively disenfranchise particular groups in order to influence the result. In so far as possible, the constitution should guard against voter suppression, including by subtle means such as making voting more difficult by reducing the number of polling stations, or requiring expensive forms of identification that poorer voters might not have. The Kenyan constitution of 2010 contains a notable provision (article 83) stating that 'Administrative arrangements for the registration of voters and the conduct of elections shall be designed to facilitate, and shall not deny, an eligible citizen the right to vote or stand for election.'

The other main form of democratic decision making is the referendum. The scope for referendums varies between Westminster Model constitutions, although in general it is fair to say that Westminster Model constitutions – in contrast to other forms of democracy in continental Europe and Latin America – are 'referendum shy'. Referendums are provided for in Westminster Model constitutions, it is usually only in the context of constitutional amendments, as discussed in Chapter 8. Citizens' Initiatives of the form found in places like Switzerland and California, the abrogative referendums used in Italy, and the minority-veto referendums provided for in the constitutions of Latvia and Denmark have no parallel in any Westminster Model constitution. The closest is a provision in the state constitution of New South Wales allowing a referendum on ordinary legislation in order to resolve deadlocks between the two Houses. Parliaments in Westminster systems may nevertheless make provision by law for the holding of referendums – and in these situations, the constitutional regulation may create difficulties. When a referendum is held on a constitutional amendment, everyone knows the effect of the result: the amendment – which has already been passed by Parliament – is either approved or rejected. A referendum held on a merely statutory basis is not so clear: there is no requirement to put forward a bill or even a White Paper, and the result of the referendum – even if it is strictly advisory – is therefore difficult to assess. We have seen in the United Kingdom the problems that may arise from such poorly-regulated referendums, and it might be better if in future there was a constitutional requirement for any referendum to be on a specific bill or at least a White Paper, rather than on an ill-defined policy slogan.

Finally, a constitution must guard against the influence of money in politics, which is the negation of democratic politics. It transforms 'one person one vote' into 'one billionaire, one bought election'. It is necessary at least for the constitution to provide for the enactment of legislation to counter such trends, whether that be through caps on donations, disclosure rules, the prohibition of foreign donations, restrictions on campaign spending, or other means. Perhaps the constitution cannot spell these things out in detail – they are too fast-moving – but it can create a supportive and facilitative framework for legislation to tackle the problem. Above all, the constitution should be framed to stop the courts from ever making a decision like that in the United States in *Citizens United vs. Federal Election Commission* [2010], in which the United States Supreme Court held that campaign spending was 'speech' and therefore constitutionally protected against campaign spending regulations.[287]

12

Constitution-Building Processes

This final chapter draws on the experiences of other Westminster Model and Commonwealth democracies to consider how a new constitution for the United Kingdom might be adopted. It examines what the process of constitution-building might look like, what institutions should be responsible for negotiating and drafting the constitution and how the participants should be chosen, the process of final adoption of the agreed draft, and the scope at different stages of the process for both political consensus and public engagement.

The design of constitution-making processes has been a subject of increasing academic study since Jon Elster's work on constitution-building in post-Communist Central and Eastern Europe in the 1990s.[288] Elster argues that participants in a constitution-building process may be motivated by 'reason', 'interest' and 'passion', and pursue their goals through a mixture of 'arguing' (seeking to persuade others) and 'bargaining' (seeking to cut deals with others). He also identifies different types of 'constitution-making body' as the main institution in which this arguing and bargaining takes place. The constitution-making body can range from a large elected Constituent Assembly to a small appointed constitutional commission; it might also serve as an interim legislature, or be confined only to constitution-making duties.[i]

The constitution-making body may be subject to what Elster calls 'upstream' and 'downstream' constraints. Upstream constraints are those that apply at the early stages of constitution-building, before the constitution-making body sets to work: they constrain the arguing and bargaining by setting the agenda, by ruling some things in and out, and

---

[i] Although Elster's work has been expanded upon or questioned by subsequent scholars, the basic framework and terminology of constitution-building as a subject of study continues to owe much to him.

by determining who is included in the process. For example, an Act of Parliament appointing the members of a constitutional commission and setting out its terms of reference would be an upstream constraint on the decisions of the commissioners. Downstream constraints are those imposed by the need to get approval for the constitution-making body's decisions, be it from the legislature or in the form of a referendum. Occasionally, as in the 1994–96 constitution-building process in South Africa, judicial certification of the constitution may be required to ensure compliance with conditions set at the upstream stage.

Constitution-building processes can be 'open' (based on wide public participation) or 'closed' (restricted to smaller elite and expert actors). They can also be 'partisan' (dominated by one party) or 'cross-party' (based on broad agreements between parties). It is possible for a constitution-building process to be 'open' and yet 'partisan', as when a ruling party seeks to appeal to the people directly, through public consultations and referendum, without any cross-party consensus. Likewise, a relatively 'closed' process can nevertheless be based upon a consensus between all or most relevant political parties. This results, broadly speaking, in four types of constitution-building process: (i) 'imposed' processes ('partisan' and 'closed'); (ii) 'populist' processes ('partisan' but 'open'); (iii) 'consensual' processes ('cross-party' but 'closed'), and (iv) 'inclusive' processes ('cross-party' and 'open').

There is a growing public demand in constitution-building processes around the world to keep the politicians as far as possible out of the process and to adopt open processes – either using 'crowd-sourcing' techniques through online platforms and mass participation (such as in Iceland), or else creating randomly selected Citizens' Assemblies that bypass party politics in favour of direct deliberation by ordinary people (as in Ireland). This demand is understandably fuelled by mistrust of political parties and of politicians, and by a desire for a more authentic expression of democracy. Naturally, this desire is most keenly felt at the very times when constitution is most likely to take place: after a crisis or scandal of sufficient magnitude to implicate the whole political class and to undermine the legitimacy of the constitutional order.

However, constitution-building is not a process from which the political leadership should be excluded, but one in which they should be encouraged to engage. There is no shame in admitting that most working and enduring constitutions are 'elite pacts' between political leaders. In a democracy, these leaders generally represent different sections of the population (whether defined by party, interest, class or region) and have the legitimacy to act on behalf of their voters. Research by Abrak Saati suggests that reaching an inter-elite consensus is more important, in terms of improving and sustaining democratic outcomes, than widespread public participation.[289] According to Jonathon Wheatley and Carlos Mendes public participation can be beneficial if brought to bear at early stages of the process (e.g. in setting the agenda through public consultation), but holding a referendum at the end of the process, signifying majority approval, is no substitute for consensus among political leaders.[290]

Constitutions are also social contracts, expressing general public consensus: what the people stand for and will not stand for. Their democratic legitimacy comes from widespread public approval. Elite consensus may be vital, but a 'stitch-up' from which the people are excluded will be rejected. On the other hand, a constitution calls for technical expertise in its writing – from political scientists who can advise on the likely effects of various design choices and from lawyers and legal drafters who can help ensure that the wording of the document is sufficiently watertight. Thus constitution-building is a three-way process involving 'elites', 'everyone' (the general public) and 'experts'. Jostling in the middle of these three we find 'civil society': interest groups, trade unions, professional bodies, non-profit organizations, and campaigning organizations of all types, who interact with, and seek to influence, the others.

In many cases, there is a fourth, external dimension. Assuming that the United Kingdom would wish (or be forced by economic necessarily) to re-engage in European institutions, the reports of the Venice Commission, which acts as a gatekeeper for compliance with the 'European values' of democracy, human rights and the rule of law, could not lightly be ignored. Moreover, there are several international or inter-governmental organizations that provide advice, support and technical assistance to countries undergoing major constitutional change. The United Kingdom might make good use of the services of the Commonwealth Secretariat, the Commonwealth Parliamentary Association, the Forum of Federations, and the International Institute for Democracy and Electoral Assistance, among others.

Constitution-building processes engage these sets of participants in different ways at different stages of the process. Elster's model of public participation is like an hourglass: thick and open at the top and bottom, squeezed and narrow in the middle. It would be reasonable, for example, for the public to be involved at the upstream stage, either in electing the members of a Constituent Assembly or in giving their approval by referendum to the general direction of the constitution-building process. It would also be reasonable for the public to have a final say on the constitution – again, potentially, by referendum.

Yet there are crucial stages in the middle, particularly where difficult political bargains have to be reached, where it may be necessary for small groups of top-level political leaders to negotiate late into the night in proverbial 'smoke-filled rooms'. The closed negotiating core of the process is legitimated by the democratic inputs into the upstream and downstream constraints; the negotiators are political elites, but they have democratic legitimacy to act and can be held democratically answerable.

Beyond Elster's hourglass design, recent processes have developed more of a concertina shape, alternately broadening out to the general public and narrowing down to political elites as different stages of the process unfold. For example, the first stage might be an inter-elite agreement, perhaps in the form of a round-table agreement between party leaders, that will set the agenda for the process; experts and civil society might then be engaged. Then an expert commission will be set up, operating under terms of reference agreed at the round table. That commission might then consult with civil society and the general public – through surveys, the circulation of drafts or memoranda for comment, hearings in which persons are invited to give evidence before the commission, town hall meetings, or in a myriad of other ways. From this a draft might result, which is put to Parliament; perhaps further arguing and bargaining will take place as it passes through Parliament, with crucial decisions being taken between party leaders in a special constitutional committee set up for the purpose. Finally, the agreed draft as passed by Parliament might be put to a referendum; political leaders, experts and civil society will all have their say in the referendum campaign, but the final decision will rest with the public. This hypothetical example is not, of course, to be taken as a norm or standard, but merely as an illustration of how various participants make take centre stage at different phases of the process.

Finally, there is a vital difference between, on the one hand, the sort of constitution-building process where everything is on the table, and a more limited constitutional review process where specific issues can be identified for surgical amendments. In Ireland, very 'open' processes involving Citizens' Assemblies have worked in part because they were dealing with discrete issues (such as same-sex marriage) that did not affect the distribution of political power. Citizens' Assemblies, which lack the legitimacy that comes from an electoral mandate, might be unsuitable for complex constitutional settlements where combinations of institutional choices must be negotiated, and strategic trade-offs made. When everything is up for grabs, excessive public participation can even be counter productive. It is not only a matter of public ignorance giving rise to unworkable proposals, but also the risk of overloading the process and blocking decision making by an excess of public demands. This is not to deny the need for democratic legitimacy or genuine public engagement. It is simply to warn against the fetishization of 'crowd-sourcing', when consensus between elected political leaders may – in particular, contexts, for certain issues, and at some stages of the process – be more beneficial.

Constitution-building in Westminster Model democracies

Constitution-building in the Westminster tradition has taken many forms, with many specific variations, but four broad approaches can be identified: (i) conventions of members deputed from colonial legislatures; (ii) bi-partisan conferences of national political leaders convened by the British before granting independence; (iii) constituent assemblies elected directly or indirectly; and (iv) small constitutional commissions with an appointed, expert membership.

The first widely used constitution-building technique was to bring together delegates of several pre-existing colonial legislative bodies in order to negotiate the terms of a union, and then for the product of those negotiations to be translated into an Act of the Imperial Parliament. The constitutions of the three large old dominions, Canada in 1864–67, Australia in 1899–1901 and South Africa in 1909, were negotiated in this way. Of course, this approach presupposed both a desire for union and the existence of colonial legislatures which have sufficient democratic legitimacy to be able to engage in such an important constituent task.

The British North America Act 1867, which remains the basis of the present Canadian Constitution, was adopted as an act of the Imperial Parliament, with the British government giving active support to Canadian Confederation. The substance of the Act, however, was grown on Canadian soil. It had been agreed by Canadian politicians – delegates from the legislatures of the various provinces – meeting first in Charlottetown, Prince Edward Island in September 1864 and then in Quebec City, Quebec, in October of that year.[291] The 72 'Quebec Resolutions', arising from the latter conference determined the overall shape of the Canadian Constitution. Although a further conference of provincial delegates with British officials took place in London in 1866, it made only relatively minor changes to the settlement reached at Quebec, and the role of the Imperial Parliament was to give effect in law to what the Canadians had agreed.[292]

In Australia a similar process, driven by conventions of delegates from the Australian colonial legislatures, was adopted. The first was the National Australasian Convention, held in 1891, at which the general outlines of what was to become the Australian Constitution were agreed. This was followed by the Australasian Federal Convention of 1896–97, which made amendments to the proposal. In comparison to Canada, the Australian process was more 'open', with the delegates to the latter Convention being directly elected by the people, and the draft constitution being submitted to a referendum in the several colonies. After initial rejection by New South Wales, the draft constitution was amended and resubmitted to a second referendum. On the basis of that approval, it was formally enacted in London.[293]

The 1909 constitution of the Union of South Africa was developed by a National Convention consisting of delegates from the legislatures of its constituent parts – the self-governing British colonies and the former Boer republics. The Convention consisted of 30 members: twelve from the Cape, eight from the Transvaal, and five each from Natal and the Orange River Colony, with three observers from Southern Rhodesia, with a numerical balance between delegates of governing parties and those of the opposition.[294] Having been agreed at the National Convention, the constitution was then approved by the legislatures of the constituent colonies – unanimously in the case of the Transvaal and Orange Free State, and overwhelmingly, with just two votes against, in the Cape; in Natal, a referendum was organized, with around three-quarters of the votes cast being favour of the constitution, on a 58 per cent turnout.[295] This process was necessary to provide the inter-elite political agreement and the public support necessary to forge a viable and acceptable constitutional text. The next step was to enact the constitution in the form of an Act of Parliament at Westminster. Those excluded from that deal – which in South Africa's case included the non-white races – sent a delegation to London to lobby on their behalf, but were unable to influence the content of the constitution as it went through the formalities of the legislative process.[296]

The second widely used constitution-building technique in the Westminster tradition was the 'Constitutional Conference' – or, as it was sometimes called, an 'Independence Conference'. This technique, typical of the New Commonwealth Constitutions adopted from the 1950s to the 1980s, lay behind the Constitutions of places as diverse as Jamaica (1962), Kenya (1963), Malta (1964), Fiji (1970) and Tuvalu (1978), among many others. The precise details of the process varied with each case but was usually entwined with the transition to independence.

The trigger was usually the election of a pro-independence majority to the colonial legislature. The Chief Minister, or other responsible leader of the legislative majority, would then apply to the British government for independence. A conference would be convened to discuss the terms on which independence would take place. These Constitutional Conferences typically included British government officials together with delegates of the main political parties (Government and Opposition) represented in the legislature of the colony applying for independence. In some cases, representatives of other major interest groups were also invited or consulted. Usually these conferences were held at Lancaster House or Marlborough House in London. A successful conference would result in the publication of a report, outlining the terms of the 'independence constitution' and perhaps setting the date and other terms for the transition to independence.[ii] An Independence Act would then be passed by the British Parliament, with the Constitution, as agreed by the conference, usually issued as an Order-in-Council under the terms of the Act.

Despite the presence of the British officials in these Constitutional Conferences, it would be wrong to assume that the resulting constitutions were simply imposed by them. Colonial Office officials hosted these conferences and supported them through the provision of legal advice and secretariat functions. They actively participated in the conferences, sometimes to protect what they perceived to be British strategic or economic interests, and sometimes to ensure fair play and to encourage the parties to reach a more balanced and consensual constitutional settlement, rather than letting the majority dictate terms. In many cases, for example, the British actively supported the adoption by newly independent countries of bills of rights.[297] Yet genuine negotiations between the national Government and Opposition parties took place at these conferences to decide the form that their future constitution would take. The resulting constitutions were usually based on some genuine cross-party agreement.

Moreover, national politicians at these Constitutional Conferences did not have an entirely free hand. They were constrained by domestic public opinion, either through upstream elections held before the Constitutional Conference to give them a mandate, or through

---

[ii]   The Report of the Jamaica Independence Conference 1962, and Annex C to the Lancaster House Agreement (Report of the Southern Rhodesia Constitutional Conference 1979), are examples of the typical structure, content, and level of detail, of such a report.

downstream elections in which the parties would have to justify their actions to the people. The Constitution of Jamaica, for example, was not 'pre-fabricated' by the British Colonial Office, nor merely 'handed to' Jamaica, but 'made by Jamaicans for Jamaicans'.[298] In some cases (e.g. Malta) a referendum was also held on the final constitutional settlement.

The third constitution-building technique was to establish a Constituent Assembly. A Constituent Assembly is a large representative assembly vested with constitution-making powers. A Constituent Assembly may be indirectly elected from provincial legislatures as in India (1947–50) and Pakistan (1947–56), or directly elected by the people as in South Africa (1994–96) and Nepal (2007–16).[iii] Either way, it contains the foremost national leaders. As an elected body with a popular mandate, Constituent Assembly does not merely formulate recommendations to be enacted by another Parliament, but itself adopts the constitution in the name of the people. It might also act as an interim legislature during the transition period.

Constituent Assemblies, unlike the less visible conferences or conventions, embody a public 'founding moment' in which the truly re-creative power of national sovereignty can be expressed. The Constituent Assembly of India, for example, was a transformative institution that set out to create not only a new constitution, but a new, re-constituted Indian national identity. In the words of Jawaharlal Nehru, the Indian Constituent Assembly represented: 'a nation on the move, throwing away the shell of its past political and possibly social structure, and fashioning for itself a new garment of its own making.'[299] Likewise in South Africa, the nation that emerged from the Constitutional Assembly in 1996 did not merely have a new constitution, it became – through the very public process of agreeing that constitution – a new nation, with a new identity.

Constituent Assemblies are risky. Once things are poured into that sovereign cauldron of constituent power, there is no way of knowing what will emerge, or when. Pakistan's delayed and interrupted constitutional process is a counterpoint to the Indian experience. It took nearly a decade after independence – until 1956 – for Pakistan to give itself a constitution. That constitution was short-lived, and in the

---

[iii] Nepal is an interesting case of the migration of constitutional ideas. It was never part of the British Empire, but its cultural and geographical proximity first to British India and then to independent India has made it quite receptive to Westminster-style institutions. The current (2015) constitution clearly shows – albeit indirect – signs of Westminster influences.

following decades it proved difficult to maintain a consensus at both elite and mass levels around any constitutional settlement.[300]

South Africa in the 1990s mitigated this risk by developing an 'interim constitution', produced by the second Convention for a Democratic South Africa (CODESA II) – a round-table process involving the main political parties, who met to agree principles for reform before the first multiracial elections. This interim constitution established the Constitutional Assembly (which consisted of both Houses of the interim Parliament), which was responsible for developing the final constitution. It limited the Constitutional Assembly's sovereignty by including a set of 34 'Constitutional Principles', agreed at CODESA II, to which the final constitution had to conform – with the Constitutional Court ensuring compliance.[301]

The fourth form of constitution-making body is the constitutional commission. Rather like a Royal Commission, this might consist of a small number of members appointed by the government on the basis of their experience and expertise. Typically, a senior judge will be appointed as chair, while the other commissioners might be eminent lawyers, civil servants or former ministers. Lacking any kind of democratic mandate, the authority for a commission of this type comes from the eminence of its members and the esteem in which they are held. Their actions are bound by terms of reference, prescribed by the authority establishing them; usually, this will be limited to conducting inquiries and making recommendations, which are expressed in the form of a report. Constitutional change may then follow on the basis of that report, but only through the intermediate hands of another institution, such as Parliament.

The Federation of Malaya (later Malaysia) provides the best example of constitution-building by commission in the decolonization era. The commission, which reported in 1957, consisted of five members. They were chosen from across the Commonwealth: two from the United Kingdom (including the chair, Lord Reid, and Sir Ivor Jennings), and one each from Australia, India and Pakistan; a sixth member was initially appointed from Canada, but withdrew, ostensibly on 'medical grounds'.[302] There was, notably, no Malaysian member of the commission. It was, tellingly, the Alliance Party – a multiracial party that had won 51 of the 52 seats in the Legislative Council – that insisted on a non-Malay commission, on the grounds that only external experts would treat the non-Malay minorities fairly.[303]

Constitution-building by commission was quite rare during the transition from Empire to Commonwealth. Its limitation is that an expert body, no matter how excellent its members might be, cannot provide a forum for the all-important political negotiations that are essential to reaching a lasting constitutional settlement. The operating principle of a commission is to find a *constitutional solution* objectively, based on knowledge of constitutional design and a dispassionate assessment of the country's needs, not to find a *constitutional settlement*, based on arguing and bargaining between political actors. Since there is never a solution without a settlement, a commission is only useful if that settlement has already been reached at some earlier part of the process. In Malaya, the commission was established pursuant to agreements reached at a conference, held in London in 1956, between the British authorities, the hereditary rulers of the Malay states, and the political leadership (dominated by the Alliance Party).

In addition, since a commission lacks opportunities for direct input to the process (such as would be provided, for example, by the election of a Constituent Assembly), there must be opportunities for indirect inputs from civil society through a consultative process. The Reid Commission in Malaya conducted 31 public meetings – half of them outside the capital – and received 131 memoranda from political and civil society associations and interested individuals.[304] Some of these memoranda seem to have had at least a partial or marginal influence on the recommendations of the commissioners.[305]

Although rare in transitions to independence, constitutional commissions have become a standard means of carrying out reviews or reforms of a constitution already in effect. The 1976 reforms in Trinidad & Tobago, by which the country abolished the monarchy and became a republic with a figurehead president, and the 2011 reforms in Jamaica, by which the new Charter of Fundamental Rights and Freedoms was adopted, were both based on reports presented to their Parliaments by constitutional commissions of this sort. Elsewhere in the Commonwealth, constitutional commissions have also been used to draft completely new constitutions, most recently (ongoing at the time of writing) in The Gambia.

An increasing trend is for constitution-building processes to be governed by a statutory framework. By means of a Constitutional Transition Act (or similar), the political leadership commits itself to a process – ensuring that the momentum is kept up and that the new draft constitution does not lie languishing on a civil servant's shelf. The Constitutional Transition Act would typically provide for the selection of the members of the constitution-making body (be it a convention, conference, constituent assembly, or commission). The Act would set the terms of reference of the constitution-making body, embodying any 'upstream constraints' already agreed upon. It might establish certain obligations of the constitution-making body, such as a requirement to consult with the public. It will typically establish a Secretariat to support the constitution-making body. Crucially, the Act should provide for the funding of the body, perhaps as a statutory charge on the Consolidated Fund for the duration of its existence. It should also provide for the mechanism for the adoption of the new constitution – whether it is to be passed by Parliament or referred directly to the people in a referendum.

Examples of such transitional laws include the Constitution of Kenya Review Act (Kenya) 2008, the Constitutional Review Act (Tanzania) 2011, and the Constitutional Review Commission Act (The Gambia) 2017. In countries with an existing written constitution, which has a prescribed amendment formula, the statutory framework establishing and regulating such a commission must obviously comply with those requirements for constitutional change.

This survey of constitution-building processes, by no means exhaustive, highlights two general principles. Firstly, there must always be some way of reaching a broad and inclusive settlement on the outlines of the constitution, and some way of translating that settlement into a technically competent constitutional draft that can then be legitimately adopted. Secondly, the precise means by which all that is done depends largely on context and on the nature of the 'constitutional drama' being played out. An Australian or Canadian style constitutional conference may be suitable when creating a federation. A Constituent Assembly makes sense when a massive democratic renewal is required to rejuvenate the country. A small technical Commission may be sufficient, when the settlement is already agreed – perhaps by means of a previous conference between the parties – and it is necessary only to work out the details.

Towards a constitution-building process for the United Kingdom

Lord Norton identified three conditions that must be met for constitutional reform to occur: (i) a window of opportunity; (ii) a coherent set of proposals; and (iii) clear leadership.[306] On the first point, the window of opportunity is now wide open. New constitutions, according to Jon Elster, are usually adopted in response to momentous political shifts, such as regime collapse, a revolution, severe economic troubles, defeat in war, the negotiated end of a civil war, or the achievement of independence.[307] In such circumstances of failure or crisis, new constitutions are used 'to promote values and frameworks of nation building as well as to restructure the state'.[308] For a long time, people in the United Kingdom (except Northern Ireland) thought we did not have to worry much about such things. We do now. Since 2016, British politics has lurched from paralysis to reaction, in an atmosphere of feverish polarization, crass populism, strained legitimacy, decayed institutions, oligarchic corruption and deadly incompetence. The unwritten constitution has reached a point of moral exhaustion and is ripe for replacement. In such circumstances, constitution-building is like dentistry when you have a toothache; it is not a pleasant experience, but necessary, and better done sooner rather than later if future pain is to be minimized.

This book has tried to contribute to the second condition. It has set out a coherent set of proposals, showing that a reforming refoundation programme, giving effect to the 'Charter 88 agenda', can be achieved by making use of tried and tested Westminster Model designs. The aim is not to necessarily prescribe solutions in detail, but to outline the main options and to suggest design choices that seem suitable and practicable in the United Kingdom's context.

For the third of Lord Norton's conditions – clear leadership – we must look to our parliamentarians. Sir Keir Starmer, elected as Leader of the Labour Party in April 2020, has made several pledges to constitutional reform, including commitments to a Constitutional Convention that will draw up plans for federalism, the replacement of the House of Lords with a Senate of 'nations and regions', and electoral reform.[309] It remains to be seen whether he will ever have the opportunity to put this agenda into effect, and if so whether he proposes a comprehensive constitutional refoundation, or just another round of piecemeal reforms.

Labour has the chance, post-Brexit and with the collapse of the Liberal Democrats,[iv] to embrace constitutional reform and to campaign strongly for a new constitutional settlement. That will be difficult enough for a Labour leader; if it is to be more than a cynical electoral ploy, it demands a serious rethink of Labour's traditionally sceptical, if

---

[iv] From being a credible third party with 57 seats when entering the coalition after the 2010 general election, the Liberal Democrats were reduced to a rump of eight seats in 2015 and twelve seats in 2017. Having been swelled to 21 seats by several defections of pro-European MPs from both Labour and the Conservatives, the party was cut down to 12 seats in the 2019 general elections. Thus the performance of the Liberal Democrats over the last three general elections resembles the record of the Liberals as a marginal third party during the 1945–79 era of two-party dominance.

not actively hostile, approach to constitutional change.[310] Even more difficult – but no less essential – will be to build a movement for constitutional refoundation that transcends party lines and can lead to a new constitutional settlement with a sufficient degree of cross-party support. It is impossible to say more than that on the immediate political situation – here is not the place for political punditry, and any political prediction could be out of date before the book goes into print. The enduring point, however, is that successful constitutional change must always be driven by political leaders who understand it, are committed to it, and can mobilize support for it. If such leadership can be found, it is exceedingly difficult; if it cannot be found, it is impossible.

Assuming that a new Prime Minister comes to office, fresh from an election victory in which constitutional refoundation was a manifesto commitment, how in practical terms might the process of adopting a written constitution for the United Kingdom proceed? The first formal step would be to introduce a Constitutional Transition Bill. As described in the previous section, this would provide for the creation of a constitution-making body, its composition terms of reference, timetable of operations, secretariat support, funding and other incidentals. The bill would also prescribe the mechanism for the adoption of the constitution, specifying whether it would require approval by a referendum or by a parliamentary super-majority.

This bill would be passed by an ordinary majority in the Parliament in the usual way, but any pains taken to broaden parliamentary support, even at this initial stage, would be worthwhile. The publication of the bill might therefore be preceded by a pre-legislative stage in which the government seeks to build some cross-party consensus on the membership of the constitution-making body, its terms of reference, and the overall shape of the process.[v]

The more specific are the terms of reference of the constitution-making body, the less fret there will be about where the process will end up. It would be wise to commit in advance to certain core principles or key design choices – as was done, for example, in Malaya and South Africa (1994–96). For example, the constitutional transition bill might prescribe that the constitution must be democratic and parliamentary, that it must incorporate the European Convention on Human Rights, that

---

[v] Assuming the initiative for constitutional refoundation is taken by a Labour Government, it might be impossible to bring the bulk of Conservatives on side, but every effort should be made to reach out to other parties – particularly the Liberal Democrats, the Green Party, the Scottish National Party, Plaid Cymru and the Democratic Unionist Party.

there should be a bicameral Parliament at least one House of which must be directly elected by proportional representation, that it should establish a federal scheme based on four equal nations, that the independence of the judiciary and civil service should be assured. These baselines would constrain the constitution-making body, but also empower it by giving it an explicit – and politically backed – statutory mandate to fulfil.

Getting such a Constitutional Transition Act onto the statute book would itself be a considerable challenge. It would have to get through the gauntlet of government indifference, civil service obstruction, a reactionary tabloid press, and the scepticism of legal and political academics wedded to the old ways of parliamentary sovereignty. Nevertheless, to focus on passing a Constitutional Transition Act – rather than focusing on the resulting constitution itself – does at least make the goal seem achievable. If Parliament could pass the Blair-Brown reforms, then it can – given sufficient vision and commitment from the political leadership – pass a Constitutional Transition Act to initiate the process of constitutional refoundation.

In terms of the composition and selection of the constitution-making body established by the Constitutional Transition Act, much will depend on the preliminary question of whether the Union is to continue. If it is, the constitution-making body would have to be composed in such a way as to represent the constituent nations. This leads to two subsidiary issues: firstly, what compromise can be reached, in the numerical balance of the delegations, between the principles of equality-of-nations and equality-of-population; secondly, whether delegates are to be directly elected by the people or should be indirectly elected by existing legislatures.

On the first point, the key requirement is that England should not be able to dominate the other parts of the Union. The composition of the constitution-making body is therefore related to the decision-making rule. One might imagine, for example, a Constituent Assembly of 70 members: 35 from England, 15 from Scotland, and 10 each from Wales and Northern Ireland. With a two-thirds majority vote decision-making rule, this would mean that nothing could be agreed without England, but that England would not be able to impose any decision without the consent of at least one of the other three nations. England and Scotland together would have sufficient votes, as would England, Wales and Northern Ireland together, but England and either Wales or Northern Ireland would be a few votes short. This assumes, of course, that members vote as national blocs; in practice they are more likely to vote as party blocs, but the principle still stands.

On the second point, direct election would give the constitution-making body its own popular mandate. It would force parties to take public positions on constitutional issues and might encourage greater public engagement in the constitution-building process. However, we are not in a situation, like that of India in 1947–50 or South Africa in 1994–96, where the Constituent Assembly could replace Parliament as an interim legislature; it would have to sit beside Parliament, and it is unlikely that first-rank politicians would give up their places to seek election to it. Even if the politicians were to allow it to exist, it might become a sideshow.

An indirectly elected body, chosen by and from among existing parliamentarians, is probably the best that can be done under the circumstances. In that case, the Scottish, Welsh and Northern Irish delegates might be elected by electoral colleges consisting of all members of the House of Commons representing each of those nations, together with the members of their devolved legislatures, while the English delegates might be elected by MPs from English constituencies. The delegates should be chosen according to an inclusive formula, set out in the Constitutional Transition Act, that ensures cross-party representation. For example, for every ten members, five could be elected from the majority party in each nation, three from the largest opposition party, and two from the minor parties. Such a body would be likely to contain front-bench politicians, including those with ministerial experience; we must assume that the Prime Minister, the Attorney-General, and the Minister for Constitutional Transition would be delegates, as would the Leader of the Opposition, their shadow Cabinet counterparts, and the First Minsters and Ministers of Constitutional Affairs of the devolved administrations.

The vital point is that the constitution-making body should not be a mere 'conference' or 'convention' with a remit to discuss and reach political agreements, nor a 'commission' to produce a report with recommendations, but a real Constituent Assembly with the authority – granted to it by the Constitutional Transition Act – to draft a new written constitution. We need a new constitution, not another long-ignored report like those of Jenkins and Wakeham.

The Constituent Assembly needs a chairperson. The chairperson has to lead and drive the process, being absolutely committed to its successful outcome, without being partisan. To save wrangling in the Assembly, it might be as well for the chairperson to be named directly by the Constitutional Transition Act, with a former Speaker of the House of Commons being an obvious choice.

Rules of procedure for the Constituent Assembly should also be laid down by or under the Constitutional Transition Act. To facilitate cooperation and consensus, these might owe more to the rules of an enlarged Select Committee than to the rules of the whole House – with members being able, for example, to speak from their seats rather than having to rise to speak, and with scope for non-members to be questioned. The Constituent Assembly might be divided into committees, each dealing with particular aspects of constitutional design (Rights, Principles and Citizenship; Crown, Government and Parliament; Nations, Regions and Local Government; Judiciary and Independent Commissions, and so on), but at its core would have to be a small drafting committee, in which the whole constitutional scheme would be harmonized.

The Constituent Assembly would have to be supported and assisted by a Secretariat. As the Constituent Assembly would be a political body, in which the arguing and bargaining takes place between political leaders who might have very little constitutional knowledge, a primary function of the Secretariat would have to provide the 'expert' element to guide and inform its deliberations. There should be within the Secretariat a team of constitutional advisors, able to give technical, legal and comparative constitutional design assistance. Most of these advisors should not be drawn from the United Kingdom, because people are needed who have experience of working with written constitutions; an Australian and a Canadian would be useful, an Indian and a West Indian absolutely indispensable. The second function of the Secretariat would be to engage with 'everyone', through public outreach and civic education. There would have to be a means of soliciting comments and suggestions from the public and civil society, and of reporting on these to the Assembly. The Secretariat would also have a logistical function, with a third department responsible for the practical administration of the Constituent Assembly. The whole organization should be under the direction of a Chief Secretary – perhaps a former Clerk to the House of a large Commonwealth Parliament – who would report directly to the Chairperson of the Assembly.

It would be extremely helpful if the government could give momentum to the process by proposing its own draft constitution to the Constituent Assembly. It is much easier to work on adjusting and improving a draft than to start with a blank sheet of paper. Another good way of proceeding would be to invite each party to set out their heads of proposals and to examine the areas where these overlap. Once political agreement on the substance of the constitution is reached, the drafting committee would work with the Secretariat to produce the final text. That final text would then be put to a confirmatory vote of the Constituent Assembly; if passed by a two-thirds majority vote, as prescribed by the Constitutional Transition Act,[vi] the new constitution would be enacted by the Queen and would come into effect as the supreme and fundamental law on the appointed day.

One further consideration concerns the political and logistical management of concurrent activities. Elster famously likened constitution-building to 'rebuilding a ship at sea'.[311] At the same time as the ship of state is being rebuilt from her legal-institutional keel, she must keep on sailing. The state must continue to function during the constitution-building process: to protect its borders, to maintain the rule of law and public security, to collect taxes and to provide public services. This poses a difficult challenge, not least because the period of constitutional transition is likely to be characterized by what Peter Russell describes as 'mega-constitutional politics', when constitutional change absorbs the energy, passion and political resources of political leaders, causing other domestic and economic issues to be pushed down the agenda.[312] Conversely, daily political issues can choke constitutional transition efforts and cause pro-reform alliances to pull apart, as happened in 2018 in Sri Lanka and the Maldives.[313] This is another reason why having a Constitutional Transition Act in which the process is laid out is so important. Creating a separate parallel body, with its own chairperson and Secretariat, and its own statutory authority to draft the constitution, enables ordinary government and constitution-building to proceed in parallel. Even if many of the same people are Members of Parliament and members of the Constituent Assembly, each forum has its own function, its own ways of working, and its own sitting times, to better focus the mind.

There are no right way to organize a constitution-building process, although there are perhaps plenty of wrong ways. That sketched out here is merely illustrative of how a process in the United Kingdom might bring together elites, experts and everyone, and might produce a constitution that reflects a genuine cross-party and four-nation

---

[vi] In South Africa there was a rule enabling the draft constitution to be submitted to the people in a referendum, and approved by a majority vote, if a two-thirds majority could not be reached in the Constitutional Assembly. The Constitutional Transition Act might provide for a similar rule in the United Kingdom; however, the concerns about the suitability of Union-wide referendums in a federal state, addressed in Chapter 8, could not be avoided. To be legitimate, the Constitution would have to be approved by majorities in all four nations. Those opposed to reform might see this high threshold as an opportunity to sabotage the process.

constitutional settlement, that is technically sound and workable, and that also has public and democratic legitimacy.

Beyond the constitution: democracy, culture and civic virtue

In closing the book, two final points remain to be made. The first is that constitutional renewal alone cannot solve every problem. It is important, even necessary, but it cannot be a panacea.

Perhaps the most pressing problems are economic and ecological. We live in an age of 'falling living standards and profound social and economic inequality',[314] with 'mounting poverty and economic insecurity' coexisting alongside 'great concentrations of wealth'.[315] The resulting consolidation of oligarchic and corporate power, and decline of labour power, distorts democracy,[316] and makes it harder to mitigate the economic impacts of climate change. The brunt resource extraction and wealth appropriation is borne by the poorest, but everyone – society as a whole – is made worse off in consequence.[317] Relative deprivation (a sense of not doing as well as one could and should because the game is rigged) sparks disaffection.[318] In the United Kingdom this was exacerbated by the rigorous application of austerity policies, resulting in cuts to public services and benefits applied at a time of falling wages, rising unemployment and rising food and energy prices. This produced a sense of fatalistic betrayal – that 'they' no longer care about 'us', and that to talk of the 'common good' is almost hopeless. To this grim list, we must add pandemics and global depression, which have exposed weak governance capacity and highlighted structural economic inequalities.

While the United Kingdom's constitutional crisis is unique, there are warning signs of a wider 'crisis of democracy' affecting much the world, including in countries with written constitutions on the lines proposed in this book. The symptoms of this wider crisis include falling electoral turnouts;[319] frustration with political systems that seem unresponsive to people's needs;[320] loss of trust in political leaders and institutions;[321] increasing willingness to accept military rule or other non-democratic alternatives;[322] the rise of far-right parties and new forms of authoritarian national populism;[323] the erosion of conventional 'soft guardrails' of democracy;[324] the hallowing out of political discourse through overreliance on the technocratic rationale of managerial capitalism;[325] the disintegration of political culture, with a decline in the mass-membership organizations such as political parties, trade unions and churches that once gave form and substance to collective political action;[326] the corruption, debasement, avarice, venality and licentiousness of the governing class;[327] the polarization of society into adversarial 'tribes' lacking a common identity or interest;[328] and the collapse of the civic virtues that were once held to be essential to a democratic polity, such as tolerance, integrity, truthfulness and responsibility.[329]

A bad constitution may exacerbate all these problems, and a good constitution might provide a sound democratic framework in which to solve them, but no constitution is a ticket to paradise. Like South Africans before their new constitution was adopted in 1996, we need to understand the need for major constitutional change and put our effort into it; if it happens, then like South Africans after 1996 we will need patience and realistic expectations.

The second point is that democracy makes moral demands and assumes a certain set of civic values. The Westminster Model of democracy, in particular, expects a lot of its leaders. A Prime Minister with the support of a working parliamentary majority, even if constrained by a written constitution, has broad powers – over the executive, over Parliament, and over their own party – that call for qualities of good leadership and good stewardship, with a sense of public duty, responsibility and self-restraint. It is a system, even when written down in a supreme and fundamental law, that does not rely on a mechanistic calculation of interests, but on people doing the right thing and caring that the right thing be done.

Democracy assumes that the people are competent to make decisions about government – at least to the degree of being able to choose intelligently at a general election between a few viable choices of party, each with its leader as a potential Prime Minister and its manifesto as a potential programme for government. It assumes that people care about public affairs, and that they have some sense of responsibility for how they vote. It assumes moreover that the people can get relevant, accurate information on public affairs. This is not to say that everyone should have uniformity of opinion – far from it – but it is to say that there has to be some value to truth itself. Democracy also assumes that people are of equal moral worth as fellow citizens – there are diverse gifts, of course, and differences of talent, knowledge, wisdom and expertise – but ultimately we are members of one body-politic, all the parts of which are equally valued.

These assumptions are grounded upon certain socio-cultural values, which were historically rooted in Christianity even if they have since been absorbed into a largely secularized culture.[330] It is not clear how well, or for how long, a democracy can flourish if those underlying values are abandoned. In the absence of that ethical foundation, there is a danger that democratic institutions will be morally hollowed out, eroding their ability to discern and promote the common good, and deteriorating into a clash of personal rivalries and factional interests. Democracy does not require us to set all personal considerations aside, but it does ask us to moderate our desires, to co-ordinate with others and to compromise for the sake of wider public interests; it invites us to be active citizens, contributing in small, ordinary ways to the good of our neighbours, our town, our country and our world.[331] The constitution can recall these values to mind, putting them before us so that we do not lose sight of them. It cannot, however, work well in the absence of these values; nor can words on a page alone sustain these values, without moral leadership. Constitutional renewal points to the need for a deeper ethical revival in public life.

References

1 Bulmer, W.E. (2016) *Constituting Scotland: The Scottish National Movement and the Westminster Model* (Edinburgh: Edinburgh University Press), p 45.

2 Jennings, I. (1956) *The Approach to Self-Government* (Cambridge: Cambridge University Press), pp 12–13.

3 David Cameron, former Prime Minister of the United Kingdom, Address to Both Houses of the Parliament of Jamaica, 30 September 2015.

4 King, A. (2000) 'Does the United Kingdom Still Have a Constitution?' in *The Hamlyn Lectures* (London: Sweet & Maxwell).

5 Levitsky, S. and Ziblatt, D. (2018) *How Democracies Die* (NY: Crown).

6 Elkins, Z., Ginsburg, T. and Melton, J. (2009) *The Endurance of National Constitutions* (Cambridge: Cambridge University Press).

7 Barnett, A. (2019) 'D-Day and the constitution: why Britain needs a written constitution', *Open Democracy*, 5 June 2019.

8 Benn, T. and Hood, A. (1993) *Common Sense: A New Constitution for Britain* (London: Hutchinson).

9 IPPR (1991) *The Constitution of the United Kingdom* (London: IPPR).

10 De Smith, S.A. (1964) *The New Commonwealth and its Constitutions* (London: Stevens and Sons), p 254.

11 Ryrie, A. (2017) *Protestants: The Radicals who Made the Modern World* (London: William Collins), p 340.

12 Jennings (1956) *The Approach to Self-Government*, p 12.

13 Coffey, D. (2019) 'Brexit and the Commonwealth: Lessons from Comparative Legal History', IACL-AIDC Blog, 12 November, https://blog-iacl-aidc.org/2019-posts/2019/11/12/brexit-and-the-commonwealth-lessons-from-comparative-legal-history

14 Adams, J.C. and Barile, P. (1966) *The Government of Republican Italy* (Boston: Houghton Mifflin).

15 Birch, A.H. (1967) *British System of Government* (London: Routledge).

16 Marquand, D. (1997) *The New Reckoning: Capitalism, States and Citizens* (Oxford: Polity); (2004) *Decline of the Public: The Hollowing Out of Citizenship* (London: Polity).

17 Blond, P. (2010) *Red Tory: How the Left and Right Have Broken Britain and How We Can Fix It* (London: Faber and Faber).

18 Crewe, I. and King, A. (1995) *SDP: The Birth, Life, and Death of the Social Democratic Party* (Oxford: Oxford University Press).

19 1983 Liberal-SDP Alliance Election Manifesto, www.libdems.co.uk/manifestos/1983/1983-liberal-manifesto.shtml

20 Bulmer (2016) *Constituting Scotland: The Scottish National Movement and the Westminster Model.*

21 Erdos, D. (2009) 'Charter 88 and the Constitutional Reform Movement: A Retrospective', *Parliamentary Affairs*, 62(4), pp 537–551 (p 529).

22 House of Commons Research Paper 98/112, *Voting Systems: The Jenkins Report*, 10 December 1998, https://researchbriefings.files.parliament.uk/documents/RP98-112/RP98-112.pdf

23 Royal Commission on the Reform of the House of Lords (2000) *A House for the Future.*

24 Information Commissioner's Organisation, 'What is the Freedom of Information Act?' https://ico.org.uk/for-organisations/guide-to-freedom-of-information/what-is-the-foi-act/

25 Amnesty International (2018) 'Eight reasons why the Human Rights Act makes the UK a better place', 8 October, www.amnesty.org.uk/eight-reasons-why-human-rights-act-has-made-uk-better-place-british-bill-of-rights; Gardbaum, S. (2013) *The New Commonwealth Model of Constitutionalism: Theory and Practice* (Cambridge: Cambridge University Press).

26 Mill, J.S. (1972) 'Consideration on Representative Government' [1867] in H.B. Acton (ed), *J.S. Mill: Utilitarianism, On Liberty and Considerations on Representative Government* (Everyman Classics), p 367.

27 McCormick, N. (1991) 'An Idea for a Scottish Constitution', in W. Finne, C. Himsworth and N. Walker (eds), *Edinburgh Essays in Public Law* (Edinburgh: Edinburgh University Press).

28 *The Economist* (2019) 'The next crisis: The Brexit referendum and the British constitution', 30 May, www.economist.com/briefing/2019/05/30/the-brexit-referendum-and-the-british-constitution

29 Political and Constitutional Reform Committee: Written evidence submitted by Canon Kenyon Wright CBE, May 2012, https://publications.parliament.uk/pa/cm201213/cmselect/cmpolcon/371/371we02.htm

30 O'Toole, F. (2018) *Heroic Failure: Brexit and the Politics of Pain* (NY: Apollo).

31 King, A. and Crewe, I. (2013) *The Blunders of Our Governments* (London: Oneworld).

32 United Nations Human Rights Council (2019) Visit to the United Kingdom of Great Britain and Northern Ireland: Report of the Special Rapporteur on extreme poverty and human rights, https://undocs.org/A/HRC/41/39/Add.1

33 Armstrong, S. (2017) 'Want, disease, ignorance, squalor and idleness: are Beveridge's five evils back?' *The Guardian*, 10 October, www.theguardian.com/society/2017/oct/10/beveridge-five-evils-welfare-state

34 Goodhart, D. (2017) *The Road to Somewhere: The Populist Revolt and the Future of Politics* (London: Hurst & Co).

35 Blond (2010) *Red Tory: How the Left and Right Have Broken Britain and How We Can Fix It*; Milbank, J. and Pabst, A. (2016) *The Politics of Virtue* (London: Rowman & Littlefield).

36 Paine, T. (1791) *Rights of Man*, Part 2, Chapter V.

37 Seldon, A. (2009) *Trust: How We Lost it and How to Get it Back* (London: Biteback).

38 Clegg (2017) *Politics: Between the Extremes*, p 251.

39 Runciman, D. (2014) *The Confidence Trap: A History of Democracy in Crisis from WWI to the Present* (Princeton: Princeton University Press).

40 Blick, A. and Hennessey, P. (2019) 'Brexit and the Melting of the British Constitution', The Constitution Society, https://consoc.org.uk/wp-content/uploads/2019/07/Blick-and-Hennessy-Brexit-and-the-Melting-of-the-British-Constitution.pdf

41 Sparrow, A. (2018) 'Most English Tory voters would be happy to see UK break up as price of Brexit, survey suggests', *The Guardian*, 8 October, www.theguardian.com/politics/blog/live/2018/oct/08/labour-and-tory-mayors-unite-to-demand-they-take-back-control-of-regional-spending-after-brexit-politics-live; Thompson, S. (2019) 'Poll: Most Tories would sacrifice union with Northern Ireland for Brexit', *The Irish Times*, 18 June, www.irishnews.com/news/brexit/2019/06/18/news/poll-most-tories-would-sacrifice-union-with-northern-ireland-for-brexit-1644668/

42 Russell, M. and Grover, D. (2017) *Legislation at Westminster: Parliamentary Actors and Influence in The Making of British Law* (Oxford: Oxford University Press).

43 European Union (Withdrawal) (No. 3) Bill 2019, House of Commons, https://publications.parliament.uk/pa/bills/cbill/2017-2019/0321/19321.pdf

44 Walker, P. (2018) 'Breaking vote pairs has dire consequences', *The Independent*, 20 July, www.theguardian.com/politics/2018/jul/20/breaking-vote-pairs-dire-consequences-michael-heseltine-jo-swinson)

45 Taylor, R. (2019) ' "She's dead of course!" The British constitution, Brexit and human rights', LSE, 3 July, https://blogs.lse.ac.uk/brexit/2019/07/03/shes-dead-of-course-the-british-constitution-brexit-and-human-rights/

46 Fitzjames Stephen, J. (1873) 'Parliamentary Government', Part 1, December 1873, http://fitzjames-stephen.blogspot.com/2016/09/parliamentary-government.html

47 Booth, R. (2019) 'Racism rising since Brexit vote, nationwide study reveals', *The Guardian*, 20 May, www.theguardian.com/world/2019/may/20/racism-on-the-rise-since-brexit-vote-nationwide-study-reveals

48 Cobain, I. and Taylor, M. (2016) 'Far-right terrorist Thomas Mair jailed for life for Jo Cox murder', *The Guardian*, 23 November, www.theguardian.com/uk-news/2016/nov/23/thomas-mair-found-guilty-of-jo-cox-murder

49 Schofield, K. (2019) 'MPs advised to share taxis home amid fears of Brexit-related attacks', Politics Home, www.politicshome.com/news/article/excl-mps-advised-to-share-taxis-home-amid-fears-of-brexitrelated-attacks

50 Slack, J. (2016) 'Enemies of the People', *Daily Mail*, 4 November.

51 Anonymous ('The Civil Servant') (2019) 'Dominic Cummings' war on the British civil service will undermine democracy', *The Guardian*, 1 August, www.theguardian.com/commentisfree/2019/aug/01/boris-johnson-dominic-cummings-whitehall-democracy-civil-servants

52 Booth, 'Racism rising since Brexit vote, nationwide study reveals', 20 May 2019.

53 Temelkuran, E. (2019) *How to Lose a Country: The 7 Steps from Democracy to Dictatorship* (London: Fourth Estate).

54 Jones, D.J.V. (1975) *Chartism and the Chartists* (London: Allen Lane).

55 Dicey, A.V. (1915) *Introduction to the Study of the Law of the Constitution*, 8th edition (London: Macmillan and Co), pp 39–40.

56 Blick and Hennessey (2019) 'Brexit and the Melting of the British Constitution'.

57 IPPR (1991) *The Constitution of the United Kingdom*.

58 Lord Bolingbroke (1733) 'Dissertation on Parties', quoted in King (2001), 'Does the United Kingdom still have a constitution?', p 80.

59 King (2001) 'Does the United Kingdom still have a constitution?', p 1.

60 Constitution Act (Canada) 1982, s. 51.

61 Elkins, Ginsburg and Melton (2009) *The Endurance of National Constitutions*, p 39.

62 Palmer, M. (2006) 'Using Constitutional Realism to Identify the Complete Constitution: Lessons from an Unwritten Constitution', *American Journal of Comparative Law*, 54, p 595.

63 Palmer (2006) 'Using Constitutional Realism to Identify the Complete Constitution: Lessons from an Unwritten Constitution', p 608.

64 Palmer (2006) 'Using Constitutional Realism to Identify the Complete Constitution: Lessons from an Unwritten Constitution', p 621.

65 Canadian Supreme Court judgment: Reference re Secession of Quebec, [1998] 2 S.C.R. 217.

66 Van Loon, R.J. and Whittington, M.S. (1987) *The Canadian Political System: Environment, Structure and Process* (New York: McGraw Hill), p 173.

67 Bulmer, W.E. and Hind, D. (2017) 'Democratic Socialism: Why the Left should demand a new Constitution', New Socialist, 15 August, https://newsocialist.org.uk/democratic-socialism-why-the-left-should-demand-a-new-constitution/

68 Bulmer, W.E. (2015) *A Constitution for the Common Good*, 2nd edition (Edinburgh: Luath Press).

69 *Steve Thoburn v Sunderland City Council* [2002] EWHC 195 (Admin).

70 *R (Miller) v The Prime Minister* [2019] UKSC 41 Para. 39.

71 *R (Miller) v The Prime Minister* [2019] UKSC 41 Para. 55.

72 Pettit, P. (1982) *Republicanism: A Theory of Freedom and Government* (Oxford: Oxford University Press).

73 Thornhill, C. (2011) *The Sociology of Constitutions: Constitutions and State Legitimacy in Historical-sociological Perspective* (Cambridge: Cambridge University Press).

74 De Smith, S.A. (1961) 'Westminster's Export Models: The Legal Framework of Responsible Government', *The Journal of Commonwealth Political Studies*, 1(1), pp 2–16.

75 Ghai, Y.-P. (2010) 'Chimera of constitutionalism: State, economy and society in Africa', Research Seminar, Faculty of Law, The Chinese University of Hong Kong, p 3. www.up.ac.za/media/shared/Legacy/sitefiles/file/47/15338/chimera_of_constitutionalism_yg1.pdf

76 Thornhill (2011) *The Sociology of Constitutions.*

77 Lerner, H. (2011) *Making Constitutions in Deeply Divided Societies.* (Cambridge: Cambridge University Press).

78 Gargarella, R. (2010) *The Legal Foundations of Inequality* (Cambridge: Cambridge University Press).

79 Paine (1791) *Rights of Man* (Part 2, Chapter IV).

80 Paine (1791) *Rights of Man* (Part 2, Chapter IV).

81 Paine (1791) *Rights of Man* (Part 2, Chapter IV).

82 Paine (1791) *Rights of Man* (Part 2, Chapter IV).

83 King, J. (2018) 'The Democratic Case for a Written Constitution', UCL Inaugural Lecture, 27 April, www.ucl.ac.uk/laws/news/2018/apr/professor-jeff-king-inaugural-lecture-democratic-case-written-constitution

84 Bellamy, R. (2009) *Political Constitution: A Republican Defence of the Constitutionality of Democracy* (Cambridge: Cambridge University Press).

85 King (2018) 'The Democratic Case for a Written Constitution'.

86 Burke (1775) Speech to Parliament on Reconciliation with the American Colonies.

87 Brezezinski, M. (1998) *The Struggle for Constitutionalism in Poland* (New York: MacMillan).

88 Parau, C.E. (2013) 'Romania's Transnational Constitution' in Galligan, Dennis and Mila Versteeg (eds) *Social and Political Foundations of Constitutions.* (Cambridge: Cambridge University Press).

89 Ghai (2010) 'Chimera of constitutionalism: State, economy and society in Africa', p 5.

90 *Minerva Mills Ltd. and Ors. v. Union Of India and Ors.* [AIR 1980 SC 1789]

91 Ginsburg, T. (2013) *Constitutions in Authoritarian Regimes* (Cambridge: Cambridge University Press).

92 Couso, J., Lovera Parmo, D., Guiloff, M. and Coddou, A. (2011) *Constitutional Law in Chile* (Alphen aan den Rijn, The Netherlands: Kluwer Law International).

93 Report of the Constitutional Commission (Trinidad and Tobago) (1974) www.ttparliament.org/documents/1101.pdf

94 Barrow-Giles, C. (2010) 'Regional Trends in Constitutional Developments in the Commonwealth Caribbean', paper prepared for the Conflict Prevention and Peace Forum, www.cpahq.org/cpahq/cpadocs/Cynthia%20Barrow.pdf

95 Butler, A. and O'Connell, R. (1998) 'A Critical Analysis of Ireland's Constitutional Review Group Report', *Irish Jurist New Series*, 33, pp 237–65.

96 Maynor, J.W. (2003) *Republicanism in the Modern World* (Oxford: Polity); Honohan, I. (2002) *Civic Republicanism* (London: Routledge); Bellamy, R. (2009) *Political Constitution: A Republican Defense of the Constitutionality of Democracy* (Cambridge: Cambridge University Press).

97 Tate, N. and Vallinder, T. (eds) (1995) *The Global Expansion of Judicial Power* (New York: New York University Press); Stone-Sweet, A. (2012) 'Constitutional Courts', in M. Rosenfeld and A. Sajó (eds) *The Oxford Handbook of Comparative Constitutional Law* (Oxford: Oxford University Press).

98 Harris, C. (2015) *Magna Carta and its Gift to Canada: Democracy, Law and Human Rights* (Toronto: Dundurn).

99 Harrington, J. (2004) 'The Challenge to the Mandatory Death Penalty in the Commonwealth Caribbean', *The American Journal of International Law*, 98(1), pp 126–40.

100 Amnesty International (2002) 'State Killing in the English-speaking Caribbean: A Legacy of Colonial Times', 22 April, www.amnesty.org/en/docume nts/AMR05/003/2002/en/)

101 Levitsky, S. and Ziblatt, D. (2018) *How Democracies Die*; also Muller (2007) *What is Populism?* (Philadelphia, PA: University of Pennsylvania Press).

102 Cats-Baril, A. (2020) 'Coalitions for constitutional change: Sri Lanka's constitutional crisis and the Maldives' 2018 elections', *Annual Review of Constitution Building 2018* (Stockholm: IDEA).

103 Beard, C. (1913) *An Economic Interpretation of the Constitution of the United States* (New York: Dover); Dahl (2003) *How Democratic is the American Constitution?* (New Haven: Yale University Press).

104 Bulmer (2015) 'Exclusionary constitutionalism: Developments in Chile and Hungary', *Annual Review of Constitution Building 2014*.

105 Gargarella (2010) *The Legal Foundations of Inequality*.

106 Lagassé, P. (2019) 'The Crown and Government Formation: Conventions, Practices, Customs, and Norms', *Constitutional Forum*, 28(3).

107 Milbank and Pabst (2016) *The Politics of Virtue*.

108 Magna Carta (1215), Article 1.

109 Wade, H.W.R. (1980) *Constitutional Fundamentals*, Hamlyn Trust Lectures (London: Stevens & Co.), pp 24–9.

110 Oliver, P.C. (2005) *The Constitution of Independence: The Development of Constitutional Theory in Australia, Canada, and New Zealand* (Oxford: Oxford University Press).

111 Alder, J. (1989) *Constitutional and Administrative Law* (London: Macmillan) pp 72–3.

112 Oliver, P. (2005) *The Constitution of Independence: The Development of Constitutional Theory in Australia, Canada, and New Zealand* (Oxford: Oxford University Press).

113 Kumarasingham, H. (2013) *Political Legacies of Empire* (London and New York: Tauris), pp 2–3.

114 Wilson, G. (1994) 'The Westminster model in comparative perspective', in J. Budge and D.H. McKay (eds) *Developing Democracy: Comparative Research in Honour of J.F.P. Blondel* (London: Sage), p 190.

115 Lijphart, A. (1999) *Patterns of Democracy: Government Forms and Performance in Thirty-six Countries* (Yale: Yale University Press).

116 De Smith (1961) 'Westminster's Export Models: The Legal Framework of Responsible Government', p 3.

117 Judge, D. (2005) *Political Institutions in the United Kingdom* (Oxford: Oxford University Press), pp 25–7.

118 Blick (2016) *The Codes of the Constitution* (Oxford: Hart).

119 Patapan, H., Wanna, J. and Weller, P. (eds) (2005) *Westminster Legacies: Democracy and Responsible Government in Asia and the Pacific* (Sydney: University of New South Wales Press).

120 Patapan, Wanna and Weller (eds) (2005) *Westminster Legacies: Democracy and Responsible Government in Asia and the Pacific*; Blick (2016) *The Codes of the Constitution*.

121 Bulmer (2016) *Constituting Scotland: The Scottish National Movement and the Westminster Model*, p 21.

122 Wolf-Phillips, L. (1984) 'A Long Look at the British Constitution', *Parliamentary Affairs*, 37(4), pp 385–402, https://doi.org/10.1093/pa/37.4.385

123 Thornhill (2011) *A Sociology of Constitutions*.

124 Jennings (1956) *The Approach to Self-Government*, pp 21–2.

125 Hearnshaw, F.J.C. (1920) *Democracy and the British Empire* (London: Constable and Co. Ltd), pp 133–5.

126 Patapan, Wanna and Weller (eds) (2005) *Westminster Legacies: Democracy and Responsible Government in Asia and the Pacific*.

127 Kumarasingham (2013) *Political Legacies of Empire*.

128 Glover, M. and Hazell, R. (2008) 'Introduction: forecasting constitutional futures', in R. Hazell (ed) *Constitutional Futures Revised: Britain's Constitution to 2020* (Basingstoke: Palgrave Macmillan); also see Bulmer (2016) *Constituting Scotland: Constitutions and State Legitimacy in Historical-sociological Perspective.*

129 De Smith (1961) 'Westminster's Export Models: The Legal Framework of Responsible Government', p 4.

130 Glover and Hazell (2008) 'Introduction: forecasting constitutional futures'; also see Bulmer (2016) *Constituting Scotland: Constitutions and State Legitimacy in Historical-sociological Perspective.*

131 De Smith (1964) *The New Commonwealth and its Constitutions*, pp 107–108.

132 De Smith (1964) *The New Commonwealth and its Constitutions*, p 109.

133 De Smith (1964) *The New Commonwealth and its Constitutions*, p 109.

134 De Merieux, M. (1982) 'The codification of constitutional conventions in the Commonwealth Caribbean Constitutions', *International and Comparative Law Quarterly*, 31(2).

135 De Smith (1964) *The New Commonwealth and its Constitutions*, pp 82–90.

136 Evatt, H.V. 'The King and His Dominions' (p 304), cited in de Smith (1964) *The New Commonwealth and its Constitutions*, p 83.

137 De Smith (1964) *The New Commonwealth and its Constitutions*, p 95.

138 De Smith (1964) *The New Commonwealth and its Constitutions*, p 83.

139 Evatt, 'The King and His Dominions' (p 306), cited in de Smith (1964) *The New Commonwealth and its Constitutions*, p 83.

140 De Smith (1964) *The New Commonwealth and its Constitutions*, p 108.

141 De Smith (1964) *The New Commonwealth and its Constitutions*, p 108.

142 De Smith (1964) *The New Commonwealth and its Constitutions*, p 109.

143 Jennings (1956) *The Approach to Self-Government.*

144 De Smith (1964) *The New Commonwealth and its Constitutions*, p 109.

145 De Smith (1964) *The New Commonwealth and its Constitutions*, p 108.

146 De Smith (1964) *The New Commonwealth and its Constitutions*, p 109.

147 Arter, D. (2004) *The Scottish Parliament: A Scandinavian Style Assembly?* (London, and Portland, OR: Frank Cass).

148 De Smith (1961) 'Westminster's Export Models: The Legal Framework of Responsible Government', p 9.

149 Furnivall, J.S. (1960) *The Governance of Modern Burma*, 2nd edition (New York: Institute of Pacific Relations), p 1.

150 Bulmer (2015) *A Constitution for the Common Good.*

151 Lerner, H. (2011) *Making Constitutions in Deeply Divided Societies* (Cambridge: Cambridge University Press).

152 McCarthy, A. and Keogh, D. (2008) *The Making of the Irish Constitution of 1937* (Blackrock: Mercier Press).

153 Khosla, M. (2012) *The Indian Constitution* (Oxford: Oxford University Press).

154 Singh, M.P. (2013) *V. N. Shukla's 'Constitution of India'* (Lucknow: Eastern Book Company), p A-21.

155 Charter of the Commonwealth (2013) https://thecommonwealth.org/sites/default/files/page/documents/CharteroftheCommonwealth.pdf

156 Kashyap, S.C. (2001) *Our Constitution: An Introduction to India's Constitution and Constitutional Law* (National Book Trust: India); see also *Kesavananda Bharati v. State of Kerala* (1973) 4 SCC 225 (para 116).

157 Parkinson, C. (2007) *Bills of Rights and Decolonization: The Emergence of Domestic Human Rights Instruments in Britain's Overseas Territories* (Oxford: Oxford University Press).

158 Gardbaum, S. (2001) 'The New Commonwealth Model of Constitutionalism', *American Journal of Comparative Law*, 49, p 707.

159 Bulmer, W.E. (2019) *Emergency Powers*, International IDEA Constitution Building Primers (Stockholm: IDEA).

160 Sinclair, T.A. (trans.) (1962) *Aristotle: The Politics* (London: Penguin).

161 Sunstein, C.R. (1999) 'Social and Economic Rights – Lessons from South Africa: New Developments in World Constitutionalism', University of Chicago Law School; 11 Constitutional Forum 123.

162 Constitution of Tuvalu, 1986, Preamble and Section 29.

163 The Constitution of Ireland, Art. 44.1 (as originally enacted); these provisions were removed by the Fifth Amendment of the Constitution Act 1972.

164 Constitution of Ireland 1937 (as amended), Preamble.

165 Constitution of Malaysia 1956 (as amended to 2010), art. 3.

166 Constitution of Sri Lanka 1972, art. 6 and art. 18(1)(d).

167 Constitution of Fiji, 2013: article 4.

168 Dawood, A. (2017) 'Religion-State Relations', International IDEA Constitution-Building Primer, no. 8, 2nd edition (Stockholm: IDEA).

169 Constitution Act (Canada) 1982, Part 1.

170 Patrick, J. (2006) 'Church, State, and Charter: Canada's Hidden Establishment Clause', *Tulsa Journal of Comparative and International Law*, 14(1), pp 25–52.

171 Jennings, I. (1965) 'Status of Gibraltar', in H. Kumarasingham (ed) (2014) *Constitution-Maker: Selected Writings of Sir Ivor Jennings*, Camden Fifth Series, Volume 46 (Cambridge: Cambridge University Press).

172 De Smith, S.A. (1949) 'The London Declaration of the Commonwealth Prime Ministers, April 28, 1949', *The Modern Law Review*, 12(3), pp 351–4.

173 Adams, J.C. and Barile, P. (1972) *Government of Republican Italy* (Boston, MA: Houghton Mifflin).

174 Constant, B. (1988) 'Principles of politics applicable to all representative governments', in B. Fontana (ed) *Constant, Political Writings* (Cambridge: Cambridge University Press), pp 171–305.

175 Bagehot, W. (1867) *The English Constitution* (London: Fontana, 1963).

176 Twomey, A. (2008) *The Veiled Sceptre: Reserve Powers of Heads of State in Westminster Systems* (Cambridge: Cambridge University Press), pp 93–7.

177 Blackstone, W. (1765) *Commentaries on the Laws of England* (Oxford: Clarendon).

178 Bagehot (1867) *The English Constitution*.

179 Saunders, C.A. (2011) The *Constitution* of *Australia*: A *Contextual Analysis* (Oxford and Portland, Oregon: Hart), p 11.

180 Blick (2019) *The Codes of the Constitution*, pp 97–8.

181 De Smith (1964) *The New Commonwealth and its Constitutions*.

182 Parliament of Australia Senate Briefs (2020) *Ministers in the Senate* (February), www.aph.gov.au/About_Parliament/Senate/Powers_ practice_n_procedures/Senate_Briefs/Brief14

183 Parliament of Australia Senate Briefs (2020) *Ministers in the Senate* (February).

184 Russell and Gover (2017) *Legislation at Westminster.*

185 Ministers of State Act 1952, No. 1, 1952, Compilation no. 11, www.legislation.gov.au/Details/C2018C00020)

186 Bulmer (2016) *Constituting Scotland.*

187 Russell and Gover (2017) *Legislation at Westminster.*

188 Rosenblum, N. (2020) 'Parliamentarism Recidivus', *The New Rambler*, https://newramblerreview.com/book-reviews/political-science/parliamentarism-recidivus

189 Bagehot, W. (1873) *The English Constitution*, 2nd edition, p 56, https://socialsciences.mcmaster.ca/econ/ugcm/3ll3/bagehot/constitution.pdf

190 Killey, I. (1989) 'Peace, Order and Good Government: A Limitation on Legislative Competence', *Melbourne University Law Review*, 24, pp 24–55.

191 Khan, M. (1975) 'The Constitution of Fiji', PhD Thesis, University of Auckland, p 215; *Ibralebbe v The Queen* [1964] A.C. 900.

192 Poole, T. (2010) 'The royal prerogative', *International Journal of Constitutional Law*, 8(1), *R v Secretary of State for Foreign and Commonwealth Affairs*, ex p Bancoult (No 1) [2000] EWHC Admin 413.

193 Lord Judge's speech at King's College London, 'Ceding power to the executive; the resurrection of Henry VIII', April 2016, www.regulation.org.uk/library/2016_Henry_VIII_powers-Lord_Judge.pdf

194 Rosenbluth, F. and Shapiro, I. (2018) *Responsible Parties: Saving Democracy from Itself* (New Haven: Yale University Press).

195 Lijphart (2011) *Patterns of Democracy*.

196 Rose and Macallister (1990) *The Loyalties of Voters* (Newbury Park, CA: Sage).

197 Rosenbluth and Shapiro (2018) *Responsible Parties*.

198 Ellis, A., Reilly, B. and Reynolds, A. (2005) *Electoral System Design: The New International IDEA Handbook* (Stockholm: IDEA).

199 House of Commons Research Paper 98/112 (1998) *Voting Systems: The Jenkins Report*, 10 December, https://researchbriefings.files.parliament.uk/documents/RP98-112/RP98-112.pdf

200 Livingston, E. (2017) 'Electoral reform is a feminist issue', *Open Democracy*, 7 June, www.opendemocracy.net/en/5050/electoral-reform-feminist-issue/

201 Mahadew, A. (2019) 'Reforming Mauritius's electoral system: More gender and less communal representation?', CONSTITUTIONNET, 25 February, http://constitutionnet.org/news/reforming-mauritiuss-electoral-system-more-gender-and-less-communal-representation

202 Bagehot (1873) *The English Constitution*.

203 Lloyd George, D. (1910) *Better Times: Speeches by the Hon. D. Lloyd George, MP* (London: Hodder & Stoughton), p 143.

204 *Reform and Proposals for Reform since 1900* (House of Lords Briefing Note), March 2000, https://publications.parliament.uk/pa/ld199798/ldbrief/ldreform.htm

205 Russell, M. (2013) *The Contemporary House of Lords: Westminster Bicameralism Revived* (Oxford: Oxford University Press).

206 Independent Advisory Board for Senate Appointments (2019) 'Assessment criteria: Merit-based criteria established by the Government'.

207 Legislative Council Act (New Zealand) 1891 (54 & 55 VICT 1891 No 25)

208 Legislative Council Abolition Act (New Zealand) 1950.

209 Constitution of Barbados, 1966: section 36.

210 O'Brien, D. (2014) *The Constitutional Systems of the Commonwealth Caribbean: A Contextual Analysis* (London: Hart Publishing), p 149.

211 Constitution of Malaysia, art. 45.

212 Constitution of Ireland, art. 18.

213 'The Maltese Senate: 1921–1933', Maltese History and Heritage, https://vassallohistory.wordpress.com/parliament/the-senate-since-1921/

214 Constitution of Fiji, 1970: sections 45, 67 and 68.

215 Constitution of Malaysia, art. 45.

216 Constitution of Iraq (1925), art. 31.

217 Royal Commission on the Reform of the House of Lords (2000) *A House for the Future.*

218 House of Commons' Political and Constitutional Reform Committee (2015) *A New Magna Carta.*

219 Royal Commission on the reform of the House of Lords (2000) *A House for the Future.*

220 Webber, J. (2015) *The Constitution of Canada: A Contextual Analysis* (London: Hart).

221 Constitution of Australia, 1901: Section 57.

222 South Africa Act, 1909: Section 63.

223 Constitution of India, 1950: article 108.

224 Constitution of Trinidad and Tobago, 1976: section 65.

225 Constitution of Belize, 1981: section 79.

226 Constitution of Grenada, 1973/1991: section 48.

227 Constitution of Barbados, 1966: section 56.

228 Gallagher, M. (2010) 'The Oiraechtas: President and Parliament', in J. Coakley and M. Gallagher (eds) *Politics in the Republic of Ireland*, 5th edition (Abingdon: Routledge), pp 198–229.

229 Office of the Parliamentary Counsel: 'Queen's or Prince's Consent', September 2018, https://assets.publishing.service.gov.uk/government/uploads/system/uploads/attachment_data/file/742221/Queen_s_and_prince_s_consent_pamphlet__September_2018___accessible_.pdf

230 Booth, R. (2013) 'Secret papers show extent of senior royals' veto over bills', *The Guardian*, 15 January, www.theguardian.com/uk/2013/jan/14/secret-papers-royals-veto-bills

231 Lagassé, P. (2013) 'On Crown Consent', https://lagassep.com/2013/08/13/on-crown-consent/

232 Lagassé (2013) 'On Crown Consent'.

233 Lagassé (2013) 'On Crown Consent'.

234 House of Commons (2019) *The Role of Parliament in the UK Constitution: Authorising the Use of Military Force*, Public Administration and Political Affairs Committee Inquiry, www.parliament.uk/business/committees/committees-a-z/commons-select/public-administration-and-constitutional-affairs-committee/inquiries/parliament-2017/authorising-use-military-force-inquiry-17-19/publications/

235 Bulmer, W.E. (2019) 'Her Majesty's Precarious Opposition: "Clean Sweep" Elections and Constitutional Balance in Commonwealth Caribbean States', *Annual Review of Constitution Building*, International IDEA (Stockholm: IDEA).

236 House of Lords Select Committee on the Constitution, *Referendums in the United Kingdom* (I IL 2009–10), Ch.6, para. 206. See also Tierney (2012) *Constitutional Referendums: The Theory and Practice of Republican Deliberation* (Oxford: Oxford University Press).

237 Joint Committee on Parliamentary Privilege (1999) *Parliamentary Privilege First Report*, April, https://publications.parliament.uk/pa/jt199899/jtselect/jtpriv/43/4303.htm

238 House of Commons Library (2020) *Commons Opposition Day debates since 1992*, 27 February, https://researchbriefings.parliament.uk/ResearchBriefing/Summary/SN06315#fullreport

239 House of Commons (2009) *Rebuilding the House*, House of Commons Reform Committee, First Report of Session 2008–09, https://publications.parliament.uk/pa/cm200809/cmselect/cmrefhoc/1117/1117.pdf

240 Lagassé, P. (2019) 'The Crown and Government Formation: Conventions, Practices, Customs, and Norms', *Constitutional Forum*, 28(3).

241 Muirhead draft; see Bulmer (2016) *Constituting Scotland*, Appendix A.

242 O'Brien, P. (2010) 'Committee to examine Oireachtas powers of investigation', *Irish Examiner*, 22 October, www.irishexaminer.com/ireland/politics/committee-to-examine-oireachtas-powers-of-investigation-134241.html

243 Hansard, Wednesday 9 January 2019, vol. 652, https://hansard. parliament.uk/Commons/2019-01-09

244 Marshall, G. (1986) 'Constitutional Conventions: The Rules and Forms of Political Accountability', *The University of Toronto Law Journal*, 36(2), pp 221–5.

245 Headlam-Morley, A. (1928) *The New Democratic Constitutions of Europe* (Oxford: Oxford University Press).

246 For a full account of this incident and its constitutional implications, see Twomey (2008) *The Veiled Sceptre*.

247 Twomey (2008) *The Veiled Sceptre*.

248 Twomey (2008) *The Veiled Sceptre*.

249 Fixed Term Parliament Act 2011, Section 6.

250 Twomey (2008) *The Veiled Sceptre*, p 593.

251 The Canadian Press (2010) 'Gov. Gen. Jean explains 2008 prorogation', CBC, 29 September, www.cbc.ca/news/canada/ gov-gen-jean-explains-2008-prorogation-1.879923

252 Wheeldon, J. (2014) 'Constitutional Peace, Political Order, or Good Government? Organizing Scholarly Views on the 2008 Prorogation', *Canadian Political Science Review*, 8(1), pp 102–25.

253 'Recall of Parliament', House of Commons Library, No. 1186, 13 January 2020, http://researchbriefings.files.parliament.uk/ documents/SN01186/SN01186.pdf

254 Jennings (1956) *The Approach to Self-Government*.

255 McLean, I. and McMillan, A. (2005) *State of the Union* (Oxford: Oxford University Press).

256 Hassan, G. and Shaw, E. (2019) *The People's Flag and the Union Jack: An Alternative History of Britain and the Labour Party* (London: Biteback).

257 Denham, J. (2019) 'English Identity and Labour', speech to the Young Fabians in Westminster, 8 January, www.theoptimisticpatriot. co.uk/post/182240412323/english-identity-and-labour

258 Kenny (2015) 'UKIP didn't invent English Nationalism: It's been brewing for years', Centre on Constitutional Change, www.centreonconstitutionalchange.ac.uk/opinions/ ukip-didnt-invent-english-nationalism-its-been-brewing-years

259 Ramsay, A. (2018) 'Trying to milk a vulture: if we want economic justice we need a democratic revolution', *Open Democracy*, 22 October.

260 Anderson, G. (2008) *Federalism: An Introduction* (Oxford: Oxford University Press).

261 De Smith (1964) *The New Commonwealth and its Constitutions*, p 254.

262 Elazar, D. (1987) *Exploring Federalism* (Tuscaloosa, AL: University of Alabama Press).

263 Saunders (2011) *Constitution of Australia*.

264 Webber (2015) *The Constitution of Canada*.

265 Austin, G. (1999) *The Indian Constitution: Cornerstone of a Nation*, 2nd edition (Oxford: Oxford University Press).

266 Keith-Lucas, B. (1977) *English Local Government in the Nineteenth and Twentieth Centuries* (London: The Historical Association).

267 Blond (2010) *Red Tory*; Marquand (1997) *The New Reckoning*; Marquand (2004) *Decline of the Public*.

268 Goodhart (2017) *The Road to Somewhere*.

269 Mill, J.S. (1861) *Considerations on Representative Government* (London: Parker, Son and Bourn), Chapter XV.

270 Macfadyen (2014) *Flatpack Democracy: Power Tools for Reclaiming Local Politics* (Bath: Eco-Logic Books).

271 Harding, A. (2018) 'Local Democracy in a Multi-layered Constitutional System: Malaysian Local Government Reconsidered', in A. Harding and M. Sidel (eds) *Central-Local Relations in Asian Constitutional Systems* (Oxford: Hart).

272 Mathew, G. (1994) *Panchayati Raj: From Legislation to Movement* (New Delhi: Concept).

273 Commonwealth Governance, 'Local Government of Saint Lucia', www.commonwealthgovernance.org/countries/americas/st_lucia/local-government/

274 Harding (2018) 'Local Democracy in a Multi-layered Constitutional System'.

275 Bulmer, W.E. (2014) 'Judicial Appointments', *International IDEA Constitution-Building Primer*, no. 4 (Stockholm: IDEA).

276 Rankin, J. (2019) 'Poland broke EU law by trying to lower age of retirement for judges', *The Guardian*, 5 November, www.theguardian.com/world/2019/nov/05/poland-broke-eu-law-trying-lower-age-retirement-judges-says-court

277 De Smith (1964) *The New Commonwealth and its Constitutions*, p 109.

278 Eckersley, R. and Zifcak, S. (2001) 'The constitution and democracy in Victoria: Westminster on Trial', *Australian Journal of Political Science*, 36(1), p 63.

279 Pettit, P. (2001) *A Theory of Freedom: From the Psychology to the Politics of Agency* (Cambridge and Oxford: Polity), p 169.

280 Saunders (2011) *Constitution of Australia*, p 173.

281 Bagehot (1867) *The English Constitution*.

282 Ackerman, B. (2000) 'The new separation of powers', *Harvard Law Review*, 113(3), pp 633–729.

283 de Merieux, M. (1982) 'The codification of constitutional conventions in the Commonwealth Caribbean constitutions', *International and Comparative Law Quarterly*, 3(2), pp 265–6.

284 Commonwealth Secretariat, 1998: Art. IX.

285 Blick (2019) *The Codes of the Constitution*.

286 House of Lords (2007) 'Select Committee on Communications – First Report' 25 July, https://publications.parliament.uk/pa/ld200607/ldselect/ldcomuni/171/17105.htm

287 *Citizens United v. Federal Election Commission*, 558 U.S. 310 (2010).

288 Elster, J. (1995) 'Forces and Mechanisms in the Constitution-Making Process', *Duke Law Journal*, 45, pp 364–96; (1993) 'Constitution-Making in Eastern Europe: Rebuilding the Boat in the Open Sea', *Public Administration*, 71(1–2), pp 169–217.

289 Saati, A. (2015) *The Participation Myth: Outcomes of Participatory Constitution Building Processes on Democracy* (Umeå: Statsvetenskapliga institutionen, Umeå universitet).

290 Wheatley and Mendez (2016) *Patterns of Constitutional Design: The Role of Citizens and Elites in Constitution-Making* (London: Routledge).

291 McNaught, M. (1983) *The Pelican History of Canada* (Harmondsworth, Middlesex: Pelican), p 126.

292 McNaught (1983) *The Pelican History of Canada*, p 130.

293 Saunders (2011) *Constitution of Australia*.

294 Lacour-Gayet, R. (1977) *A History of South Africa* (New York: Hastings House), p 238.

295 Lacour-Gayet (1977) *A History of South Africa*, p 241.

296 Lacour-Gayet (1977) *A History of South Africa*, p 242.

297 Parkinson (2007) *Bills of Rights and Decolonization*.

298 Henry, M. (2017) 'Jamaica 55: The Making of The Constitution', *The Jamaica Gleaner,* 30 July, http://jamaica-gleaner.com/article/focus/20170730/martin-henry-jamaica-55-making-constitution

299 Bhargava, R. (2018) 'Why we need a Constitution', *The Hindu*, 8 July, www.thehindu.com/opinion/columns/why-we-need-a-constitution/article24361253.ece

300 Waseem, M. (2015) 'Constitutionalism and extra-constitutionalism in Pakistan', in M. Khosla and M. Tushnet (eds) *Unstable Constitutionalism: Law and Politics in South Asia* (Cambridge: Cambridge University Press), pp 124–58.

301 Arato, A. (2016) *Post Sovereign Constitution Making: Learning and Legitimacy* (Oxford: Oxford University Press).

302 Jennings, I. (1956) 'The Malayan Saga: Diary from the Reid Commission, 1956–7' (25 June 1956), in H. Kumarasingham (ed) (2014) *Constitution-Maker: Selected Writings of Sir Ivor Jennings*.

303 Parkinson (2007) *Bills of Rights and Decolonization*, pp 74–82.

304 Report of the Federation of Malaya Constitutional Commission ('Reid Commission Report') (1957) Colonial Office No. 330 (HMSO: London).

305 Parkinson (2007) *Bills of Rights and Decolonization*, pp 87–92.

306 Norton, P. (2000) 'Reforming Parliament in the United Kingdom', *Journal of Legislative Studies*, 6(3).

307 Elster (1995) 'Forces and Mechanisms in the Constitution-Making Process'.

308 Ghai (2010) 'Chimera of constitutionalism', p 3.

309 Electoral Reform Society (2020) 'Keir Starmer announces support for constitutional convention and proportional representation', 31 January.

310 Dorey, P. (2008) *The Labour Party and Constitutional Reform: A History of Constitutional Conservatism* (Palgrave: MacMillan).

311 Elster, J., Offe, C. and Preuss, U.K. (1998) *Institutional Design in Post-Communist Societies: Rebuilding the Ship at Sea* (Cambridge: Cambridge University Press), p 27; Elster (1993) 'Constitution-Making in Eastern Europe: Rebuilding the Boat in the Open Sea'.

312 Russell, P. (1993) *Constitutional Odyssey: Can Canadians Become a Sovereign People?* (Toronto: University of Toronto Press).

313 Catz-Baril, A. (2019) 'Sri Lanka and Maldives', *Annual Review of Constitution Building 2018*, International IDEA (Stockholm: IDEA).

314 Church of Scotland (2012) *A Right Relationship with Money*, Report of the Special Commission on the Purposes of Economic Activity, (Edinburgh: Church of Scotland).

315 Fishkin, J. and Fortbath, W.E. (2014) 'The Anti-Oligarchy Constitution', *Boston University Law Review*, 94(671), University of Texas, Public Law Research Paper, No. 561.

316 Fishkin and Fortbath (2014) 'The Anti-Oligarchy Constitution'.

317 Wilkinson, R. and Pickett, K. (2009) *The Spirit Level: Why More Equal Societies Almost Always Do Better* (London: Penguin).

318 Eatwell and Goodwin (2018) *National Populism: The Revolt Against Liberal Democracy* (London: Penguin).

319 World Bank (2017) *Annual Report*, p 228, ubdocs.worldbank.org/en/908481507403754670/Annual-Report-2017-WBG.pdf

320 Sandel, M. (2016) 'The energy of Brexiteers and Trump is born of the failure of elites', *New Statesman*, 13 June.

321 Seldon, A. (2009) *Trust: How We Lost it and How to Get it Back* (London: Biteback).

322 Feierherd, G., Schiumerini, L. and Stokes, S. (2018) 'When Do the Wealthy Support Redistribution? Inequality Aversion in Buenos Aires', *British Journal of Political Science*, 50, pp 793–805.

323 Eatwell, R. and Goodwin, M. (2018) *National Populism: The Revolt Against Liberal Democracy* (London: Penguin).

324 Levitsky and Ziblatt (2018) *How Democracies Die*.

325 Marquand (2004) *Decline of the Public*.

326 Putnam, R.D. (2000) *Bowling Alone: The Collapse and Revival of American Community* (New York: Simon & Schuster); Manin, B. (1997) *The Principles of Representative Government* (Cambridge: Cambridge University Press).

327 Bobbio, N. and Viroli, M. (2003) *The Idea of the Republic*, translated by A. Cameron (Cambridge and Oxford: Polity), p 95.

328 Chua, A. and Rubenfeld, J. (2018) 'The Threat of Tribalism', *The Atlantic*, October.

329 Viroli, M. (2002) *Republicanism*, translated by Shugaar (New York: Hill & Wang); Rosenfeld, S. (2018) *Democracy and Truth: A Short History* (Philadelphia: University of Pennsylvania Press); Carter, S. (1998) *Civility: Manners, Morals, and the Etiquette of Democracy* (Basic Books).

330 Holland, T. (2019) *Dominion: The Making of the Western Mind* (London: LittleBrown).

331 Viroli, M. (2002) *Republicanism* (New York: Hill & Wang) pp 75–8.

Index

Note: page numbers in **bold** type refer to Tables. Those followed by 'n' and a Roman numeral refer to Notes.

Representation of the People Act
    1884 141
Representation of the People Act 1971,
    Barbados 45
Representation of the People
    Acts 44nii, 46, 71
representation role of Parliament 136, 137
Republic of Ireland *see* Ireland (Republic
    of Ireland)
Republic of Ireland Act 1948 111
republics 111–13
'responsible party government' 78
Rhodes, R.A.W. 82
right of House to determine its
    proceedings 177, 178
rights
  fundamental rights and
      freedoms 99–103
  religious 99
  restriction of in emergencies 102
  in Westminster Model
      constitutions 64–5
Rights ('7 Rs' of written constitutions) 43
Rights of Man, The (Paine) 7, 51–3
Roadmap ('7 Rs' of written
    constitutions) 43
Roman Catholicism 106–7
Romania, Constitution of 1923 57
Rosenbluth, Frances 142, 145
rotten boroughs 141, 145
Roundheads 91
royal assent 8, 163–6
  refusal of 87niii, 163–4
Royal Commission on the Constitution
    (Kilbrandon Commission),
    1972 17
royal consent 166–7
Royal Victoria Order 120
Russell, Lord John 7
Russell, Peter 9, 247

S
Saati, Abrak 232–3
Saint Lucia
  Constitution of
    abolition of local democracy 215
    dissolution of parliament (section
        55) 191
    House of Assembly 141nii
    Leader of the Opposition (section
        67) 185
    prorogation of parliament (section
        55) 195
    royal assent 164
    section 47(2) 87niii
same-sex marriage, prohibition of in
    Constitution of Ireland 64

Samoa, Constitution of
  gender quota (article 44) 148
  Head of States' powers and functions
      (section 40) 121
  Judicial Service Commission (article
      72) 219
  lack of second chamber 156
  legislative role of Parliament (article
      43) 140
  religion-state relations 106
  as a republic 112
Saudi Arabia
  Fundamental Law of Saudi Arabia 60
Scarman, Lord (Leslie Scarman) 6
Scheduled Castes and Tribes,
      India 84, 148
Scotland
  Brexit referendum vote 27–8
  'Claim of Right' 20, 175
  devolution 19–20, 21–2
    1979 referendum 17
  draft constitution 2002
    number of ministers 132
  Gaelic and Scots language equality 211
  independence 28, 175, 197, 199
  judicial appointments 219
  judicial tenure (section 95, Scotland Act
      1998) 221
  Presbyterianism 106
  pressure for political change, 1960s
      onwards 17
  proposal for State Parliament in federal
      United Kingdom 210–11
  religion-state relations 106, 109
  Scottish identity 200
  see also United Kingdom
Scotland Act 1998 21, 44nii, 221
Scots language equality 211
Scottish Constitutional
      Convention 19–20, 21
Scottish Federation of Small Businesses 20
Scottish National Party (SNP) 17, 21–2,
      91, 132, 201, 243nv
Scottish nationalism 201
Scottish Parliament 16, 206
  appointment of First Minister 23
  electoral system 142, 146
  Scandinavian-inspired practices in 88
Scottish Provisional Constituent
      Assembly 179
Scottish Trades Union Congress 20
Scottish Unionists 200
SDP-Liberal Alliance (Alliance) 19
secession 175
second chambers 84–5, 90, 149–63
  directly elected 151, 155–6, 159
  and federalism 207